THE EVOLUTION OF
CULTURAL ENTITIES

PROCEEDINGS OF THE BRITISH ACADEMY · 112

THE EVOLUTION OF CULTURAL ENTITIES

Edited by
MICHAEL WHEELER, JOHN ZIMAN
& MARGARET A. BODEN

Published for THE BRITISH ACADEMY
by OXFORD UNIVERSITY PRESS

Oxford University Press, Great Clarendon Street, Oxford OX2 6DP

Oxford New York

*Athens Auckland Bangkok Bogotá Buenos Aires Cape Town
Chennai Dar es Salaam Delhi Florence Hong Kong Istanbul Karachi
Kolkata Kuala Lumpur Madrid Melbourne Mexico City Mumbai Nairobi
Paris São Paulo Shanghai Singapore Taipei Tokyo Toronto Warsaw*

*and associated companies in
Berlin Ibadan*

*Published in the United States by
Oxford University Press Inc., New York*

*© The British Academy, 2002
Database right The British Academy (maker)*

*British Library Cataloguing in Publication Data
Data available*

ISBN 0–19–726262–7

ISSN 0068–1202

*Typeset by J&L Composition Ltd, Filey, North Yorkshire
Printed in Great Britain
on acid-free paper by
Creative Print and Design Ltd,
Ebbw Vale*

Contents

Notes on Contributors

Margaret A. Boden is Professor of Philosophy and Psychology at the University of Sussex, and a Fellow of the British Academy. She is interested in the philosophy of mind, psychology, and AI/A-Life. Her work is highly interdisciplinary, reflecting her own academic background: she holds independent qualifications in medical sciences, philosophy, and psychology. Her first two books were *Purposive Explanation in Psychology* (1972) and *Artificial Intelligence and Natural Man* (1977/87); and the two latest are *The Creative Mind: Myths and Mechanisms* (1990) and *Dimensions of Creativity* (ed.) (1994). She is now writing a history of cognitive science.

Susantha Goonatilake was trained in electrical engineering and in sociology. Among his books are *Merged Evolution: The Long Term Implications of Information Technology and Biotechnology* (1999) and *Evolution of Information: Lineages in Genes, Culture and Artefact* (1992). He is presently attached to the Center for Studies of Social Change, New School for Social Research, New York.

C. A. Hooker, FAHA, is Professor of Philosophy at the University of Newcastle, Australia. With doctorates in each of physics and philosophy, he has always taught intelligent systems design and assessment to engineers as well as teaching philosophy subjects. His research focuses on understanding complex adaptive dynamical systems, from physical foundations through biological and neuro-cognitive organisation to economic and social dynamics and policy, publishing across this range and in related areas (20 books authored/edited, 100+ papers). The goal is to develop a naturalistic, dynamical systems based understanding of life, including mind, science, ethics, and culture.

Tim Ingold, FBA, FRSE, is Professor of Social Anthropology at the University of Aberdeen. He has carried out ethnographic research among Saami and Finnish people in Lapland, and has written extensively on the comparative anthropology of hunter-gatherer and pastoral societies, evolutionary theory, human-animal relations, and human ecology. He has edited *Tools, Language and Cognition in Human Evolution* (with Kathleen Gibson, 1993), the *Companion Encyclopedia of Anthropology* (1994) and *Key Debates in Anthropology* (1996). His current research interests in the anthropology of technology and in aspects of environmental perception form the subject of his latest book, *The Perception of the Environment: Essays on Livelihood, Dwelling and Skill* (2000).

Eva Jablonka is a professor in the Cohn Institute for the History and Philosophy of Science and Ideas in Tel-Aviv University. Her background is in molecular genetics, but her teaching and research interests now include evolutionary biology, epigenetics, animal behaviour, the philosophy of biology, and the history of genetics. Her books include: a textbook, *Evolutionary Biology* (in Hebrew, 1994–7, for the Open University of Israel); *The History of Genetics* (in Hebrew, 1994); *Epigenetic Inheritance and Evolution: The Lamarckian Dimension* (1995; co-authored with Marion Lamb), and *Animal Traditions: Behavioural Inheritance in Evolution* (2000; co-authored with Eytan Avital).

Adam Kuper is Professor of Social Anthropology at Brunel University. His most recent books are *The Chosen Primate* (1994), *Among the Anthropologists* (1999) and *Culture: The Anthropologists' Account* (1999).

Brian J. Loasby, a Cambridge graduate, held appointments at the Universities of Aberdeen, Birmingham and Bristol before joining in 1967 the new University of Stirling, where he is now Emeritus Professor. He was elected Fellow of the British Academy in 1994. The prime focus of his work is the growth and organisation of knowledge, within economics and economic systems, ranging from the history of thought to business management, with increasing emphasis on cognitive and evolutionary aspects. His book *Knowledge, Institutions and Evolution in Economics* (Routledge 1999) was joint winner of the Schumpeter Prize in 2000.

Mary Midgley is a professional philosopher whose special interests are in the relations of humans to the rest of nature (particularly in the status of animals), in the sources of morality, and in the relation between science and religion (particularly in cases where science becomes a religion). Until retirement she was a Senior Lecturer in Philosophy at the University of Newcastle on Tyne in England, where she still lives. She is a widow. Her husband was another philosopher, Geoffrey Midgley, and she has three sons. Her best-known books are: *Beast and Man, Evolution as a Religion, Science as Salvation, Wickedness,* and, most recently, *Science and Poetry*.

Richard R. Nelson is George Blumenthal Professor of International and Public Affairs at Columbia University. Over his career he has also taught at Yale University, Carnegie Mellon University, and Oberlin College. He has been a senior staff member of the Presidents Council of Economic Advisors, and a researcher at the Rand Corporation. His central research interests have been on long-run economic change, with a particular focus on how technology advances over time, and the nature and function of economic institutions. These interests led him some years ago to develop, along with Sidney Winter, an evolutionary theory of economic change. He has written extensively on technological advance, and topics in science and technology policy.

Henry Plotkin is Professor of Psychobiology in the Department of Psychology at University College London. He is the author of *Darwin Machines and the Nature of Knowledge*, *Evolution in Mind*, and *The Imagined World Made Real*, and has edited and co-edited three other books. His principal interests are the evolution of intelligence and culture, and the relationship between the social and biological sciences.

W. G. Runciman is a Senior Research Fellow in Sociology at Trinity College, Cambridge, and President of the British Academy. His books include *Relative Deprivation and Social Justice* (1966), *A Treatise on Social Theory* (Vol. I, 1983; Vol. II, 1989; Vol. III, 1997), and *The Social Animal* (1998). He is a foreign honorary member of the American Academy of Arts and Sciences, and holds honorary degrees from the Universities of Edinburgh, Oxford, and York.

Joan Solomon has a strong background in science teaching, and initiated the first Science Technology and Society (STS) course for comprehensive schools. She became Lecturer in Research at Oxford University, and carried out commissioned research on Teaching the History of Science, Discussion of Issues in School Science and other topics. She is now Visiting Professor and Senior Research Fellow at the Open University. Her books include *Teaching Science Technology and Society*, *Getting to Know about Energy in School and Society* and, co-edited with Glen Aikenhead, *STS Education: International Perspectives on Reform*.

Gunther Teubner is Professor of Private Law and Legal Sociology, University of Frankfurt, and Centennial Visiting Professor, London School of Economics. His research fields include social theory of law and comparative private law. He is the author of *Law as an Autopoietic System* (1993), *Droit et réflexivité* (1994), and *Il diritto policontesturale* (1999). He has also edited/authored *Paradoxes of Self-Reference in the Humanities, Law, and the Social Sciences* (1991), *State, Law, Economy as Autopoietic Systems* (1992), *Environmental Law and Ecological Responsibility* (1995), *Global Law without a State* (1998), and *Die Rückgabe des Zwölften Kamels* (2000).

Michael Wheeler is Lecturer in Philosophy at the University of Dundee. Previously, he has held teaching and/or research posts at the Universities of Sussex, Oxford, and Stirling. His published work includes studies of situated, embodied, and dynamical systems approaches to cognition, representational explanation in scientific psychology, neo-Cartesian and neo-Heideggerian interpretations of cognitive science, the conceptual foundations of evolutionary psychology, philosophical issues in artificial life and evolutionary robotics, and the nature and plausibility of the idea that genes code for phenotypic traits. His first book, *Reconstructing the Cognitive World: The Next Step* is forthcoming with MIT Press.

John Ziman is Emeritus Professor of Physics of the University of Bristol and a Fellow of the Royal Society. He was brought up in New Zealand, studied at Oxford, and lectured at Cambridge, before becoming Professor of Theoretical Physics at Bristol in 1964. After taking voluntary early retirement from Bristol in 1982 he has worked unofficially, and written extensively, on various aspects of the social relations of science and technology. His latest book, *Real Science: What It Is and What It Means*, was published in 2000. Since 1994 he has been the Convenor of the Epistemology Group, which studies the evolution of knowledge and invention.

Preface

Ever since Darwin, scholars in different disciplines have noted that very diverse cultural entities, such as languages, laws, firms, theories, etc. seem to 'evolve' through sequences of variation, selection, and replication, in many ways just like living organisms. This analogy between cultural and biological change has frequently been remarked, but seldom explored and analysed in detail. Is it 'just a metaphor', or can modern evolutionary theory help us to understand the dynamics of a variety of different cultural domains—linguistic, legal, economic, and so on?

Most of the papers published here are revised versions of talks given at a discussion meeting on this specific theme, held on 14–15 April 1999 at the British Academy, in London. This meeting was organised by Margaret Boden and John Ziman, and was sponsored jointly by the British Academy and the Epistemology Group. This volume also contains contributions invited from other scholars interested in the same subject. These somewhat varied texts were collected, collated, and edited for publication by Michael Wheeler. We are grateful to the British Academy and to Oxford University Press for their ready assistance in getting this material into print.

This work forms part of a long-term programme on the Evolution of Knowledge and Invention, initiated in 1994 by the Epistemology Group with the generous support of the Renaissance Trust. In effect, it is a natural extension of the studies reported at length in *Technological Innovation as an Evolutionary Process* (John Ziman [ed.], Cambridge University Press: 2000). It will be obvious to the reader that the 'evolutionary paradigm of rationality' has a significant role to play throughout the human sciences. At the same time, it raises a variety of complex but related issues in every cultural context where it is applied. By fostering discussion between scholars from a wide range of research traditions, this volume should have a significant influence on the evolution of all of them.

M. W.
University of Dundee
J. Z.
University of Bristol
M. A. B.
University of Sussex

Introduction:
Selectionist Reasoning as a
Tool of Thought

JOHN ZIMAN

THE EVOLUTIONARY PARADIGM OF RATIONALITY

A NEW MODE OF METASCIENTIFIC reasoning is developing. The underlying rationale of Charles Darwin's explanation of the 'Origin of Species' is being applied to many other examples of historical change. The 'evolutionary paradigm of rationality' (Kantorovich 1993) can be summed up in the formula (Campbell 1977):

'BVSR' = Blind Variation + Selective Retention.

A *Darwinian* process operates by the repeated application of a mechanism for *selecting*, *retaining* (and typically *replicating*) a proportion of the entities in an existing population containing *variants* whose characteristics are typically 'random'—that is, not preordained to satisfy the criteria of selection.

Selectionist reasoning applies to the changing membership of a *population*, rather than to changes that might be occurring in any particular member of that population. In the typical limit of a large population, evolutionary change is always effectively continuous, although it may be very rapid over short periods. One of the striking features of a Darwinian process is that it is *adaptive*. Over a period of time it results in a population whose members are more 'fit'— that is better able to satisfy the criteria of selection. It thus explains the dynamical response of a population to changes in these criteria, for example through environmental change.

Evolutionary reasoning is essentially *naturalistic*, and not formally deductive. Its underlying metaphysics is *selectionism*, as distinct from, say, 'instructionism'. It is causative, but being dependent on a stochastic factor—the chance of a particular variant appearing at a significant moment of selection —it logically excludes strict determinism. It is thus capable of explaining historical processes retrospectively, but never of predicting their outcome.

BIO-ORGANIC EVOLUTION

The salient exemplar of a Darwinian process is, of course, the evolution of biological organisms by natural selection. Needless to say, *bio-organic evolution* has been studied in great detail, empirically and theoretically. Many of its characteristic features are very familiar in practice and reasonably well understood in principle. The whole subject is dominated by the immense scientific literature on topics such as speciation, adaptive fitness, heritability, recombination, lineages, taxonomies, etc.

As a consequence, accounts of Darwinian processes and phenomena in other systems, such as the history of ideas, are often presented in the language of bio-organic evolution, as if the resemblance were no more than an 'analogy' or 'metaphor'. The key factor in widening the field of application of evolutionary reasoning is the realisation (Campbell 1974) that this is a general mode of historical change, of which the evolution of biological organisms is only one example. Even within an individual organism, for example, the biochemical development of the immune system and the neuro-psychological development of the nervous system (Edelman 1992) are now understood to be essentially BVSR processes in their own right.

For this reason, it is important to recognise that not all the familiar features of bio-organic systems are absolutely essential to an evolutionary mechanism of change. It is now known, for example (Jablonka and Lamb 1995), that bio-organic evolution itself is not completely *Mendelian*, that is, involving long-lasting, quasi-atomic, almost perfectly replicable *genes*—'replicators'—assembled into distinctive genotypes that code for the variant phenotypes—'interactors'—on which natural selection actually operates (Dawkins 1976). Nor does it seem necessary to have a mechanism analogous to sexual recombination, or rules barring the recombination of traits from distant lineages—and so on.

The present-day *neo-Darwinian* theory of bio-organic evolution lays great stress on *Weismannian inheritance*—that is, that there is no correlation between the genetic mechanisms for producing variants and the criteria by which they are subsequently selected. It should be emphasised, however, that this extreme degree of 'blindness' is not obviously necessary. The non-existence of *Lamarckian* mechanisms, such as the 'inheritance of acquired characteristics', is an empirical fact of biology, not an essential evolutionary feature of such systems.

ARTIFICIAL LIFE

By its very nature, evolutionary reasoning is difficult to formulate and analyse by traditional mathematical methods. But the operation of simplified BVSR mechanisms can be *simulated computationally*. Rapidly growing interest in 'artificial life' (e.g. Levy 1992) has revealed the generality of many evolutionary phenomena, even in the space spanned by a 'genetic algorithm', or the grainy two-dimensional universe of a population of 'cellular automata'. It turns out, for example, that such systems do not always evolve smoothly, but exhibit the property of 'punctuated equilibrium'—that is, long periods of apparent *stasis* interrupted by short *revolutionary* episodes of very rapid change.

More general theoretical analysis of 'complex systems' of this type suggests that they are typically *self-organising*—that is, that new modes of order may emerge as they evolve. Paradoxically, this seems to occur when the system is actually approaching a state of *chaos*, where its properties change erratically and unpredictably (Kauffman 1993).

Complexity theory thus provides an abstract formal framework for evolutionary reasoning. A number of significant phenomena, for example, can be explained in terms of the search for optima on *fitness landscapes* in many dimensions (Wright 1932). These findings not only show that many familiar features of bio-organic evolution do not depend directly on the details of biological reproduction, ecological competition, etc. They also help to decouple evolutionary reasoning intellectually from its historical origins in evolutionary biology and molecular genetics.

THE EVOLUTION OF ARTEFACTS

Primitive human artefacts such as prehistoric stone tools undoubtedly 'evolve', in the sense that specimens from successive periods show progressive changes that are obviously analogous to the succession of organisms in the fossil record —for example in the lineage leading to the modern horse. It is natural to infer that this is due to a very similar mechanism. In effect, a relatively small, unintended variation in the shape or structure of a 'standard' artefact may give it a differential advantage in practical or symbolic use, and this variation is therefore copied in the manufacture of the next generation (Basalla 1988; Mokyr 1990); this theme is dealt with at length from various points of view in Ziman (2000b).

The history of material artefacts exhibits many typical 'evolutionary' phenomena, such as 'punctuated equilibrium', which can easily be interpreted on this basis. Moreover, evolutionary reasoning demystifies invention and innovation by emphasising the social criteria for selection in 'the marketplace' in addition to the individual creativity required to generate the succesful variant. This selectivity still favours 'progress', even when the variants on which it operates are very far from 'enlightened'.

The obvious objection is that novel artefacts are the product of human *design*. Craftworkers and inventors *learn* from experience and use their *imagination*. In effect, the evolution of artefacts would seem to be more 'Lamarckian' than 'Darwinian'. Hence, it is often argued, the analogy with bio-organic evolution is invalid.

In practice, however, individual inventors vary very widely in the experiences and concepts that go into their designs. Within the general requirements and practical constraints that limit the range of 'plausible' variants, the population of these is often highly diversified. More significantly, the 'fitness' of even the most carefully designed artefact is never precisely predictable and only becomes apparent in use. Thus, although never produced completely 'blindly', technological artefacts satisfy the basic operating condition for the BVSR mechanism. Indeed, evolutionary change may be facilitated by prior rejection of obviously unfit variants, such as ones that are generally known to have been faulty in the past.

SCIENTIFIC AND TECHNOSCIENTIFIC EVOLUTION

The application of evolutionary reasoning to the history of science itself dates back almost to the time of Darwin. It is often argued (e.g. Toulmin 1972; Campbell 1974) that scientific change is a typical BVSR process, where a great variety of theories (conjectures!) are proposed, but only a few survive systematic experimental testing (refutation!), and are retained as the basis for the next cycle.

The philosophical implications of this line of argument are well known (Popper 1963 [1968], 1972). But to develop them naturalistically, they need to be coupled with the co-evolution of *epistemic institutions* (Hull 1988; Restivo 1994). Opinions differ, for example, as to whether selection operates on the theories directly, or on the scientists who advocate them, or on the research groups where they originated. Nevertheless, a systematic analysis suggests that science as a whole can be treated as a complex, *self-organising system* (Hooker 1995) incorporating many selectionist processes (Ziman 2000a).

Technological sciences such as engineering evolve along similar lines (Vincenti 1990). These produce material artefacts, which are caught up in evolutionary cycles through market selection. They are also closely linked with economic entities, such as companies, which evolve in their own dimension (Nelson and Winter 1982). *Technological innovation* is also largely the result of technoscientific research and development, where much of the action involves learning by trial and error, the testing of design concepts, and other processes governed by evolutionary reasoning (Ziman 2000b).

CULTURAL EVOLUTION

By definition, human artefacts and scientific theories are *cultural* entities. Cultural practices and social institutions are involved in their production and use. These, in turn, must change as it evolves—that is, they must *co-evolve* with it. Indeed, material artefacts are the most tangible, and scientific theories the most intangible, of the many types of cultural entity to which evolutionary reasoning is applicable. There is a long history, for example, of more or less Darwinian explanations of the evolution of natural languages (Pinker 1994). Systems of common law evolve by the selective citing of precedents. Evolutionary economics (Saviotti 1996) helps to explain change and innovation in the structures and practices of economic institutions. Patterns of social behaviour seem to change in the same way (Boyd and Richerson 1985). And so on.

However, as the other chapters in this volume show, the situation is not nearly as simple as this argument would suggest. In each cultural domain, there are particular circumstances that complicate the direct use of evolutionary reasoning to explain cultural change. There are also some general objections which need to be faced from the start.

In essence, there are obvious defects in the putative parallel between cultural and bio-organic systems. The former involve strong intentional factors, operating through memory and imagination, which are rigorously excluded from the latter. Bio-organic systems have no means comparable with writing for the exosomatic storage and subsequent revival of genotypes or phenotypes. As in the evolution of artefacts, cultural change in general is not only far from 'blind' in the Weissmanian sense: it also often involves the recombination of features drawn from several distinct traditions—as one might say, the hybridisation of organisms from 'lineages' as distant as an octopus from a giraffe, or even as an extinct dinosaur from a modern whale.

Nevertheless, it can be argued that these differences in the prior rationality and scope of 'variation' do not affect the basic BVSR mechanism of change. The most serious objection to the application of general evolutionary reasoning to cultural change is the difficulty of defining entities analogous to genes. It is often suggested (Dawkins 1976) that ideas, concepts, patterns of behaviour, etc. can be analysed into *memes*—that is, discrete elements that can exist relatively unchanged for relatively long periods, and can be replicated relatively accurately—for example, by communication from person to person.

Indeed, much is written about cultural and intellectual change in the language of memes (Csikszentmihaly 1993; Munz 1993). But are memes essential to evolutionary reasoning? It is certainly convenient and instructive to describe the emergence, survival, diffusion, and mutation of ideas in terms of such entities. It is quite obvious, however, that a meme is unlike the neo-Darwinian notion of a gene—that is, a coded stretch of DNA—in that it is an arbitrary construct that cannot be abstracted from the specific context in which it is defined. The real question is not whether memes can somehow be characterised less vaguely but whether evolutionary reasoning absolutely needs them as operational entities. In effect, it is not clear that cultural evolution has to be basically 'Mendelian'. It could just as well be 'Darwinian' and/or 'Lamarckian' as 'neo-Darwinian'.

EVOLUTIONARY EPISTEMOLOGY

A fully naturalistic approach would emphasise the continuity between the bio-organic and cultural domains. These overlap in *sociobiology*, where it is argued that human behaviour, including mental faculties and language, has biological correlates, with which it co-evolved (Barkow *et al.* 1992; Plotkin 1994). That is to say, the cognitive and perceptive capabilities of the human brain were shaped bio-organically over millions of years by selection and adaptation to social existence—and vice versa. Evolutionary reasoning is thus basic to an understanding of *epistemology*.

Indeed, this idea can be carried back to the origins of life itself. An evolving organism that is adapting to its environment is, so to speak, acquiring 'knowledge' that is incorporated in its genome and biological structure—for example, its sensory organs and its memory. Culture and science are merely continuations of this process by other means. This leads naturally to Kantian ideas about space and time. Taken to a metaphysical extreme, *evolutionary epistemology* (Lorenz 1973 [1977]; Campbell 1974; Munz 1993; Dennett 1995) would make the whole of the natural world and of human existence subject to 'universal Darwinism'.

EVOLUTIONARY REASONING AS A TOOL OF THOUGHT

For the present work, a slightly more modest claim will suffice. The notion of evolutionary reasoning as a 'paradigm of rationality' (Kantorovich 1993) presents it simply as a 'tool of thought'. Like a formalism such as the calculus, or a thema (Holton 1973) such as a field of force, it is an abstract algorithm defined by certain general conditions. Its terms are initially unspecified, but can be identified hypothetically by the 'thinker' with designated real-world entities supposed to satisfy those conditions. Thereupon, so the 'thinker' can reasonably argue, the intrinsic dynamics of the system may be expected to produce consequences of a certain kind.

As with logic itself, the force of such an argument depends on how well the necessary conditions are actually met. Evolutionary reasoning as such has no epistemological or ontological significance. Thus, the fact that it may help scholars and others to understand certain historical processes involving certain types of cultural entity does not automatically mean that this aspect of the world is somehow 'intrinsically biological' (Riedl 1984), 'irrational', 'subject to chance rather than necessity' (Monod 1970 [1972]), or even 'spiritually compelling' (Midgley 1992). Pragmatically, evolutionary reasoning is sometimes remarkably powerful: sometimes, of course, it is just the wrong tool for the job. Let's see!

REFERENCES

Barkow, J. H., Cosmides, L., and Tooby, J., eds (1992), *The Adapted Mind: Evolutionary Psychology and the Generation of Culture*. New York, NY: Oxford University Press.

Basalla, G. (1988), *The Evolution of Technology*. Cambridge: Cambridge University Press.

Boyd, R. and Richerson, P. J. (1985), *Culture and the Evolutionary Process*. Chicago, IL: University of Chicago Press.

Campbell, D. T. (1974), 'Evolutionary Epistemology', in *The Philosophy of Karl Popper*, edited by P. A. Schilpp. La Salle, IL: Open Court, pp. 413–63.

Campbell, D. T. (1977), 'Descriptive Epistemology: Psychological, Sociological, Evolutionary', Unpublished Draft of William James Lectures, Harvard.

Csikszentmihaly, M. (1993), *The Evolving Self: A Psychology for the Third Millennium*. New York, NY: Harper Collins.

Dawkins, R. (1976), *The Selfish Gene*. Oxford: Oxford University Press.

Dennett, D. C. (1995), *Darwin's Dangerous Idea*. London: Penguin.

Edelman, G. M. (1992), *Bright Air, Brilliant Fire: On the Matter of the Mind*. London: Penguin.

Holton, G. (1973), *Thematic Origins of Scientific Thought*. Cambridge, MA: Harvard University Press.

Hooker, C. A. (1995), *Reason, Regulation and Realism: Towards a Regulatory Systems Theory of Reason and Evolutionary Epistemology*. Albany, NY: SUNY Press.

Hull, D. L. (1988), *Science as a Process: An Evolutionary Account of the Social and Conceptual Development of Science*. Chicago, IL: University of Chicago Press.

Jablonka, E. and Lamb, M. J. (1995), *Epigenetic Inheritance and Evolution: The Lamarckian Dimension*. Oxford: Oxford University Press.

Kantorovich, A. (1993), *Scientific Discovery: Logic and Tinkering*. Albany, NY: SUNY Press.

Kauffman, S. A. (1993), *The Origins of Order: Self-Organization and Selection in Evolution*. Oxford: Oxford University Press.

Levy, S. (1992), *Artificial Life: The Quest for a New Creation*. London: Penguin.

Lorenz, K. (1973 [1977]), *Die Ruckseite des Spiegels: Versuch einer Naturgeschichte menschlichen Erkennis*, English translation. New York, NY: Harcourt-Brace.

Midgley, M. (1992), *Science as Salvation*. London: Routledge.

Mokyr, J. (1990), *The Lever of Riches*. New York, NY: Oxford University Press.

Monod, J. (1970 [1972]), *Chance and Necessity*, English translation. London: Collins.

Munz, P. (1993), *Philosophical Darwinism: On the Origin of Knowledge by Means of Natural Selection*. London: Routledge.

Nelson, R. R. and Winter, S. (1982), *An Evolutionary Theory of Economic Change*. Cambridge, MA: Belknap.

Pinker, S. (1994), *The Language Instinct*. London: Penguin.

Plotkin, H. C. (1994), *The Nature of Knowledge: Concerning Adaptations, Instinct and the Evolution of Intelligence*. Harmondsworth: Penguin.

Popper, K. R. (1963 [1968]), *Conjectures and Refutations: The Growth of Scientific Knowledge*, 3rd edn. New York, NY: Harper Torchbooks.

Popper, K. R. (1972), *Objective Knowledge: An Evolutionary Approach*. Oxford: Oxford University Press.

Restivo, S. (1994), *Science, Society and Values: Towards a Sociology of Objectivity*. Bethlehem, PA: Lehigh University Press.

Riedl, R. (1984), *Biology of Knowledge: The Evolutionary Basis of Reason*, translated by Paul Foulkes, 3rd edn. Chichester: Wiley.

Saviotti, P. P. (1996), *Technological Evolution, Variety and the Economy*. Cheltenham: Edward Elgar.

Toulmin, S. (1972), *Human Understanding, Vol. 1*. Oxford: Oxford University Press.

Vincenti, W. G. (1990), *What Engineers Know and How They Know It: Analytical Studies from Aeronautical History*. Baltimore, MD: Johns Hopkins University Press.

Wright, S. (1932), 'The Roles of Mutation, Inbreeding, Crossbreeding and Selection in Evolution', paper read at Sixth International Congress of Genetics, Vol. 1, pp. 356–66.

Ziman, J. M. (2000a), *Real Science: What It Is and What It Means*. Cambridge: Cambridge University Press.

Ziman, J. M., ed. (2000b), *Technological Innovation as an Evolutionary Process*. Cambridge: Cambridge University Press.

Heritable Variation and Competitive Selection as the Mechanism of Sociocultural Evolution

W. G. RUNCIMAN

I

THE APPLICATION TO HUMAN BEHAVIOUR of Darwin's fundamental insight about what he called 'descent with modification' goes back, as is well known, to Darwin himself, and in particular to the *Descent of Man* rather than the *Origin of Species*. Given how much Darwin didn't and couldn't know about population genetics, molecular biology, primate ethology, game theory, and developmental and cognitive psychology, his prescience is all the more remarkable. Not only does Part I of the *Descent*, which deals with the derivation of the 'so-called moral sense' from the 'social instincts', anticipate much of the extensive recent literature on the evolution of reciprocal altruism, but Parts II and III, which deal with sexual selection and female mate choice, open up a related topic whose importance, despite the attention given to it by R. A. Fisher (1930), has come to be fully recognised only in the last two decades of the century (Dawkins 1986: ch. 8; Miller 2000: ch. 2). But in taking Darwin's insight forward with the benefit of the advances in the relevant disciplines which have taken place since his lifetime, we must distinguish the direct application of the theory of natural selection to areas of human behaviour previously assumed to be beyond its scope from the application of the paradigm of heritable variation and competitive selection to other processes of change of which sociocultural evolution is one—or, as I shall argue, cultural and social evolution are two. Donald Campbell was perhaps the first behavioural scientist to appreciate what follows from the recognition that, as he put it in discussing Popper's philosophy of science, the natural selection paradigm can be seen as 'the universal nonteleological explanation of teleological achievements' (1974: 420)—which is why Daniel C. Dennett can plausibly credit Darwin, as he does, with 'the best single idea anyone has ever had' (1995: 21).

It follows that there are both analogies and disanalogies between biological and sociocultural evolution, but that the analogies are more significant than

Proceedings of the British Academy, **112**, 9–25, © The British Academy 2002.

the disanalogies. We are by now well used to the idea that genes can be defined in terms of 'any hereditary information for which there is favourable or unfavourable selection bias' (Williams 1966: 23), and once instructions affecting phenotype are transmitted not only from organism to organism by direct biological inheritance of sequences encoded in strings of DNA, but also from one organism's mind to another's by exosomatic imitation and learning, units of cultural selection can be defined, and their transmission modelled, in similar terms to the units of natural selection. The differences between the two processes are obvious enough. In cultural selection, the bundles of instructions can jump across lineages in a way that they cannot in natural selection; their mutations arise less from random copying error than from active reinterpretation by the receiving mind; and they can be accepted, rejected, and reaccepted over the course of the lives of the organisms whose minds are their carriers. But these differences mean no more than that heritable variation and competitive selection of information affecting phenotype can work in different ways. Mutations in heritable units of cultural selection which are replicated, diffused, and further replicated in adjacent or successive populations succeed or fail, as mutations in the units of natural selection do, according to whether or not their probability of further replication is enhanced or diminished by their environment. What is more, sociocultural, like biological, evolution is a path-dependent, non-linear process, and cultural systems, defined as complexes of extended phenotypic effects of units of cultural selection transmitted by imitation and learning, have the formal capacity for self-organisation which they share with biological systems. The wide, but neither limitless nor random, diversity of cultures and societies in the archaeological, ethnographic, and historical record is the product of an evolutionary sequence in which, under specifiable antecedent conditions, certain mutations were fit and hence selected where others were not.

That general proposition, so stated, leaves open the question how far socio-cultural selection is reducible to natural selection. But the answer to it can be left to be decided by the course of future research. We can, for example, say with confidence that Darwin was right not only about the importance of sexual selection but about the uniformity across cultures of the facial expression of the emotions (Ekman 1973, 1998), and the contributions which behavioural ecology (Smith and Winterhalder 1992), behaviour genetics (Plomin *et al.* 1997), and evolutionary psychology (Crawford and Krebs 1998) can make to the understanding of human behaviour are there for all to read. It will always be possible that natural selection turns out to be able to explain patterns of human behaviour conventionally assumed to be irreducibly cultural better than cultural anthropologists have been willing to concede. But a comprehensively reductionist programme is another matter altogether. Its implausibility becomes apparent as soon as we move away from such topics as adoption

(Silk 1980), polygyny (Betzig 1992), bridewealth (Borgerhoff Mulder 1987), dispersal (Clarke and Low 1992), or homicide (Daly and Wilson 1988) in the direction of the standard agenda of comparative and historical sociology: the rise of states and nations, the spread of the major world religions, the displacement of feudalism by capitalism, the relative prevalence of monarchic, oligarchic, and democratic forms of government, the diversity of both civil and criminal law-codes, urbanisation, bureaucracy, military participation ratios, and so on. When E. O. Wilson visited Cambridge in 1982, I took the opportunity to ask him what he thought his ideas could contribute to the solution of the problem of the origins of the Greek *polis* on which I had been working at that time (Runciman 1982). His answer was as brief as it was candid: 'Nothing.'

Wilson's position continues to be that genes 'hold culture on a leash' (1978: 167) and that 'hereditarians' are those who believe, on empirical grounds, that 'the leash is short, causing cultures to evolve major features in common' (1998: 157). But the metaphor of a 'leash' is unhelpful, if not positively misleading. There are numerous constraints imposed by biology, as by chemistry and physics, on the possible range of sociocultural variation, and it is obvious that any set of norms or form of social organisation which is sufficiently inimical to reproductive fitness will be self-extinguishing: if the Shakers could convince the whole population of the world not to procreate, there would soon be nobody left. But the speed of sociocultural evolution is so much greater, and the behavioural differences between populations which it generates are so wide, that no hypothesis grounded directly in the theory of natural selection can hope to provide the explanations that are called for in comparative and historical sociology. Wilson is quite right to point out that cultures evolve major features in common as well as major differences. But the explanation of these major features in common lies in convergent cultural evolution, not reductionist sociobiology. Once Wilson has conceded that 'to a degree that may prove discomfiting to a diehard hereditarian, cultures have dispersed widely in their evolution under the epigenetic rules so far studied' (1998: 174), he has effectively undermined his own case.

Ironically, the view that a Darwinian theory of human social behaviour must be reductively sociobiological if it is Darwinian at all is shared by the numerous anthropologists, sociologists, and philosophers on the other flank for whom the distinctive mental capacities of the human species remove human beings altogether from the workings of heritable variation and competitive selection. Their often-repeated argument is that our ability freely to choose between alternative courses of action means that our conscious purposes in themselves furnish the explanation of our behaviour. But Darwin himself was, in his own words, 'very far from wishing to deny that instinctive actions may lose their fixed and untaught character, and be replaced by others performed with the aid of the free will' (1883: 66). Nobody disputes that human beings do have conscious purposes and that they do make deliberate choices. But to ascertain what these purposes and choices are explains neither why they are what they are nor what consequences follow for the patterns of behaviour in which they are acted out. Behavioural strategies are bundles of instructions affecting phenotype which are replicated and diffused to the extent that they are fit and hence selected, and this holds no less where they are culturally transmitted, whether horizontally to an adjacent population or vertically to a succeeding one, than where they are transmitted genetically from parents to offspring.

It is, accordingly, little more than a truism to say that the diversity of human cultures is the outcome of a process of heritable variation and competitive selection of instructions affecting phenotype which have been transmitted from one person's mind to another's by imitation and learning. The difficulty is to understand the sources of mutation and the mechanisms of coding and transmission as well in cultural as we do in natural selection. Several of the issues involved are, as they are bound to be, controversial, and they have not been made any less so by the readiness of some, and reluctance of other, researchers to adopt the term 'meme' for the units of cultural selection and to accord to 'memetics' the status of a distinctive science (Blackmore 1999). Many of those who dislike 'memes' do so because of the apparent implication that the analogy with genes is closer than in fact it is. But the idea which the word encapsulates was already formulated in other terms before it was coined by Richard Dawkins (1976: 206). The anthropologist F. T. Cloak phrased it in terms of a distinction between what he called 'i-culture', by which he meant the set of cultural instructions carried in the minds of a human population, and 'm-culture', by which he meant the material structures and relationships between them brought about and maintained by the 'i-culture'. These terms have not been taken up by anthropologists and psychologists in the way that 'meme' has, but they accurately reflect the two most important implications, in this context, of Darwin's fundamental insight: first, that selective environmental pressure acts on heritable units of information through their extended phenotypic effects; and second, that (in Cloak's own words):

> the survival value of a cultural instruction is the same as its function; it is its value for the survival/replication of itself or its replica(s), irrespective of its value for the survival/replication of the organism which carries it or of the organism's conspecifics. (1975: 168)

This way of putting it not only avoids the implications which antagonise those who dislike the term 'meme', but also directs attention to the need to establish precisely where bundles of instructions affecting phenotype are encoded. This, indeed, may be one of the reasons for which archaeologists, like historians of technology, are readier than anthropologists not only to apply the neo-Darwinian paradigm to the explanation of cultural change but to explore the potentialities and limitations of the notion of 'memes' in the course of doing so (Lake 1998). It is not surprising to find an archaeologist saying 'I have found that a basic evolutionary view of cultural development as "descent with modification" is indispensable when analysing prehistoric cultural sequences' (Spencer 1990: 4) in the way that it would be to find a cultural anthropologist saying the same. By now, the literature in which it is taken for granted that cultural change can be modelled as an evolutionary process (Boyd and Richerson 1985) has expanded to the point that it is no longer a question of whether heritable variation and competitive selection are at work, but only how. To cite one striking recent example: Walter Burkert, the leading classical authority on Greek religion, in discussing what he calls the 'tracks' of biology in early religion generally, concludes that, although sociobiology may account for some widely observed forms of apotropaic and other ritual behaviour, 'Through copying and exchange, programs and information have become largely independent from the hardware and from the accidents of individual death. Information survival asserts itself side by side with and even instead of genetic survival' (1996: 24).

Once 'memes' are tacitly recognised in this way, it follows that cultural and natural selection are different evolutionary forces which are, however, acting simultaneously on the human populations studied by comparative and historical sociologists. It may well be difficult to find evidence that will enable the relative influence of each to be estimated precisely. But if, to remain with the example of religion, Christian Europe appears to contradict the sociobiological hypothesis of intensive polygyny by high-ranking males such as is found in Chinese, Islamic, Indian, and New World societies, it does not follow that there is no biologically inherited disposition in the human species so to act as to enhance the probability of replication of the agent's genes. The implication is rather that, in the particular environment of Christian Europe, memes enjoining monogamy and discouraging concubinage were culturally selected in a way that they were not elsewhere (MacDonald 1995). Much of the literature on 'gene–culture co-evolution' is addressed to patterns of cultural behaviour which seem directly inimical to reproductive fitness. But the relation between genes and memes is complex and variable: memes can act on natural selection at the same time as genes are acting on cultural selection. There is no law-like generalisation which holds across the board, even if cultural, like biological, systems exhibit formally law-like patterns in the relations between their dynamically interacting parts.

II

It is at this point, however, that the notion of 'sociocultural' evolution needs to be unpacked into two. There is, as Donald E. Brown points out (1991: 40), a persistent tendency among anthropologists not only to contrast 'cultural' and 'social' jointly with 'biological' but to use 'a culture' and 'a society' as synonyms. Nor is an insistence on retaining 'sociocultural' as a single compound term confined to anthropologists (e.g. Stuart-Fox 1999). Even Campbell does so. But behaviour-patterns acquired by imitation and learning have to be distinguished from behaviour-patterns imposed by institutional rules. This is not to say that 'social' behaviour is produced only by the direct application of coercion (although it may be), but that it is governed by rules that define the agents' roles independently of their discretion. Writers on 'gene–culture co-evolution' are, of course, perfectly well aware of institutional relations of power between the incumbents of the different roles of which societies are constituted. But they treat them as environmental constraints on cultural evolution rather than as outcomes of a separate evolutionary process. Thus, William H. Durham both argues for the recognition and analysis of 'power relations and conflicts of interest' and allows for ' "selection by imposition" or simply "imposition" ', by which he means 'the preservation of allomemes by compliance with the decisions of others' (1991: 176, 198). He also (1991: 463) charges Boyd and Richerson (1985: 9) with failing to include imposition in their list of 'conceivable processes that can change culture through time'. But he gives no hint that in the process of imposition heritable variation and competitive selection might be acting at another level on units of selection other than genes and memes.

Why not? Once institutions like markets, armies, and churches have evolved out of the informal interpersonal relationships that preceded them, social behaviour is no longer a matter only of innate instincts which are supplemented, guided, or overridden by imitation and learning. Hereditary information affecting phenotype is now encoded also in rule-governed practices which define the society's roles, and carried by pairs of interacting roles whose incumbents acknowledge their reciprocal influence on one another. To borrow the terms which James S. Coleman uses in talking about authority relationships, social, as opposed to cultural, behaviour-patterns involve 'an acting unit consisting of two individuals in place of two separate and independent units' (1990: 145). The rules that govern the practices can be coded, stored, and transmitted in a wide variety of ways (framing and re-enactment of laws, negotiation and renewal of labour contracts, publication and promulgation of religious commandments, and so on). But the carriers of the practices are not the individuals, or even the pairs of individuals, whose behaviour is the phenotypic effect of the rules but the roles which the pairs of individuals occupy and

perform. Practices need not become extinct when roles are temporarily unoc-
cupied, and the same person can occupy a number of different roles. We are no
longer in a world only of cultural socialisation where individuals conform (or
not) to instructions received from parents, teachers, peer-group members, or
role-models, but a world of, in addition, institutionally sanctioned instructions
which have to be obeyed by the role-incumbents, if they are to remain in their
roles, whatever the beliefs, norms, and values they have acquired by imitation
and learning and bring to their individual performances of them.

Accordingly, a comparative and historical sociologist seeking to explain
how human societies of different kinds come to be as they are is confronted
with the workings of heritable variation and competitive selection on three
levels. Whatever the social behaviour-pattern which is the chosen explanan-
dum, it is an evolutionary product at once of natural selection (hence,
responses evoked in accordance with biologically inherited capacities, dispositions, and susceptibilities), of cultural selection (hence, exosomatically
acquired beliefs and values and their behavioural outcomes in art, ritual, myth,
fashion, and so on), and of social selection (hence, practices imposed on the
incumbents of the political, economic, and ideological roles which carry them).
A sociologist of warfare, for example, is simultaneously observing the evoked
behaviour of young adult males genetically predisposed to initiate and respond
to violence, the acquired behaviour of members of cultures in which lethal
violence on behalf of the group is legitimated and martial skills accorded prestige, and the imposed behaviour of recruits into military roles in which they are
subjected to institutional sanctions against disobedience or desertion.

In any application of neo-Darwinian evolutionary theory, explanation
involves both a narrative of particular causes and effects and a general causal
account of the mechanism by which heritable variation and competitive selection combine to produce the particular outcome observed. The narrative is, by
definition, a narrative of adaptation to the environment from which selective
pressure has been brought to bear. But it is as important in the study of sociocultural as of biological evolution to be clear what this means. It may seem
natural, as it did to Darwin himself and others since, to think initially of adaptations in terms of benefits to the individual organisms whose behaviour is
being studied. But the adaptations which drive the evolutionary process are
benefits to the units of selection, and these benefits are defined by reference to
a relative increase in the probability of their replication brought about by functional changes in their carriers. For differential replication to arise, their carriers must be able to transmit them in the first place, and they will be better able
to do so to the extent that their inherited attributes, whether keen eyes, good
ideas, efficient routines, or anything else, are so designed as to help them obtain
resources, defend themselves against predators, form alliances with con-
specifics, and secure access to prospective mates. To that extent, successful

replication by the unit of selection depends on competitive advantage to the carrier and a 'highly non-random co-ordination between recurring properties of the phenotype and the recurring structure of the ancestral environment' (Tooby and Cosmides 1996: 123). But the criterion of success is always reproduction, not (or not merely) survival. The more daring antelopes are on average more likely—even though putting themselves at unnecessary risk— to escape the cheetahs and thereby pass on their genes; the more eloquent preachers are on average more likely to make converts and thereby pass on— even, or particularly, from the gallows or the stake—the memes encoded in their sermons and prophecies; the more formidable warriors —whose casualty rates may therefore be highest—are on average more likely to win their battles and thereby impose on their defeated enemies the practices defining the roles constitutive of their own political systems. It is always a matter of benefits relative to costs. There are cultural and social, as well as biological, parasites; reproduction, whether of genes, memes, or practices, can be at the direct expense of the carrier's relative efficiency; and optimisation of design is never more than a matter of limited and temporary competitive advantage.

Similarly, it is important to be clear about what it means to say that units of selection are, or can be, selected at the level of groups rather than of individuals. In natural selection, the once fashionable idea that altruistic behaviour could be explained by its contribution to the 'greater good' of the collectivity was effectively discredited by the demonstration that a population of altruists is always vulnerable to invasion by free-riders (Cronin 1991: ch. 12). But under some conditions, it is empirically possible for groups rather than individuals to be the carriers who, by outperforming the groups with which they are in competition, enhance the probability of replication of some genes, memes, or practices relative to others. Darwin explicitly recognised that a group (or 'tribe') with a higher proportion of 'sympathetic' (i.e. reciprocally altruistic) members 'would be victorious over most other tribes' (1883: 132), and there are strong grounds for expecting to find group selection more often in cultural than in biological evolution (Soltis *et al.* 1995; Sober and Wilson 1998: ch. 4). But already W. D. Hamilton, in discussing the Price equation for the increase in frequency of an altruistic allele in a global population under conditions where the covariance term reflecting the contribution of between-group selection outweighs the term reflecting within-group selection, conceded the possibility of modelling circumstances in which a positive group-selection term outweighs a negative individual-selection one; he merely warned that this possibility 'gives no guarantee that "altruism" can evolve by group selection: we have to consider whether the population can get into the specified state, and, if it can, whether its present state will continue' (1996: 333). In social evolution, there are still stronger grounds for expecting to find group selection at work. It is not just that practices involve reciprocal action by two or more role-incumbents: wage-labour, for example, requires both employers and employees (or, if you prefer, capitalists and proletarians). It is that where wage-labour comes to displace the practices and roles constitutive of other modes of production (Runciman 1995), it will be because collectivities such as farms, plantations, mines, ship-yards, building or transport firms, manufactories, and commercial enterprises which carry the practice and the roles defined by it take market share away from those which do not. But the broad empirical question is the same in every case: where and how does selective pressure come to bear on the phenotypic effects of the units of selection, whether biological, cultural, or social?

III

Since I have space for discussion of only one example even in outline, I have chosen the practice of venality as it was replicated and diffused in France between 1467, when the rules for the tenure of venal offices were set out in a royal decree, and 1789, when venality was formally abolished by the National Assembly—an abolition which, as so often in social evolution, did not in fact make the practice entirely extinct. The choice is for three reasons: first, because venality is a clear case of replication through social rather than cultural selec-tion; second, because its continuing replication was persistently but unsuccess-fully resisted by opponents who were both numerous and influential; and, third, because the evidence for its replication is authoritatively set out in a recent volume, on which I have relied for what follows, by a leading British historian of France (Doyle 1996).

The narrative sequence is clear and, so far as I am aware, uncontroversial, even if some of the quantitative evidence is uncertain. By the reign of Francis I, there were between 4,000 and 5,000 venal office-holders in either financial or judicial roles, and in 1522 the '*bureau des parties casuelles*' was set up under a venal treasurer to market existing offices, consider proposals for new ones, sell vacant ones, and collect fees on those changing hands. Shortly after, the 'forty-day rule' was introduced whereby offices whose incumbents died within forty days of passing them on reverted to the parts casual. The number of venal offices, including offices which involved the supervision of the holders of already existing offices, increased to the point that, by the accession of Louis XIII, there were something like 15,000 of them. In 1604, the '*paulette*' was introduced whereby exemption from the forty-day rule could be bought for an annual payment rather than a single capital sum. The Estates-General of 1614 protested against venality in vain: its token abolition in 1618 was purely tem-porary. Colbert, with the support of the young Louis XIV, succeeded in halting its growth and reducing the rise in the price of offices, but only briefly and to a limited extent. Later, in the 1770s, Maupeou resumed the attack as part of his assault on behalf of the crown against the *Parlements* but Terray then created more venal offices than Maupeou had suppressed. Necker in turn suppressed venal offices representing over 10 per cent of the estimated capital value of all of them, but most of them were restored after his resignation in 1780. By the time that the *ancien régime* was moving towards what was to be its terminal financial crisis, there were perhaps 70,000 venal offices occupied by roughly 1 per cent of adult French males, and of these over 4,000 ennobled their incumbents or their incumbents' heirs.

Venality 'seems agreed among specialists to have fulfilled the double function of raising much-needed money and providing a channel of upward social mobility for regional bourgeois and minor nobility' (Runciman 1989: 220), and to that extent might therefore seem explicable, despite all the hostility directed against it, by the 'greater good' of France. But the practice was maladaptive for the society that furnished the environment favourable to its replication. Offices which could be bought and sold were at the same time homologues of the free-holds in benefices, stewardships, commissions, or partnerships familiar from other societies and analogues of the alternative practices and roles by which governments in other societies raised their revenues in the form of taxes, tolls, duties, or tribute. But, by any measure of national efficiency, the practice of venality was bad for finance, bad for trade, bad for investment in productive assets, bad for competition, and bad for the level of competence with which the various venal roles were performed. The opponents of venality always had the better of the argument. As often happens in social evolution, a practice whose continuing replication is at first sight puzzling owed its success to a competitive advantage accruing to its carriers relative to other roles which the environment might have been expected to favour instead. Except in a few limited areas, including the navy, the bar, and the collection of direct taxes by government-appointed commissioners, institutions constituted by venal roles were unin-vadable, whatever the critics said or the policy-makers did, by alternative practices such as were relatively more favoured in other societies similar in many ways to France.

This is not to say that the mutations in the practice of venality from 1467 onwards were random with respect to adaptive value. But it was not 'directed' evolution in the sense that, for example, the Meiji reformers in Japan redesigned the institutions of their society in deliberate imitation of the more advanced capitalist economies, or even in the qualified sense that the competitive selection of heritable variants in technology (Ziman 2000: 5), or military tactics (Runciman 1998b: 15–16), or bureaucratic routines (Kracke 1953: 54), although the outcome of a deliberate process of trial and error, generates outcomes which were, and were bound to have been, unpredictable in advance. It was, rather, 'directed' in the sense that venalisation of existing roles or creation of new ones was actively promoted by agents like the private contractors known as *traitants* or *partisans* whose roles gave them a direct interest in doing so. Doyle aptly says of the system that it 'spawned lesser financial offices at every level' (1996: 10). Not every new venal role survived, any more than does every organism carrying a mutant gene or every mind carrying a mutant meme. But in the institutional environment of France's modes of production, persuasion, and coercion, venality furnishes a classic example of a practice whose extended phenotypic effects favoured its continuing replication and diffusion, despite all the opposition which it aroused and all the disadvantages which its opponents deplored.

Nor did individual incumbents of all the many venal roles necessarily benefit from being the carriers of the practice of venality, any more than all individual peacocks benefit from carrying the genes which give them their exaggerated tails or all individual cultivators on the island of Ponapae benefit from carrying the memes which cause them to grow enormous yams of limited nutritional value (Boyd and Richerson 1985: 269–70, citing Bascom 1948; cf. Bliege Bird and Bird 1997: 69, n. 8). 'Runaway' effects are observable in cultural and social as well as biological evolution, and their explanation is the same: the mutant unit of selection has a higher probability of replication despite the loss of competitive advantage to the carrier because selection for the phenotypic effect is reinforced by a frequency-dependent or conformist preference for it. In the case of venality in pre-Revolutionary France, the status attaching to the incumbency of a purchased office, even if its net pecuniary rewards were less than incumbency of alternative roles defined by different practices, made it an object of emulation in the same way as the Ponapaeans' huge but relatively un-nutritious yams. Some venal offices, particularly the higher receiverships or treasurerships, could be very lucrative. But many were not. There was often an element of conspicuous consumption in the purchase of office, not in the sense of flagrant exhibitionism so much as the signalling of a capacity and willingness to behave in a way that imposes costs which the signaller is, by implication, able to afford (Zahavi and Zahavi 1997). In an environment where this strategy turned out to be mistaken—because, as it might have been, the government was able to raise revenue more effectively through the appointed *intendants* who were often at odds with the venal office-holders—the practice of buying and selling offices might have been driven to extinction. But, as one of Louis XIV's comptrollers-general was alleged to have said, no sooner did the king create offices than God created fools to buy them. The story may be apocryphal, but it catches a significant aspect of the process whereby the probability of replication and diffusion of the practice of venality was enhanced, and its heritable variants selectively favoured, even when no more adaptive for its individual carriers than for their society as a whole.

At this point, I might fairly be asked whether, despite my claiming venality as a clear case of social rather than cultural selection, I am not after all reintroducing culture into the explanation of its success — to which the answer is yes, I am. Cultural selection is still at work in any and all human societies, just as natural selection is, and just as there is a substantial literature on 'gene–culture co-evolution' so could there be on 'meme–society co-evolution'. In French society during this period, status was culturally defined by reference to an ideology of hereditary monarchy underwritten by the Catholic Church, and memes enjoining deference to superiors were transmitted down successive populations by priests and confessors as well as parents and teachers. It is true that in the decades before 1789 there was an increasing diffusion of critical and secular doctrines among French intellectuals and their readers. But, as Doyle has pointed out elsewhere, before 1789 'Hardly anybody, and certainly not the *philosophes*, dreamed of revolution, or even would have understood the idea' (1980: 84). There was thus positive feedback between the units of cultural and social selection: the cultural environment was favourable to the replication of the practice of venality and the social environment was favourable to the replication of the meme enjoining deference to social superiors. Discontent with the workings of the system did not undermine the value attached to the wearing of the coveted red robe, a seat on the *fleur-de-lys*-covered benches of the sovereign courts, the possession of an honorific title, and association on terms of equality with fellow-members of a privileged estate. And when venality was abolished by the National Assembly on the night of 4 August 1789, it was by an unplanned and unforeseen disavowal of privileges now suddenly viewed as illegitimate by a group most of whose members owed their position in French society to the very practice which they denounced. Whatever the selective pressures in the institutional environment that had sustained it in the past, its abolition was, you might say, cultural selection with a vengeance.

It is worth remarking how this account differs from the account given from within the Marxist paradigm, which dominated French historiography for many decades. In the Marxist paradigm, the Revolution was seen as the achievement of an ascendant *bourgeoisie* which, as Marxist theory predicts, replaced a previously dominant feudal nobility. There is, it could be said, an implicit appeal to group selection in the Marxist theory: the successive pairs of classes which are the protagonists of social evolution are the competitors for control of the means of production, and, as is well known, Marx himself saw Darwin's theory of natural selection as furnishing a natural-scientific grounding for his theory of class struggle. But the Marxist theory fails on four counts. First, it is teleological in precisely the way that Darwinian theory is not: it presupposes an inescapable dialectic in which successive winners and losers are preordained. Second, it denies autonomous influence to the practices and roles constitutive of societies' modes of persuasion and coercion as well as production. Third, it directs attention away from the mutation and replication of practices which define 'bourgeois' and other roles in favour of class membership as of itself the determinant of the phenotypic behaviour of individual role-incumbents. Fourth, it makes no allowance for the possibility that the carriers of successfully replicating practices may not be members of antagonistic classes, like lord and serf or bourgeois and proletarian, but, like the venal office-holders, members of different economic classes who nonetheless share a common relationship to the incumbents of the political roles from which their own roles derive. It is true that this relationship involves a zero-sum conflict between governments and office-holders over the value of the perquisites of the offices relative to the monies paid to acquire them. But to explain the continuing replication and diffusion of venality, the specific selective pressures in the environment acting on its phenotypic effects have to be identified; and, whatever the answer may be, it will be a great deal more complex than is allowed for in Marxist theory.

A precise and detailed explanation of the origin, replication, diffusion, and eventual extinction of the practices which define the roles constitutive of the central institutions of a society is always difficult and sometimes impossibly so. In the absence of the quasi-experimental contrasts which the ethnographic and historical record so seldom provides, any proffered account risks being dismissed as a 'just-so story' which fits the evidence as well, but no better, than other alternatives. But *a* just-so story has to be the right one. Practices, like memes, are replicated if and only if their replication is favoured by their environment relative to the other bundles of instructions affecting phenotype, whether biological, cultural, or social, and the mechanism of their transmission, the medium in which their rules are encoded, the mutations in them which are successfully replicated in turn, and their rate of diffusion within the relevant population are all matters to be empirically ascertained. In the case of venality, there is more to be said than I have touched on in this chapter, or even than is covered by Doyle, including the evidence from other societies where offices were available for purchase. But a plausible selectionist hypothesis, even if it cannot be conclusively tested, is worth any amount of ostensibly a-theoretical narrative about the ideas, aims, choices, and decisions of the successive individual agents who bought, sold, created, bequeathed, brokered, inherited, modified, advertised, combined, leased, abandoned, or abolished one or more venal offices.

IV

It goes without saying that there are many questions of other kinds that can be asked about the workings of any society's constitutive roles and institutions. But if the question being asked is 'How do its institutions come to be of the kind that they are?', and if teleological explanations, whether historical-materialist, social-Darwinian, or any other sort, are no longer acceptable, then it must be right to follow up Campbell's remark and to see what can be gained from the application to both cultural and social evolution of the paradigm for non-teleological explanation of teleological effects which the theory of natural selection provides. That there is a Darwinian paradigm-shift under way across the behavioural sciences can hardly be in doubt. It may not be surprising that anthropologists and sociologists should be more resistant to it than archaeologists or linguists or game theorists or psychologists or even economists (Nelson and Winter 1982), but it would be surprising to see the resistance of anthropologists and sociologists protracted indefinitely in the face of the output of relevant findings within these more specialised disciplines which the paradigm is steadily generating.

Moreover, there are selectionists *avant la lettre* to be found in the literature of anthropology and sociology, however surprised they might be to be described as such. Sober and Wilson cite Raymond Kelly's analysis of the dominance of the Dinka by the Nuer (Kelly 1985) as a 'smoking gun of group selection in action' (Sober and Wilson 1998: 191) to be placed on a par with the detailed analysis now available of natural selection in action on Darwin's finches (Grant 1986), and I have elsewhere cited Nisbett and Cohen's analysis of the persistence of a distinctive 'culture of honour', and consequent disposition to interpersonal violence, in the American South (Nisbett and Cohen 1996) as an 'unequivocally selectionist explanation' (Runciman 1998a: 182) in which the replication of instructions affecting phenotype is linked to specific features of the ancestral environment and rival hypotheses are shown to fit the evidence much less well. More recently, I have argued that Weber's famous thesis about the part played by Protestantism in creating a cultural environment favourable to the spread of capitalism could have been both more clearly and more persuasively advanced if, instead of repudiating the concept of selection (*Auslese*) as applicable to it, he had followed up the explicitly selectionist approach to innovation and change which he briefly deployed in his sociology of law (Runciman 2001). No doubt there is a danger of reading into an earlier author's explanatory hypotheses about cultural or social change a selectionist implication that the author might well disavow. Moreover, historians, as well as anthropologists and sociologists, often use the term 'evolution' in ways that owe nothing to Darwin's fundamental notion of 'descent with modification' (Ruse 1983: 135). But in cases like those I have cited, the explanations offered can be rephrased to advantage without either loss or alteration of meaning into the language of heritable variation and competitive selection of instructions affecting phenotype.

Sceptics about the relevance of neo-Darwinian theory to human social behaviour are apt to claim that its application to sociocultural as opposed to natural selection is 'merely' metaphorical. But quite apart from the point that much of the language of science is metaphorical and none the worse for it (Dunbar 1995), in what sense is it metaphorical to say that heritable information affecting phenotype is replicated in a number of different ways down and across human populations? The idea is straightforward enough, however difficult it may be to identify the specific instructions on whose phenotypic effects the environment brings selective pressure to bear and to trace the causal sequences through which it does so. The units of selection may be competing with each other or cooperating with each other, just as their carriers may, and once this extends not only within but between the separate levels of natural, cultural, and social selection, the testing of alternative explanatory hypotheses against one another becomes correspondingly more daunting. But the task is no different from the biologist's task as described by Francis Crick (1988: 139): 'To produce a really good biological theory, one must try to see through the clutter produced by evolution to the basic mechanisms lying beneath them, realising that they are likely to be overlaid by other, secondary mechanisms.'

REFERENCES

Bascom, W. R. (1948), 'Ponapae Prestige Economy', *Southwestern Journal of Anthropology* 4: 211–21.

Betzig, L. (1992), 'Roman Polygyny', *Ethology and Sociobiology* 13: 309–49.

Blackmore, S. (1999), *The Meme Machine*. Oxford: Oxford University Press.

Bliege Bird, R. L. and Bird, D. W. (1997), 'Delayed Reciprocity and Tolerated Theft: The Behavioral Ecology of Food-Sharing Strategies', *Current Anthropology* 38: 49–78.

Borgerhoff Mulder, M. (1987), 'Adaptation and Evolutionary Approaches to Anthropology', *Man* (n.s.) 22: 25–41.

Boyd, R. and Richerson, P. J. (1985), *Culture and the Evolutionary Process*. Chicago: University of Chicago Press.

Brown, D. E. (1991), *Human Universals*. New York: McGraw Hill.

Burkert, W. (1996), *Creation of the Sacred: Tracks of Biology in Early Religions*. Cambridge, MA: Harvard University Press.

Campbell, D. T. (1974), 'Evolutionary Epistemology', in *The Philosophy of Karl Popper*, edited by P. A. Schilpp. LaSalle, IL: Open Court.

Clarke, A. L. and Low, B. S. (1992), 'Ecological Correlates of Human Dispersal in Nineteenth-Century Sweden', *Animal Behaviour* 44: 677–93.

Cloak, F. T. (1975), 'Is a Cultural Ethology Possible?', *Human Ecology* 3: 161–82.

Coleman, J. S. (1990), *Foundations of Social Theory*. Cambridge, MA: Harvard University Press.

Crawford, C. and Krebs, D. L. (1998), *Handbook of Evolutionary Psychology: Ideas, Issues, and Applications*. Mahwah, NJ: Erlbaum.

Crick, F. (1988), *What Mad Pursuit: A Personal View of Scientific Discovery*. London: Weidenfeld.

Cronin, H. (1991), *The Ant and the Peacock: Altruism and Sexual Selection from Darwin to Today*. Cambridge: Cambridge University Press.

Daly, M. and Wilson, M. (1988), *Homicide*. New York: Aldine de Gruyter.

Darwin, C. (1883), *The Descent of Man and Selection in Relation to Sex*, 2nd edn. London: John Murray.

Dawkins, R. (1976), *The Selfish Gene*. Oxford: Oxford University Press.

Dawkins, R. (1986), *The Blind Watchmaker*. London: Longman.

Dennett, D. C. (1995), *Darwin's Dangerous Idea: Evolution and the Meanings of Life*. London: Penguin.

Doyle, W. (1980), *Origins of the French Revolution*. Oxford: Oxford University Press.

Doyle, W. (1996), *Venality: The Sale of Offices in Eighteenth-Century France*. Oxford: Clarendon Press.

Dunbar, R. (1995), *The Trouble with Science*. London: Faber.

Durham, W. H. (1991), *Coevolution: Genes, Culture and Human Diversity*. Stanford, CA: Stanford University Press.

Ekman, P. (1973), 'Cross-Cultural Studies of Facial Expression', in P. Ekman (ed.), *Darwin and Facial Expression: A Century of Research in Review*. New York: Academic Press.

Ekman, P. (1998), 'Introduction', in Charles Darwin, *The Expression of the Emotions in Man and Animals* 3rd edn. London: HarperCollins.

Fisher, R. A. (1930), *The Genetical Theory of Natural Selection*. Oxford: Clarendon Press.

Grant, P. R. (1986), *Ecology and Evolution of Darwin's Finches*. Princeton, NJ: Princeton University Press.

Hamilton, W. D. (1996), 'Innate Social Aptitudes of Man: An Approach from Evolutionary Genetics', in *Narrow Roads of Gene Land I: Evolution of Social Behaviour*. New York: Freeman. [First published in 1975.]

Kelly, R. (1985), *The Nuer Conquest: The Structure and Development of an Expansionist System*. Ann Arbor: University of Michigan Press.

Kracke, E. A. (1953), *Civil Service in Early Sung China, 960–1067*. Cambridge, MA: Harvard Yenching Institute.

Lake, M. (1998), 'Digging for Memes: The Role of Material Objects in Cultural Evolution', in C. Renfrew and C. Scarre (eds), *Cognition and Material Culture: The Archaeology of Symbolic Storage*. Cambridge: McDonald Institute.

MacDonald, K. (1995), 'The Establishment and Maintenance of Socially Imposed Monogamy in Western Europe', *Politics and the Life Sciences* 14: 3–23.

Miller, G. (2000), *The Mating Mind: How Mate Choice Shaped the Evolution of Human Nature*. London: Heinemann.

Nisbett, R. and Cohen, D. (1996), *The Culture of Honor: The Psychology of Violence in the South*. Boulder, CO: Westview Press.

Nelson, R. R. and Winter, S. G. (1982), *An Evolutionary Theory of Economic Change*. Cambridge, MA: Belknap.

Plomin, R., De Fries, J. C., McClearn G. E., and Rutter M. (1997), *Behavioral Genetics*, 3rd edn. New York: Freeman.

Runciman, W. G. (1982), 'Origins of States: The Case of Archaic Greece', *Comparative Studies in Society and History* 24: 351–77.

Runciman, W. G. (1989), *A Treatise on Social Theory, II: Substantive Social Theory*. Cambridge: Cambridge University Press.

Runciman, W. G. (1995), 'The "Triumph" of Capitalism as a Topic in the Theory of Social Selection', *New Left Review* 210: 33–47.

Runciman, W. G. (1998a), 'The Selectionist Paradigm and its Implications for Sociology', *Sociology* 32: 163–88.

Runciman, W. G. (1998b), *The Social Animal*. London: HarperCollins.

Runciman, W. G. (2001), 'Was Max Weber a Selectionist in Spite of Himself?', *Journal of Classical Sociology* 1: 13–32.

Ruse, M. (1983), 'Darwin and Philosophy Today', in D. Oldroyd and I. Langham (eds), *The Wider Domain of Evolutionary Thought*. Dordrecht: Reidel.

Silk, J. (1980), 'Adoption and Kinship in Oceania', *American Anthropologist* 82: 799–820.

Smith, E. A. and Winterhalder, B., eds (1992), *Evolutionary Ecology and Human Behavior*. New York: Aldine de Gruyter.

Sober, E. and Wilson, D. S. (1998), *Unto Others: The Evolution and Psychology of Unselfish Behavior*. Cambridge, MA: Harvard University Press.

Soltis, J., Boyd, R., and Richerson, P. J. (1995), 'Can Group-Functional Behaviors Evolve by Cultural Group Selection? An Empirical Test', *Current Anthropology* 36: 473–94.

Spencer, C. S. (1990), 'On the Tempo and Mode of State Formation: Neo-Evolutionism Reconsidered', *Journal of Anthropological Archaeology* 9: 1–30.

Stuart-Fox, M. (1999), 'Evolutionary Theory of History', *History and Theory* (Theme Issue) 38: 33–51.

Tooby, J. and Cosmides L. (1996), 'Friendship and the Banker's Paradox: Other Pathways to the Evolution of Adaptations for Altruism', *Proceedings of the British Academy* 88: 119–43.

Williams, G. C. (1966), *Adaptation and Natural Selection*. Princeton, NJ: Princeton University Press.

Wilson, E. O. (1978), *On Human Nature*. Cambridge, MA: Harvard University Press.

Wilson, E. O. (1998), *Consilience: The Unity of Knowledge*. London: Little, Brown.

Zahavi, A. and Zahavi, A. (1997), *The Handicap Principle: A Missing Piece of Darwin's Puzzle*. Oxford: Oxford University Press.

Ziman, J. (2000), 'Evolutionary Models for Technological Change', in J. Ziman (ed.), *Technological Change as an Evolutionary Process*. Cambridge: Cambridge University Press.

Between Development and Evolution:
How to Model Cultural Change

ONE OF THE FASCINATING CULTURAL PROCESSES studied by historians of ideas is the transfer of concepts, metaphors, and models, from one discipline to another. During such 'ping-ponging' of ideas, or 'cross-fertilisation' as it is more commonly called, ideas become transformed. They become changed in the accepting discipline and in their movement back to the 'source discipline' they carry new connotations and new meanings, opening up new possibilities and imposing new limitations, to become transformed again, and continue in their back-and-forth migration. Such conceptual migration has been particularly important and notable in the history of biology and the social sciences. Since the middle of the eighteenth century, we have seen the journeying of concepts between the two incipient disciplines of biology and sociology. One example of an important concept that has ping-ponged is 'division of labour', which was taken from Adam Smith's economical writings into biology by Milne-Edwards, and re-introduced, somewhat transformed, back again into the social sciences. Another is 'open-ended progress', a concept initially worked out by the French ideologues and taken up by Lamarck and other biologists. Somewhat later, and throughout the nineteenth century, 'evolution' became the major organising concept in both disciplines, moving incessantly from biology to the social sciences and back again, being transformed in the process and taking many forms in both disciplines.

Today we are again witnessing an intense and ongoing process of such conceptual migration with respect to the Darwinian model of evolution. As during the last third of the nineteenth century, when Herbert Spencer was the major and most imaginative agent of the back-and-forth migration of evolutionary ideas, Darwin's selection theory is generalised and applied across the board, to many disciplines. According to Darwin's selection theory, in any world that is limited in resources, interacting entities with the properties of multiplication, heredity, and heritable variation that affects the chances of multiplication, will evolve by natural selection (Maynard Smith 1986). How the processes of heredity, multiplication, and the generation of variation actually occur is not

Proceedings of the British Academy, **112**, 27–41, © The British Academy 2002.

specified in this general version of the theory. It is this generality which gives selection theory its potential applicability to the study of cultural evolution.

As in the late nineteenth century, Darwinian theory today is applied to the world of physics (mainly to cosmology), to chemistry (mainly to pre-biotic evolution), and to the study of social behaviour and symbolic culture. Within biology, stabilisation due to cybernetic constraints and system properties is also described as an instance of selection, as is the stabilisation, through positive and negative reinforcement of patterns of behaviour, which occurs during many forms of learning. The conceptual migration from biology to the social sciences is not, however, limited to a general model of selection. The migration of assumptions and models from the modern, more specific, genic version of neo-Darwinian theory, where Darwin's theory is best elaborated, is also evident. The generation of variation, for example, is assumed to be 'blind', or random, like genetic variation in neo-Darwinian theory; a distinction similar to the phenotype/genotype distinction is commonly assumed, rephrased as the distinction between instructions and product. Recently, the use of a unit similar to the basic unit of genetics, the gene, has become fashionable. This unit is the meme, a unit of culture (Dawkins 1976, 1982), which carries many of the gene's properties, and is liberally applied to cultural evolution (Blackmore 1999).

If we are to examine the adequacy of the application of biological-evolutionary models such as the genic neo-Darwinian model to cultural evolution, we need to understand what historians, sociologists, and anthropologists, who are the scholars most knowledgeable about the evolution of culture, see as the most important properties of cultural change. It is beyond the scope of this paper to attempt a review of this subject, but I shall try to point to some widely accepted opinions, which any model of the evolution of culture must accommodate. Most people accept that cultural evolution is a process that occurs concurrently at several levels of psychological and social organisation. The individual inventor, the group, and the RD unit in a company, can all be agents of variation. Selection can occur in the brains of inventors, within firms, and in the market. Moreover, the generation of selectable variation and the selection processes at the different levels are usually intimately intertwined, so a clear distinction between the generation of variation and its selection is commonly impossible. This is because the processes underlying the generation of variation are very complex, and, in addition to functional engineering constraints and criteria, both the processes themselves and the variations produced are socially constructed. Social construction is always important, but has different roles in different cultural systems. It plays a central role in the generation, transformation, and maintenance of complex artefacts and cultural behaviours. Social construction is sometimes explicitly based on the projection of a desired future on to the present, with elaborate future goals directing both the generation of variation and its selection (for an overview of the processes involved in the case of technological evolution, see Ziman 2000).

Although I find the general framework of selection theory very useful for thinking about cultural change as well as about the evolution of other aspects of the world, I claim that the genic, neo-Darwinian model is inadequate for understanding cultural evolution. The attempt to define a gene-like unit, and the assumption that the 'copying' and the functional state of the unit can be detached, do not fit what we know of cultural evolution. Moreover, in cultural evolution, transmissible variation is guided or 'Lamarckian', since it often arises in response to the environment. I believe that this guided facet of variation involves three aspects, or layers: first, a lot of variation is *targeted*, so that the initial generation of variation is not entirely random (although there is usually an element of randomness in the formation of variation within the targeted set). Second, and in addition, the targeted variation is often developmentally, ecologically, and socially *constructed and edited* before it is transmitted to the next generation. This is clearly observed during the processes of individual and social learning, but construction through learning is only one type of construction. Third, some cultural variation in humans is also *future-oriented* in the sense that a culturally constructed virtual future reality (a utopia, a plan for building a new machine) is directing the construction of present new variation. This aspect seems to be an exclusively human aspect of guidedness, which is related to the human ability to think and communicate with symbols.

Given these obvious limitations in the classical genetic models, is it possible to modify some of its assumptions and form a modified but still recognisable genetic-like model of cultural evolution? I think that the picture that emerges when the major assumptions of the classical genetic model are changed leads to a different notion of what evolution entails. It leads to a view that denies that there is a categorical distinction between evolution and development, and looks instead at processes of adaptive change that are dominated to varying degrees by selective and instructive processes. There is a continuum from almost purely selective processes to almost purely instructive ones. Processes of cultural evolution are somewhere halfway between the two extremes on this continuum.

I shall first briefly discuss some of the properties of the genetic system to illustrate the problems it poses for modelling cultural change, and then highlight some of the properties of the other inheritance systems that we recognise today (the epigenetic, the behavioural, and the symbolic) from a perspective that focuses on variation production and variation construction (Jablonka 2000b). The additional ways that mould and guide variation, which have emerged as organisational complexity has increased, shed light on the nature of cultural evolution and suggest better models for it.

THE GENETIC INHERITANCE SYSTEM

Since the genetic inheritance system is the usual model for cultural evolution, let us look at its fundamental properties. The unit of the genetic system, the gene, is made of DNA, a long, linear molecule whose sequence of nucleotides can be transformed into functional RNA and proteins, as well as participate in the regulation of such transformations. The organisation of information in DNA is said to be 'modular' (or 'digital'): it is decomposable into modules drawn from a standard set (the modules are the nucleotides A, C, T, G), and it is also alterable module by module. The information is said to inhere in the sequence of the DNA. The modular nature of the information allows many combinations—a molecule with ten linearly linked nucleotides has more than a million possible variant sequences. The enzymatic machinery that replicates the DNA is largely indifferent to its sequence organisation. Thus a DNA sequence that has beneficial effects will be replicated with the same fidelity as one with deleterious effects or one that is completely non-functional. Copying is unaffected by functionality and expression. In the same way, a photocopier copies a Shakespeare sonnet with the same fidelity as a page from Hitler's *Mein Kampf*, or a random assemblage of letters.

Another important property of the genetic system is the distinction between the hereditary potential and its actualisation. Describing the hereditary material in the Aristotelian terms of potentiality and actuality allowed Wilhelm Johannsen, an admirer of Aristotle, to make the distinction between genotype and phenotype. He asserted that only the hereditary potential—the genotype—is transmitted through biological inheritance, whereas it is the phenotype—the actual product of the interaction of the genotype with the environment—which functions, is alive, and is the target of selection. The phenotype, however, is not inherited in a biological sense (Johannsen 1911). In today's molecular terms it means that it is the DNA sequence rather than the direct effect of the DNA sequence on development that is inherited. With minor reservations, there is wide agreement concerning these two properties of DNA—the independence of the fidelity of copying of a DNA sequence from past or future expression, and the transmission of potentiality rather than actuality. It is generally accepted that variations that occur in DNA are random with respect to the selecting environment. Variations in DNA sequence are assumed to be the products of the meiotic reshuffling of genes, or the consequences of mistakes of the replication machinery, of chemical and physical insults to the DNA, or of the movement of mobile genetic elements.

How useful then, is the genetic system as a model for cultural evolution? All the properties of the molecular gene—the independence of copying from function and development, the phenotype/genotype distinction, and the randomness of variation—have also been applied to a unit of culture that Dawkins called a meme (1976, 1982). The meme is a unit of information, a representation of an idea or a practice. It is thought of as the neural circuit in the brain that underlies a particular behaviour. It has been claimed that it is the neural representation rather than the whole behaviour that is 'replicated' during cultural evolution, and that memes are alternatives that 'compete' with each other. In order to avoid the stigma of Lamarckism, when considering new learnt behaviours or cultural practices the focus has been solely on the non-guided aspect of the generation of new behaviour. The evolved, instructive processes have been ignored (see, for example, Cziko 1995).

The problem with the gene-inspired meme is that the features that are assumed to be fundamental for both gene and meme do not fare well when we think about cultural practices. First, the transmissibility of a cultural practice or product is not independent of various aspects of its function and development. Second, variation is not random, it is highly targeted; and, third, this targeted variation is often heavily 'edited' or reconstructed before it is passed on.

Let us first consider transmissibility, and look at a very simple example of behavioural/cultural transmission, the transmission of a learnt song. The chance that my son will learn a song that I know depends on how much I like this song (which in turn depends on when I learnt it, from whom and under what circumstances, how its semantic meaning pleases me, etc.), on how often I sing it, how it fits with the kind of music my son is familiar with, how my singing pleases my son, how many other people sing it to him, and so on. The mere fact that I know the song does not in itself ensure a fixed probability of transmission. The way and the chance of transmitting the song are dependent on the particular features of the song, on the development and background of the 'models' and the 'target' of instruction, and on the existing modes of its transmission. And, of course, a song that has not been sung is not going to be passed on in a latent form like a recessive gene. The song will not be perpetuated if not displayed *unless* there is an independent system of symbolic transmission of the song in the form of notes and words that is independent of the display, or if there is another autonomous system of transmission, such as recording. If we think about the evolution of local dialects in song-birds, where neither symbolic notation and transmission nor recording technologies exist, it becomes even more clear that variations in products and processes are not transferred unless displayed. A learnt yet non-sung song is not passed on among the song-birds.

Consider another example, the transmission of a new medical practice in a non-literate society. Imagine that a new medicinal plant that gets rid of lice has been found, and a practice to extract its juice and apply it has been developed. The chances that the new practice will be transmitted to the next generation depend on the beneficial effects of the plant, on the number of occasions that the local people have been afflicted with the lice and have used it, on the authority and the teaching ability of the healer, on the methods of passing on the new practice (demonstration, words, or both), on the complexity of the task, on the number of individuals who are in the social position to learn the use of the plant from the healer, and so on. What is clear is that the selective forces that determine how successful the practice is for the discoverer and for other individuals also affect the social learning of the practice and the process of transfer across generations. Unlike the genetic case, the *transmissibility* of the 'unit' is not independent of the agents' development, the practice's actual display, the social context, and its selective benefit.

If we think about a similar example in animals, where many species use medicinal plants and seem to acquire and pass on the practice through social learning, we may see even more clearly that it is the actual display of the behaviour, as well as its context and consequences, that affects the transfer of the new practice. Thus, if the practice has been beneficial to an individual several times, she is likely to repeat it when individuals of a younger generation are present and they may learn it from her by example. The beneficial effects of the practice also reinforce practising, and bolster memory, thus enhancing the probability that the practice will be repeated and passed on. In this case, where there is no oral tradition and no independent instruction, a hardly practised practice is unlikely to be passed on. Thus transmission is not independent of actual display, and it is the actual display rather than the instruction for it, that is passed on. The study of animal traditions, which are being found in increasing number of bird and mammal species, shows the generality of this conclusion (Avital and Jablonka 2000). Separating the representation of the behaviour in the nervous system (where memes are supposed to dwell) from the motor aspect of the behaviour (the 'implementation part') is misleading, because the transmissibility of the behaviour, which is what we are interested in, depends in such cases on the interplay between the neural representation and the motor display of the practice. It is not just that the motor display depends on the neural representation; *the neural representation will not be transmitted without the motor display*.

The difference between genes and cultural practices is not confined to animal traditional practices or to illiterate societies. In our highly technological and literate society, where there are several channels for transmitting instructions, including the symbolic one, processes of transmission usually involve the simultaneous transmission of tacit knowledge. Many types of knowledge are tacit, embodied in prevailing routines adapted to current social and environmental conditions. The transfer of such knowledge involves demonstration of displays and products, as well as instructions. For example, although detailed manuals for laboratory techniques in molecular biology exist and are widely used, the successful transmission of a technique from one lab to another involves, in most cases, either sending students to the lab in which the technique has been developed or where it is successfully practised, or the importing of specialists who already know the technique into the 'naive' lab. Transmission occurs through active training involving some adjustment to prevailing local conditions, which is only partially verbal. The transfer of military technology to Israel between 1933 and 1967 involved the transfer of products, manuals, and the training of workers and managers. Although we do have cultural systems where instructions-only can be, and are, copied, other modes of transmission—by actual training and demonstration and by product copying—are often as important, and sometimes more important, than transfer through independent instruction (manuals, etc.). It is quite clear from many available case studies that different types of information and different types of transmission are involved in most cases of technological transfer (Ziman 2000).

Let us now look at the other property of the genetic system—the blindness of heritable variation. Obviously, for real novelty to be produced there must be a source of randomness in its generation. But how random is random? In the immune system, one of the favourite examples for the victory of selectionist models over instructionist ones, some of the secondary variation in the gene coding for immunoglobulin protein in B cells is somewhat targeted, not blind. It occurs preferentially in the hyper-variable regions that are involved in the recognition of antigens. These regions become 'hot spots' for mutation following the initial, often weak binding of antigens to the antibodies on the cell surface. These targeted mutations increase the chance that mutation will lead to a gene coding for an antibody with even better affinity for the antigen. The fact that mutations occur preferentially in these particular, functionally important regions of the gene, rather than in the whole gene or even the whole genome, is obviously a clever, economical, and evolved property of the system. Of course the mutations in these 'hot spots' are not necessarily those that are adaptive. They are random. *But this randomness is highly constrained: it is targeted only to the relevant region.* The argument that goal-oriented variation does not occur is clearly wrong, even for the genetic system. Instead of looking for a needle in a large haystack, evolution has targeted the search to a particular little region in the haystack. Similar processes elevating the mutation rate specifically in the sequences coding for protein domains that are relevant for future function have been described in various pathogenic micro-organisms. For example, a high rate of mutation in the pathogen *Haemophilus influenzae* occurs precisely in the region in its genome that codes for surface proteins that interact with the host. A high level of mutations in this region helps the bacterium to avoid the immune system of the host (Moxon *et al.* 1994). Moreover, in some cases variation appears not only in a sub-set of relevant genes, but also in a sub-set of the relevant environments (Wright *et al.* 1999). From an evolutionary perspective, this targeted generation of variations makes sense, since a cellular system for recognising recurrent types of environmental stress followed by a regulated restructuring of the genome as a response, is adaptive (Jablonka *et al.* 1998). It is difficult to decide how to think about the origin of such new variations. Are they evolutionary or developmental? Their trans-generational transmission and the role of selection suggest that they are evo-lutionary, while the partially guided nature of the variation shows that instructive, developmental processes are at work. The distinction between evolution and development is blurred here—there is continuity.

The targeted nature of behavioural and cultural novelties is much more familiar than targeted genetic variation. With culture there are heuristics and gut feelings governing experimentation, aesthetic judgements about what is appropriate and promising. And the mind is oriented in a certain subject-guided direction based on past history. Thus, when designing a new type of car, it is an a priori constrained set of variations on the subject of cars and vehicles (rather than ritual dances) that is produced in the brains of the designer/s. The mind has evolved in a way that ensures that an attempt to solve a new problem will not start with random firing in the brain. How ideas will change and recombine during creative learning depends on factors that are more or less closely associated with the problem. All these factors target variation. Useful variation is not just a random and lucky mistake. It is also the product of an evolved developmental system that targets luck. Since learning is part of development, and the new products and methods of learn-ing can be transmitted, evolution entails both selective and instructive processes.

Something else that moulds and designs this partially guided behavioural and cultural variation is active, context-specific, editing. In both animals and man, a new (already targeted) invention is not just uncritically applied and transmitted, it is experimented upon and transformed through individual and social learning so that it better fits the functions it serves. It is usually transmitted only after such a process of editing, and it undergoes further editing and updating in subsequent generations. For example, a new medical practice will be altered to fit the corpus of other practices, and a song trans-mitted to the young generation is changed by the prevailing style of singing. If we use the mutation metaphor, it is as if the 'mutation' is not only par-tially targeted, but after its targeted production and before its transmission to the next generation, it is also edited and modified according to the needs of the organism. It is therefore guided in two ways: its origin is targeted and, after it has originated, it is usually edited and modified. Such 'editing' can occur with respect to genetic mutations if it is thought of as any selective or selective-like process that occurs among the lower-level units that make up a higher-level individual and affect its heredity and evolution. This type of process occurs in plants, where there are many mutations in somatic cells, followed by selection among the somatic cell variants. Since in plants somatic cells can contribute to the germ line, and hence can be transmitted to the next generation, this process may culminate in the transmission of the variations that best serve the interests of the individual plant in which the somatic mutation and selection processes have occurred. From the perspective of the individual plant, the somatic mutation/selection process is a developmental construction process.

It should be clear from this section that I believe that, in order to use the genetic system as a 'reference' for cultural evolution, we have to abandon the classic neo-Darwinian assumptions about heredity and evolution, and concentrate instead on more 'Lamarckian' genetic models, assigning a central role to targeted genetic variation and to somatic selection. However, even if we do that, the genetic system is still not a very good model for the cultural one. Its modular mode of organisation, the fixed transmissibility of variation, and the assumption that phenotypes cannot be transmitted, make it an unsuitable model of cultural transmission and evolution. I think that other, simpler systems of inheritance and evolution can be more informative. The epigenetic inheritance systems described below bring out the targeted aspects of variation production and the non-modular organisation of information transmission that are characteristic of cultural evolution. They can therefore clarify these features in cultural evolution.

CELLULAR INHERITANCE: THE INHERITANCE OF INDUCED CELLULAR PHENOTYPES

Epigenetic inheritance systems (EISs) are the systems responsible for the transmission of the functional phenotypes of cells in cell lineages: for the fact that cells with the same DNA, like kidney and liver cells, have different phenotypes, which are transmitted through cell division. Kidney cells and liver cells 'breed true' (Jablonka and Lamb 1995). I shall very briefly describe the EISs, focusing on three main properties of these systems that are most relevant for our discussion: the way information is organised; the way it is copied or reproduced; and the way in which new variation it is generated (Jablonka 2000a, 2000b).

The first type of epigenetic inheritance system is the steady-state system. It is based on positive feedback loops. At its simplest, a gene produces a product as a result of induction by an external developmental or environmental stimulus, and this product stimulates further activity of the gene (positive self-regulation), even when the original external inducing stimulus has disappeared. Thus, once the gene is switched on, the cell lineage continues to produce the product unless its concentration falls below some critical threshold value. Two genetically identical cells can be in two alternative states—'gene on' and 'gene off'—and both states are self-perpetuating. The states of activity and inactivity are reproduced as an automatic consequence of cell division. Their generation is part of development, yet they can be faithfully transmitted through the cell lineage for many generations. The information reproduced in each such individual cycle is not modular—it cannot be parsed into independently transmissible units. It can be said to be holistic—it inheres in the dynamic activity of the whole self-perpetuating cycle. Although each cycle can have only two states (on or off), if a cell has twenty different and independent self-perpetuating cycles, more than million variant cell states are possible. New developmental conditions can induce changes in the activity states of several cycles in cells, producing several vari-ant states, which can then be selected. Thus the environment both induces a set of vaguely adaptive variants and also fine-tunes the adaptation by select-ing the most appropriate ones. Both the reproduction of the activity states in daughter cells and the generation of variations in this system are part of the cell's development, and it is the phenotype (a dynamic activity state, a process) that is reproduced.

The second type of EIS is that of structural inheritance, where existing cell structures serve as templates for the formation of new similar structures. For example, in ciliated protozoa, genetically identical cells can have different patterns of cilia on their cell surfaces and these different patterns are inherited. Prions, the protein agents responsible for 'mad cow disease' and several other degenerative diseases of the nervous system, seem to be passed on through such structural templating. In this system, there can be several self-perpetuating stable states whose structure can be affected by environmental conditions, and whose transmission can be part of cell division (although they can also be transferred from cell to cell by an infective type of process, as the prionic diseases testify). There is no autonomous system of transmission independent of the structural properties of the system. The reliability of transmission will be specific to each protein complex and depend on its unique architectural properties. In this EIS too, variation may be guided, induced by specific conditions in the cell. There is no autonomous and specialised copying system that is independent of the properties of the transmitted structures: each is transmitted with a fidelity depending on its own idiosyncratic molecular prop-erties. Copying is part of development, and when it is induced (guided), so is variation.

In the third EIS, chromatin marking, states of chromatin that affect gene expression are reproduced. Genetically identical cells can have variant and self-perpetuating chromatin marks, that is, protein complexes associated with DNA or DNA modifications such as cytosine methylation. In the methylation system there is an independent copying machinery that can copy patterns of methylation irrespective of their function and the states they produce (Jablonka and Lamb 1995). Methylation patterns can be changed by the environment, so some variation is guided. With chromatin marks, it is difficult to decide whether it is the genotype or the phenotype that is transmitted, because the distinction is very blurred in this case. As in all the other systems, when variation is targeted, its generation is part of development.

With all EISs, the generation of new variation is often highly targeted, since when variation is induced it is a very specific set of genes or gene products that is affected. When gene activity or protein structure is so affected, it is part of the physiological development of the cell as it interacts with its environment. The induced pattern of gene activity can be modified and edited by subsequent developmental and environmental stimuli, to adjust it to the changing needs of the developing individual. 'Copying' (or more properly the reproduction processes that ensure the faithful transmission of variant functional or structural states) is also not independent of general growth and multiplication processes. What is transmitted in the steady-state and structural EISs is not 'instructions', but rather the entity itself: the feedback loop or the protein complex. With the chromatin-marking EIS, the functional state is not determined solely by the chromatin-marking pattern. The expression of the DNA sequence carrying the chromatin marks also depends on environmental factors. Variation in marks therefore leads to a variation in the probability the DNA sequence will be expressed; it does not determine whether or not the gene is actually active. Usually it is a potential for gene expression rather than the actual activity state that is transmitted by the chromatin-marking system.

This discussion of EISs shows that our notion of information, its organisation and its transmission need not be based on the familiar models of DNA or written language. EISs suggest that *transmission may be a developmental process that is function-dependent*. There need not be a copying system that is independent of function, that will 'copy' information without regard to what this information does. Moreover, the generation of variation may be highly targeted. With EISs, *random variation occurs within rather narrow limits, which are prescribed by the developmental process*. This is of course very similar to what we see in cultural systems. Since the epigenetic systems are much simpler, and we are beginning to understand them in considerable biochemical detail, I believe the analysis of epigenetic inheritance and evolution may afford some insight into the parallel aspects of cultural evolution. But, like the genetic system, the EISs do not provide the best parallel for the editing/constructing level of guided variation. The 'editing' of variation can be seen very much more readily when the transmitted information is learnt. The study of socially learnt and transmitted variations in behaviour, where social construction of behaviour is ubiquitous, allows better scrutiny of this aspect of variation design.

TARGETING AND EDITING LEARNT VARIATION

In social non-human animals such as birds and mammals that live in groups with overlapping generations, information is transferred between generations through social learning. Social learning occurs when the presence of experienced individuals increases the probability that naive ones will learn the same pattern of behaviour. It does not exclude a-social learning. New patterns of behaviour, first acquired either by a-social learning (often in new challenging conditions) or through social learning from individuals from other species, can be transmitted to the next generation through social learning and lead to local group traditions.

In whatever way a new pattern of behaviour is first acquired, it is obviously highly targeted. First, there are simple rules that organise the perceptions, emotions, and learning processes (Schlicht 1998). These rules allow animals to construct clear perceptual and cognitive categories, anticipate that a regularity experienced for a long time will continue, and so on. Second, the type of information an animal may acquire by learning is structured by past evolutionary history: some types of behaviour are learnt easily in one species but not in others, and the time and context of learning is also often species-specific (Shettleworth 1998).

An even more conspicuous aspect of learning is its constructed nature. An ongoing process of trial and error is involved in most types of learning. Pleasing (usually adaptive) behaviour patterns are usually repeated, and painful or unpleasant ones (that are usually dangerous or are otherwise maladaptive) are avoided. This is a kind of selection process, occurring at the level of the behaviour pattern, which leads to the formation of the animal's repertoire of habits. As a newly learnt behaviour is repeated, it is adjusted through further learning so that it better fits with the behaviours and preferences of the individual performing it, and with the environment in which it is performed. When the pattern of behaviour involves social interaction, the reactions of the interacting individuals shape the behaviour. For example, in birds that practise long-term monogamy, the male and female seem to get better at performing their joint social and breeding activities. Any behaviour that involves social partners is shaped by those partners: in many cases the behaviours of individuals are standardised and streamlined to fit the local group behaviour (Avital and Jablonka 2000). In other cases, a new behaviour may be adopted into a group but, as it is transmitted among individuals and between generations, it undergoes modifications to fit the changing social needs of both individuals and the group.

The generation of a behavioural variant, its subsequent modification, and its transmission to young group members are parts of behavioural development. But of course they are also parts of behavioural evolution. Animal traditions evolve and become transformed by additional learning and selection. We cannot consider the development and evolution of traditions separately. The evolution of local traditions in animals is based on both instructive and selective processes, and both processes are concurrently part of development and of evolution.

The transmission and selection of behavioural variants illustrate another facet of variation which is important in cultural evolution. Through their activity and behaviour, organisms actively construct the ecological and social niche that they occupy, and often this 'niche construction' ensures that the environmental conditions in which they have lived will be regenerated and experienced by their descendants (Odling-Smee 1988, 1995). For example, caching seeds by birds is a habit that may be reinforced through the effect it has on the local environment. By caching seeds, birds provide themselves with a source of food for harsh winters, but since some of the cached seeds germinate, caching also provides new plants that will form seeds and create future caching opportunities (Smith and Reichman 1984). A more 'cultural' example is the propagation of dialects in some bird groups. The existence of the dialect of the previous generation of birds is the condition for the acquisition of this dialect by the younger generation. Ecological or social niche construction thus ensures that the ecological and social milieu is transmitted. The conditions eliciting the ancestral variant pattern of behaviour are reconstructed, and selection occurs for the maintenance of the type of behaviour that fits the constructed niche.

Variations in human culture obviously involve two of the 'layers' of guidedness discussed in the introduction: they are targeted and they are edited/constructed. But, as far as we know, it is only in human learnt behaviour that the third layer, the layer that makes guided variation future oriented, is seen. Humans have an additional inheritance system—that involving symbolic representation—in which symbols are transmitted. This way of transmitting information alters the nature and the complexity of human cultural evolution. Most importantly, from the point of view stressed in this paper, it allows the construction of variation on the basis of a projected future reality, a virtual reality that is the product of culture. This type of future-oriented construction is very dominant in some spheres of human cultural life. But in order to understand and assess its role, we have to consider the non-symbolic elements of information transmission that we share with other animals, and the way that these interact with our unique, symbolic, myth-oriented and future-oriented culture. The study of simpler inheritance and evolution systems, such as the epigenetic system and the system of behavioural inheritance through non-symbolic social learning, may aid our understanding in the more complex system of human cultural evolution and help us to model it. The third and uniquely human layer of guided variation may well dominate many central aspects of human cultural evolution, but it not likely to be autonomous.

The approach presented here is related to the developmental approach to evolution developed by Susan Oyama (2000), Paul Griffiths and Russell Gray (1994), and James Griesemer (2000). I came to this way of thinking from an evolutionary perspective, which focuses on the origin, construction, and transmission of heritable variations. This approach denies a categorical dichotomy between developmental and evolutionary processes, and emphasises instead the relative importance of selective and instructive processes in ontogeny and phylogeny. Since this view stresses the various guided aspects of variation production, and regards selection at lower levels of organisation (within a system comprised of several levels) as a construction process, it leads to concurrent attention to selection at different levels—the gene level, the cell level, the organism level, and the group level. Moreover, all of the different types of heritable variation—genetic, epigenetic, behavioural, and symbolic—which may have very different modes of organisation and transmission, have to be considered. This multi-level approach extends our understanding of heredity and of evolution, and is particularly appropriate for the study of human cultural evolution.

Note. I am very grateful to Marion J. Lamb for her constructive comments.

REFERENCES

Avital, E. and Jablonka, E. (2000), *Animal Traditions: Behavioural Inheritance in Evolution*. Cambridge: Cambridge University Press.

Blackmore, S. (1999), *The Meme Machine*. Oxford: Oxford University Press.

Cziko, G. (1995), *Without Miracles*. Cambridge, MA: MIT Press/Bradford Books.

Dawkins, R. (1976), *The Selfish Gene*. Oxford: Oxford University Press.

Dawkins, R. (1982), *The Extended Phenotype*. Oxford: Freeman.

Griesemer, J. (2000), 'Reproduction and the Reduction of Genetics', in P. Beurton, R. Falk, and H.-J. Rheinberger (eds), *The Concept of the Gene in Development and Evolution*. Cambridge: Cambridge University Press, pp. 240–85.

Griffiths, P. E. and Gray, R. D. (1994), 'Developmental Systems and Evolutionary Explanations', *Journal of Philosophy* 91: 277–304.

Jablonka, E. (2000a), 'Lamarckian Inheritance Systems in Biology: A Source of Metaphors and Models in Technological Evolution', in J. Ziman (ed.), *Technological Innovation as an Evolutionary Process*. Cambridge: Cambridge University Press, pp. 27–40.

Jablonka, E. (2000b), 'The Systems of Inheritance', in S. Oyama, P. E. Griffiths, and R. D. Gray (eds), *Cycles of Contingency*. Cambridge, MA: MIT Press, pp. 99–116.

Jablonka, E. and Lamb, M. J. (1995), *Epigenetic Inheritance and Evolution: The Lamarckian Dimension*. Oxford: Oxford University Press.

Jablonka, E., Lamb, M. J., and Avital, E. (1998), ' "Lamarckian" Mechanisms in Darwinian Evolution', *Trends in Ecology and Evolution* 13: 206–10.

Johannsen, W. (1911), 'The Genotype Conception of Heredity', *American Naturalist* 45: 129–59.

Maynard Smith, J. (1986), *The Problems of Biology*. Oxford: Oxford University Press.

Moxon, E. R., Rainey, P. B., Nowak, M. A., and Lenski, R. E. (1994) 'Adaptive Evolution of Highly Mutable Loci in Pathogenic Bacteria', *Current Biology* 4: 23–33.

Odling-Smee, F. J. (1988), 'Niche-Constructing Phenotypes', in H. C. Plotkin (ed.), *The Role of Behaviour in Evolution*. Cambridge, MA: MIT Press, pp. 73–132.

Odling-Smee, F. J. (1995), 'Biological Evolution and Cultural Change', in E. Jones and V. Reynolds (eds), *Survival and Religion: Biological Evolution and Cultural Change*. Chichester: John Wiley and Sons, pp. 1–43.

Oyama, S. (2000), *The Ontogeny of Information: Developmental Systems and Evolution*, 2nd rev. edn. Durham, NC: Duke University Press.

Schlicht, E. (1998), *On Custom in the Economy*. Oxford: Clarendon Press.

Shettleworth, S. J. (1998), *Cognition, Evolution and Behavior*. New York: Oxford University Press.

Smith, C. C. and Reichman, O. J. (1984), 'The Evolution of Food Caching by Birds and Mammals', *Annual Review of Ecology and Systematics* 15: 329–35.

Wright, B. E., Longacre, A., and Reimers, J. M. (1999) 'Hypermutation in derepressed operons of Escherichia coli K12', *Proceedings of the National Academy of Sciences* (USA) 96: 5089–94.

Ziman, J., ed. (2000), *Technological Innovation as an Evolutionary Process*. Cambridge: Cambridge University Press.

Between Evolution and History: Biology, Culture, and the Myth of Human Origins

TIM INGOLD

IS IT POSSIBLE TO ACCOMMODATE, within a single explanatory paradigm, the phenomena of both organic evolution and cultural change? In this chapter I shall propose just such an accommodation. This is not a matter, however, of showing how cultural or artefactual forms 'evolve', just as do organic forms, through the operation of an overarching principle of variation under selection. Countless proposals have been made to this effect, and it is not my purpose to add to them. To the contrary, I want to argue that a model of variation under selection is inadequate to grasp the generative dynamics of cultural change. For to understand these dynamics we have to focus not on the final forms of artefacts but on the activities that give rise to them, and of which they are the more or less ephemeral condensations. Moreover precisely the same, I contend, applies to organisms: their forms, too, are condensations of activity within fields of relationships. Understanding the persistence and change of form over time, whether organic or artefactual, therefore calls for nothing less than a radically alternative view of the evolutionary process itself. In brief, instead of thinking of evolution as the sequential modification, along one or more lines of descent, of the design specifications that are supposed to underwrite the construction of organisms or artefacts, we have to regard it as the unfolding of a total field of relationships—a web of life—within which forms come into being and are held in place. We can then see that what we are accustomed to call history, when speaking of human beings, is but one aspect of a total process of evolution that embraces the entire organic world. And we can see, too, that no great divide separates biological organisms from cultural artefacts: both have life-histories, both grow—or take shape—within fields of relationships, and both, through their presence in the environment, condition the development of other entities or beings to which they relate. Thus human history *is* evolutionary, cultural change *is* biological. It follows that the idea of a point of origin, at which human culture and history are conceived to have lifted off from a baseline of evolved, biological capacities, is founded upon an illusion. There is no such point.

Proceedings of the British Academy, **112**, 43–66, © The British Academy 2002.

Tim Ingold

GENOTYPE AND PHENOTYPE

Let me begin by spelling out the conception of the organism and its activity that lies at the heart of what, for convenience, I shall call the 'orthodox account' of evolutionary biology. According to this account, which is founded on a synthesis of Darwin's theory of variation under natural selection with modern population genetics, every organic life-cycle begins with the installation of a formal design specification at some particular locus within an environment. This specification, technically known as the *genotype*, is the outcome of a process of natural selection which, over innumerable previous generations, has adjusted the relative frequencies within the population of its replicable, information-bearing elements, the genes. The growth and maturation of the organism, its ontogenesis, is then understood as the process whereby the genotypic specification, by definition independent of the environmental context of development, is translated within that context into the manifest form of the *phenotype*. The majority of contemporary biologists conceive this process as one of interaction, over the course of a life-cycle, between endogenous, genetic factors and exogenous, environmental ones. Often described as the 'first law of biology', this interactionist formula creates the appearance that, from an orthodox point of view, these two sets of factors are regarded as of equivalent ontological standing, and as contributing in a certain ratio to the resultant phenotypic form. The appearance, however, is deceptive. In reality, the significance attributed by orthodox neo-Darwinism to the genes is quite different from that attributed to the environment. This is for two reasons.

First, since 'environment' nominally includes everything relevant to the development of an organism barring the genes themselves, it cannot be isolated as an interactant in the same way as can the genes. Strictly speaking, genes cannot interact *with* an environment but only *in* an environment with other entities that are, of course, also interacting with one another. In principle, then, it should be possible to focus at will on any one of these manifold interactants, and to advance an equally compelling case to the effect that the phenotypic form of the organism is the result of an interaction between *that* chosen component and its environment (Griffiths and Gray 1994). In the orthodox account, however, it is invariably the genes, rather than anything else, that are isolated as the foci of interaction. Why should this be so? The answer brings me to the second reason for the non-equivalence of genes and environment in this account. It is that genes are understood, in the first place, as units of digital information that together carry a context-independent design for the organism-to-be, whereas the environment is conceived as merely furnishing the material conditions for its realisation. I shall return below to how it was that molecules of DNA, in the nucleus of every cell, came to be seen as carriers of such a design. It is sufficient to note at this stage that, far from placing genes and environment on the same footing, orthodox evolutionary biology locates them on opposite sides of one of the most ancient and deep-seated dichotomies in the Western tradition of thought, namely, between ideal form and physical substance.

This point can be readily confirmed by means of a simple thought experiment. Imagine an organism O_1 at time T_1, and its descendant (many generations removed) O_2 at time T_2. Suppose, first, that in the period from T_1 to T_2, environmental conditions have remained unchanged, but that significant alteration has taken place in the organism's genetic constitution. Comparing O_1 and O_2, we are likely to conclude that there has been an evolution of form. But now suppose, second, that there has been no change in the organism's genes over the period T_1–T_2. Instead, it is the environmental conditions that have significantly altered. On the face of it, the differences between O_1 and O_2 are just the same as in the first case, yet on comparing them this time we conclude that no evolution has taken place at all, and that O_1 and O_2 are but outward phenotypic expressions of the same basic design. There is a technical term for this phenomenon: the environmentally induced outcome, in the second case, is said to be the 'phenocopy' of what has been produced through genetic change in the first. Crucially, however, the latter is never referred to as a 'genocopy' of the former (Cohen and Stewart 1994: 307). Now with bank notes as with works of art, a copy can be a counterfeit of the original, but not vice versa. Just so with organisms: there can be no genocopy, according to the orthodox account, since what is original to each and every organism is assumed to be its genotype. It is in the genotype that its fundamental design is supposed to reside, however much—in its phenotypic guise—it may mimic a design of another kind. And only when the genotypic design changes is evolution held to occur.

THE GENEALOGICAL MODEL

This way of thinking about the organism, as an entity whose essential nature is prefigured in advance of its life in the world, and of evolution as the gradual change in the nature of organisms linked in an ancestor-descendant sequence, has its source in a set of conventions whose range of application extends far beyond the realm of biological science. These are the conventions of what I shall henceforth call the *genealogical model* (Ingold 2000: 135–6). Since I am by trade a social anthropologist, I may perhaps be permitted to introduce this model by way of a comparison with the study of kinship. Anthropologists are used to depicting kinship relations by means of tree-like diagrams in which every line represents a link in a chain of connections running from a person's genealogical antecedents through to his or her descendants. This mode of depiction, however, has severe limitations. For the relative positions that persons occupy on a kinship chart tell us nothing about their actual placement in the world. The chart contains no clues about where they live, whom they live with, or what they do for a living. It thus presents a history of persons in the peculiar form of a history of *relatedness*, which unfolds without regard to people's *relationships*—that is, to their experience of involvement, in perception and action, with their human and non-human environments. So what does it mean, precisely, to say that one person is related to another by *descent*? What does a vertical line on a kinship chart connecting two persons, A and B, actually signify?

What is implied, in effect, is that B has derived certain rudiments of makeup and identity directly from A, as a kind of endowment, prior to embarking on a career within the arena of human relationships. Thus, concealed behind the apparently innocent graph of the line of descent is an assumption that persons are engendered, independently and in advance of their entry into the lifeworld, through the bestowal of ready-made attributes from predecessors. This assumption, which separates the generation of persons from their life in the world, lies at the core of the genealogical model. According to the model, it is descent, the passing on of the characteristics underwriting one life-cycle to the site of inauguration of another, that generates persons. Life activities themselves are *not* generative of personhood; they are rather ways of bringing already established identities and potentials into play. In other words, it is not what you do—in relating to others, building artefacts, inhabiting the land, and so on—that makes you who you are, but the received attributes that you import into these various projects. Moreover, in separating the generation of persons through descent from their activities in life, the genealogical model also splits the descent-line from the life-line. In so doing, it establishes the conventional notion of the *generation*, defined by the *Oxford English Dictionary* as 'offspring of the same parent regarded as a step in a line of descent from an ancestor'. Whereas life goes on within each generation, descent crosses from one generation to the next in a cumulative step-by-step sequence (Figure 1).

Returning from anthropology to biology, I should like to draw attention to the striking parallels between the kinship charts of anthropologists and the rather similar-looking diagrams often constructed by evolutionary biologists to illustrate the phylogenetic connections of species. Reproduced in Figure 2 is Darwin's original diagram from *The Origin of Species*—the only diagram, in fact, in the book. What do the dotted lines in the figure actually mean? They are lines of what Darwin, rather accurately, called 'descent with modification'. Each horizontal band is supposed to represent an interval of a thousand generations, such that any line of descent spanning this interval could be traced through a thousand organisms, each differing ever so slightly from the one preceding. Phylogeny, as it is depicted here and in countless textbooks of evolution ever since, is merely genealogy writ large. And in charting the phylogenies of

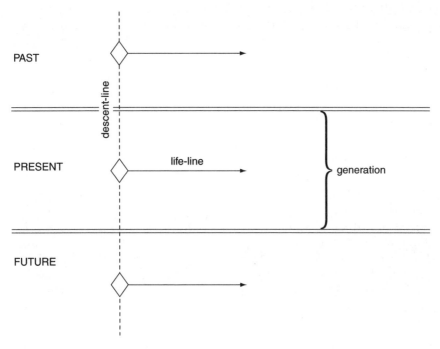

Figure 1. The relation between descent-line, life-line, and generation, according to the genealogical model. From Ingold (2000: 136).

species the concept of descent serves, just as it does in charting the genealogies of persons, to isolate a suite of heritable characteristics, passed down the line from predecessors, prior to their expression in the life-history of each individual. The species-specific attributes of the organism, in other words, are fixed from the outset as a set of design features, independently of the circumstances it actually encounters during its growth and maturation. Here, too, the effect of the genealogical model is to split descent-lines from life-lines, a split that is reinforced by the doctrine, attributed to August Weismann, that only the characteristics of the genotype, and not those of the phenotype, are transmissible across generations. Thus the division between life-history and genealogy in the anthropology of persons has its precise counterpart in the division between ontogeny and phylogeny in the biology of organisms.

One of the founding premises of the orthodox view in evolutionary biology is that the ontogenetic development of the individual organism is a separate matter from the evolution of the species to which it belongs. To be sure, what an organism does during its life is both a consequence of, and may have consequences for, the evolution of its kind. Its life-cycle is not, however, a part of that evolution. In its Darwinian conception, evolution is

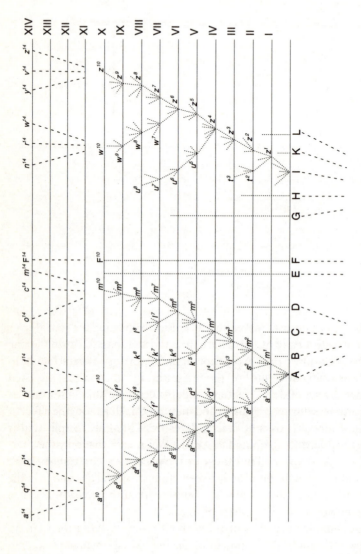

Figure 2. Darwin's schematic depiction of evolutionary phylogeny, in *The Origin of Species*. According to Darwin's explanation of the figure, A to L represent the several species of a genus. The dotted lines indicate their fortunes over the next 10,000 generations (each horizontal band represents a thousand generations). In the upper part of the diagram the phylogenetic lines are continued in a condensed and simplified form for another 4,000 generations. Some species, such as A and I, undergo considerable diversification. Others, such as F, undergo none at all. The vast majority of lines, however, end in extinction. From Darwin (1950 [1859]: 90–1).

not a life process. Evolution takes place across generations, life is expended within each generation—in the project of forwarding the heritable components needed to get it restarted in the future (Ingold 1986: 105–6, 1990: 216). Thus every organism is supposed to be generated with its own unique genotypic specification, virtually complete (though materially not yet begun) at the point of conception, and nothing that it ever does in the course of its life-cycle will change this. Just as, on a kinship chart, a person's position is shown to be fixed by descent without regard to his or her life activity in the world, so also, on the tree of evolutionary phylogeny—or 'descent with modification'—the positioning of a species has nothing to do with the environmentally situated activities of its individual members. Every organism is what it is by virtue of descent, regardless of what it does. The phylogenetic tree, in short, is a tree of genotypes, not of phenotypes, and its constituent lines do not connect real organisms in a lived-in world but virtual organisms in a continuum of abstract time and space.

THE RELATIONAL MODEL

Now for anyone who holds, as I do, that an organism exists only by way of its life activity in the world, this conception of evolutionary phylogeny is decidedly problematic. However, by turning once again to the parallel case of the social anthropological study of kinship we can begin to discern the outlines of an alternative approach. Certainly, for anthropologists, the conception of kinship embodied in the figure of the genealogical line has been the source of no end of trouble. The difficulty arises because among many, if not most, of the peoples with whom anthropologists have worked, all kinds of persons who have no direct genetic connection can be kin, including even non-humans such as particular animals, trees, or features of the landscape. Western anthropologists, primed with the genealogical model, have classically attempted to deal with such anomalous cases by placing them in a special category of 'fictive' kinship which is modelled on, but nevertheless fundamentally distinct from, the real kinship founded in genealogical connection. But the people themselves, for whom there is no anomaly, are telling us something quite different. It is that persons are not constituted, as the genealogical model implies, in advance of their entry into the lifeworld, but rather undergo continual formation throughout their lives, within the contexts of their involvements in specific social and environmental relationships.

Kinship, then, is not about the transmission of intrinsic person-specifications, but about the ways in which other agencies and entities in the environment contribute—through their presence, their activities, and the nurturance they provide—to this formative process. In many societies, for

example, the trees of the forest are considered to be persons who provide suste-
nance and shelter for human beings much as human parents do for their children: the forest, thus, is a parent too (Bird-David 1990; Rival 1998). With the
passage of time, trees develop in strength and stature, as do humans. But their
respective lives do not merely proceed in parallel; rather, they are intimately
intertwined, as they are with those of other inhabitants of the forest. One could
say of trees and humans what Alfred Schutz once said of human parents and
their children, that they 'grow older together' (Schutz 1962: 16–17). Indeed
more than that, they are *grown*. By this I mean that there is more to growth than
the autonomous realisation of pre-specified developmental potentials. At
issue, rather, is the generation of being within what could be called a sphere of
nurture. Through their involvement in the human sphere of nurture, trees grow
people, just as people grow one another (and trees). An ancient tree that has
presided over the passage of many human generations might be regarded as an
ancestor of all those who have grown up under its shelter. These human generations have followed the tree into the world, and have drawn support from it. In
that sense they are successors. But they are *not* descendants, in the sense implied
by the genealogical model.

To grasp this understanding of the kinship of both human and non-
human beings as fellow inhabitants of the lifeworld, we need to ground our
thinking in an alternative model. I call this the *relational model*. On a chart
of genealogical relatedness, as I have shown, the life of each person is collapsed into a single point, which is connected to other such points by lines of
descent. A relational model presents us with precisely the opposite picture.
There are no lines of descent linking successive 'generations' of persons.
Rather, persons are continually coming into being—or undergoing generation—in the course of life itself. To put it in a nutshell, whereas in the
genealogical model life is encompassed within generations, in the relational
model generation is encompassed within the process of life. But this also
entails a radically different conception of the person. According to the
genealogical model, every person is a unique entity whose make-up is a function of specifications received from predecessors, prior to involvement with
other entities of like or unlike kinds. By contrast, the relational model
situates the person in the lifeworld from the very start, as a locus of self-
organising activity: not a generated entity but a site where generation is
going on (the difference between thinking of the person as an 'entity' and as
a 'site' is explored by Harré [1998: 3–5]). Another way of expressing the contrast is to say that the formation of persons is a matter not of procreation
but of *progeneration*.

The conventional term, procreation, captures the sense of begetting
implied when we say that one thing is descended from another. It suggests a
one-off event: the making of something absolutely new out of elements derived

from immediate antecedents. By progeneration, on the other hand, I refer to the continual unfolding of an entire field of relationships within which different beings emerge with their particular forms, capacities, and dispositions. The procreated entity is already complete before its life begins: the design is in place, merely awaiting its fulfilment in the world. But the progenerative process is perpetually going on. As temporally developing loci of growth and activity, persons are—as John Shotter puts it—'always *incomplete*' (1991: 389). Life, for them, is open-ended, always on the verge of new possibilities of being. Moreover, as a principle of progeneration, life is not contained within the span of any particular individual, in the interval between initial conception and final death, nor, therefore, does it have to be restarted, generation after generation, in order to keep a society going. The birth of any person, or the death of another, may call for a reconfiguration of the relational field, but the unfolding of that field—life itself—continues. Actual events of birth and death, therefore, punctuate the progenerative process instead of either opening it or bringing it to a close. Life, with a relational model, does not start or stop. To borrow a phrase from Gilles Deleuze and Félix Guattari, it is a question of 'coming and going rather than starting and finishing' (1988: 25).

From a relational perspective, then, persons should be understood not as procreated entities, connected to one another along lines of genealogical connection or *relatedness*, but as loci of progenerative activity variously positioned within an all-encompassing field of *relationships*. And whereas a person's genealogical position, as I have shown, is determined independently of their location in the lifeworld, every locus within the relational field is itself an emplacement in the world—a site, as Rom Harré puts it, 'from which a person perceives the world and a place from which to act' (1998: 3). Now while each person is at the centre of their own field of perception and action, the position of this centre is not fixed but moves relative to others. As it does so, it lays a trail. Every trail, however erratic and circuitous, is a kind of life-line, a trajectory of change and development. Thus the growth of the person may be understood as a movement along a *way of life*, conceived not as the enactment of role-specifications received from predecessors, but literally as the negotiation of a path through the world. It is from this movement that people draw not just their perceptual orientations but the very substance of their being, while reciprocally contributing to the substantive make-up of others. Such contributions are given and received throughout life, in the contexts of a person's ongoing relationships with human and non-human others. And it is at the points where the life-lines of different persons cross or commingle that these exchanges occur.

EVOLUTION AND DEVELOPMENT

Having set out the main outlines of the relational model, I now want to propose that this model is applicable not only to persons, in the context of the study of kinship, but also, and more generally, to organisms, in the context of the study of their development and evolution. Everything I have said above about the generation of persons applies equally to the generation of organisms. They too, I contend, are loci of progenerative activity, emergent within a life process, and undergoing growth and development along the paths of their relationships with others. To demonstrate this contention I need to pick up the threads of my critique of orthodox neo-Darwinism from where I left off a moment ago. I had reached the point of showing that the phylogenetic tree is a tree of genotypes. Its very construction, therefore, rests on the assumption that for any particular organism, there is some way in which information specifying the range of possible courses that its development could take (the so-called 'reaction norm' of the genotype) can get into the organism before any development has actually occurred. Much of the excitement surrounding the unravelling of the structure of the DNA molecule was fuelled by the belief that it could provide the vehicle for informational transfer that the theory required. This belief, however, is founded upon an illusion.

I do not mean to deny, of course, that every organism starts life with its complement of DNA in the genome. But if the genome is to carry a formal design specification, shaped up through natural selection, from one locus of development to another, then there must be some systematic correspondence between the elements of this specification and the actual DNA of the genome *that is independent of any developmental context*. The existence of such a correspondence has generally been assumed, but has never been demonstrated (Cohen and Stewart 1994: 293–4). The source of the assumption, as Lily Kay (1998) has elegantly demonstrated, lies in a simple confusion concerning the meaning of information, between the conventional sense of the term as the semantic content of messages passing between senders and recipients, and the very specialised sense in which it was invoked by information theorists. In this latter sense, as these theorists were at pains to point out, information has no semantic value at all. Any sequence of digits, however random, counts as information, if the substitution of one digit for another in the sequence can have stochastic effects. The point, however, was lost on the molecular biologists who—having realised that the DNA molecule qualifies as a form of digital information in the technical, information-theoretic sense—jumped to the conclusion that it could therefore be regarded as a *code* that carries a genotypic 'message', in the form of a design specification for constructing an organism of a certain type, from one site of development to the next.

Needless to say, this confusion is still more prevalent today than in those heady days when the structure of DNA was first unravelled. It is, in my view, the Achilles' heel of the entire neo-Darwinian paradigm. For only if the conditions of ontogenetic development are, so to speak, 'nailed down', can DNA possibly be said to carry any kind of message. To put this another way, the modern biological understanding of DNA as a vehicle for the transmission of encoded information presupposes, but does not explain, the trans-generational stability of organic form (Oyama 1992: 224). In practice, what happens is that biologists seek to redescribe the observed phenotypic characteristics of organisms as the outputs of a formal system of epigenetic rules (much as linguists seek to redescribe spoken utterances as outputs of a generative syntax). These rules are then read 'in' to the genome, so that development can be seen as the 'reading off' of a programme or specification that is already there, and that is imported with the genome into the site of inauguration of a new life-cycle. In short, as an account of the evolution of form, neo-Darwinian theory rests on a simple circularity. That is one reason why it has proved so hard to refute.

At root, the issue comes down to one about copying. The orthodox account has it that the formal characters of the incipient organism are copied along with the DNA, in advance of its interaction with the environment, so that they can then 'interact' with the environment to produce the organism. I would argue, to the contrary (and as illustrated schematically in Figure 3), that copying is itself a process that goes on within the context of organism–environment interaction. In other words, the 'missing link' between the genome and the formal attributes of the organism is none other than the developmental process itself. There is, then, no design for the organism, no genotype—except, of course, as this might be retrospectively constructed by the observing biologist. Organic form, in short, is *generated*, not expressed, in development, and arises as an emergent property of the total system of relations set up by virtue of the presence and activity of the organism in its environment. And if that is so—if the forms and capacities of organisms are properties not of genes but of developmental systems—then to account for their evolution we have to understand how these systems are constituted and reconstituted over time.

These arguments are not new. One of their most influential proponents in recent years has been Susan Oyama (1985). The nature of an organism, as she points out, 'is not genotypic . . . but phenotypic', and therefore 'depends on developmental context as profoundly and intimately as it does on the genome. . . . Evolution is thus the derivational history of developmental systems' (Oyama 1989: 5). Yet however much she has been at pains to distinguish her views from orthodox interactionism, her critics continue to confuse the two, claiming that there is nothing in a developmental systems approach that is not perfectly consistent with the premises of neo-Darwinian evolutionary biology (an example is Dunbar 1996). Some kind of mental block prevents these critics from realising that to regard form as emergent within the developmental

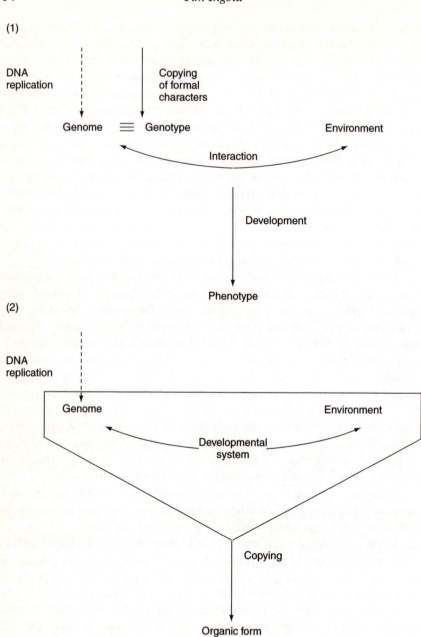

Figure 3. Two theories of copying: (1) in the orthodox, neo-Darwinian account, a design for the organism is copied with the DNA of the genome, which is then 'brought out' in the course of its development within an environmental context; (2) in the 'developmental systems approach' proposed here, the process of copying is equivalent to that of the organism's development in its environment. From Ingold (2000: 396).

process is anything other than a version of gene–environment interactionism. The source of this block seems to lie in an assumption that organisms are *effects* of genetic and environmental *causes*. However the reality, as Daniel Lehrman warned many years ago, is more complex. For the interactions from which the development of an organism proceeds are not between genes and environment, but between *organism* and environment. At every moment of the developmental process, formal structures or behavioural dispositions already established in the course of previous interaction are implicated, through further interaction, in the generation of new ones (Lehrman 1953: 345). And it is not in any of the components of the interacting systems, taken individually, that the constraints on the process are to be found, but rather in the relations among them (Oyama 1993: 8). Thus it is simply not possible to apportion causality between genetic and environmental factors. 'The web of causality', as Esther Thelen writes, 'is intricate and seamless from the moment of birth' (1995: 94). Causation is not a relation between things—genes and environmental factors on the one hand, organisms on the other—that are external to one another, but is immanent in the developmental process itself. Or to put it another way, organisms are both cause and effect of themselves (Goodwin 1988: 108).

Having said that, however, my claim that the genotype does not exist is likely to remain contentious, to say the least. Let me, then, make my position absolutely clear. I do not doubt the existence of the genome, or that it sets in train processes that are crucial to the development of the organism at every stage of its life-cycle. Nor, moreover, do I deny that the composition of the genome changes across generations through a process of variation under natural selection. What I *do* deny is that the DNA sequence in the genome encodes a context-independent design specification, and with it, the idea of natural selection as a design agent. Genes, after all, are but segments of molecules that may or may not have unspecified consequences for the organisms they are in. It is perfectly possible, as Cohen and Stewart have demonstrated, for two quite different creatures to have precisely the same DNA in the genome. Not only can creatures evolve without any genetic change at all, they can also retain a more or less constant form despite considerable modification at the genetic level (Cohen and Stewart 1994: 309). Thus natural selection, leading to changes in the composition of the genome, occurs *within* evolution, but does not explain it. Nor does it even furnish a partial explanation, since to determine what part is due to natural selection, and what part is not, would require an apportionment of causal responsibility for the development of form between genes and environmental experience. And this, as I have shown, cannot sensibly be done. Only by going beyond the theory of evolution through variation under natural selection, and by considering the properties of dynamic self-organisation of developmental systems, can we hope to discover the possible consequences of those changes that *can* be explained by natural selection for the evolutionary process itself.

THE MEANING OF EVOLUTION

By adopting a developmental systems approach we can begin to see how organisms might be understood—like persons—not as procreated entities but rather as loci of growth, of the progenerative unfolding of the entire field of relationships within which each comes into being. It is in this unfolding that the source of their differentiation lies. This, however, calls for a way of thinking about evolution quite different from that to which we have become accustomed from orthodox accounts of evolutionary phylogeny. What, then, is the meaning of evolution from a developmental, or relational, point of view? In a nutshell, it is the process in which organisms come into being with their particular forms and capacities and in which, through their environmentally situated actions, they establish the conditions of development for their successors (Ingold 1998: 95).

In its focus on the unfolding of an entire field of relationships rather than the changing composition of discrete, pre-specified entities, this conception of evolution is, in essence, a topological one, utterly opposed to the statistical conception built into the textbook definition of evolution as 'changing gene frequencies in populations of organisms'. The kind of population thinking exemplified in this latter definition is fundamental to the neo-Darwinian paradigm, as Ernst Mayr, one of its principal architects, has long insisted (Mayr 1982: 45–7). But even opponents of neo-Darwinism, driven perhaps by the powerfully objectifying force of the notion of 'system', seem to find it hard to resist cutting the world of living organisms into pieces and counting up the bits. As John Shotter has pointed out, the demand of orthodox science for accounts to be systematic makes it hard for us to comprehend 'a *poetics* of relationships . . . which leaves their precise nature open'. We tend to assume that everything of importance already exists, somewhere in the system, only awaiting discovery, and thus fail to recognise the creativity of those processes of growth and development that are going on all around us in the very world that, through our own participation, we seek to know (Shotter 1991: 380–1).

Herein, indeed, lies the source of my one significant disagreement with the developmental systems approach as it has been expounded in the writings of Susan Oyama and her collaborators, Paul Griffiths and Russell Gray. While rejecting the gene-centred informational account of neo-Darwinism and the dualisms to which this gives rise, of genotype and environment, nature and nurture, form and substance, and so on, these writers seek to retain the fundamental Darwinian logic of variation under natural selection. Only for them, the units of selection are not genes, nor individual organisms, but developmental systems. Thus, for Oyama, selection is the 'outcome of the differential propagation of developmental systems', leading to evolutionary changes in their constitution and distribution (1993: 13–14). And for Griffiths and Gray, evolution occurs because variant developmental processes or life-cycles 'differ in their capacity to replicate themselves' (1994: 300). The effect of applying this logic is once again to rupture the continuity of the relational field, to substitute self-replicating entities for loci of creative growth, and—most fundamentally—to *put life back into things*, albeit of a rather more inclusive nature than the individual organism bounded by its skin. Ontogeny, it appears, is wrapped up within each generation of a developmental system, whereas phylogeny is change in developmental systems across generations. This is to fall right back into the presumptions of the genealogical model, and to reduce an approach that could revolutionise the way we think about organisms and their evolution to little more than a footnote to Darwin.

In the view I have presented here, to the contrary, an organism's life-cycle is not bracketed off from the evolutionary process but is the very crucible from which it unfolds. This explodes, once and for all, the conventional dichotomy between ontogenetic development and phylogenetic change. The life of organisms, instantiated in their activity, is not a derivative output of already evolved capacities but the active process of their formation. In what they do, in their modes of life, organisms set up the conditions not only for their own future development but also for that of others to which they relate. In this regard they figure not just as passive objects of evolutionary change but as creative agents, producers as well as products of their own evolution. This, however, means taking an unorthodox view not only of evolution but also of life itself. We can no longer think of organisms as 'living things', as though life were a qualifying attribute of objects—more often than not identified with some feature of molecular composition like DNA or carbon chemistry. Rather, every organism should be understood as the embodiment of a particular way of being alive, of a *modus vivendi*. Life, if you will, is the creative potential of a dynamic field of relationships within which specific beings emerge and take the forms they do, each in relation to the others. In that sense, life is not so much *in* organisms as organisms are *in* life (Ingold 1990: 215).

THE LIFE-HISTORIES OF ARTEFACTS

It is now time to turn from organisms and persons to artefacts. What assumptions are entailed in rendering an account of the evolution of cultural entities in terms of the genealogical model? And what are the implications of adopting our alternative, relational model for understanding the dynamics of culture change? Recall that the founding premise of the genealogical model is the split between the descent line and the life-line—a split that translates, in the biological context, into that between phylogeny and ontogeny. In the case of artefacts, the counterpart to ontogeny is the process that leads from an initial conception or plan in the mind of the maker to the final form of the object. And the counterpart to phylogeny is the transmission, across generations of makers, of the elements of design. The making of artefacts, however, is commonly held to differ from the growth of organisms on the grounds that the design specifications underwriting the construction process are—in the case of artefacts— exterior to the objects themselves (Monod 1972: 21). Whereas the genetic programme is 'inside' the organism, the construction blueprint is 'outside' the artefact. Thus the forms of artefacts, it is supposed, are imposed from without, rather than disclosed from within. It follows that there can be no genealogies of artefacts as such; lines of descent connect the minds of makers, not the things they make. They are lines along which is transmitted the knowledge required to make these things. This knowledge is distinguished from the resultant artefactual forms much as, in biology, the genotype is distinguished from the phenotype. Indeed the elements of which it is composed have often been conceived as particles of transmissible cultural information—or 'memes'—analogous to genes.

Now the power of the theory of variation under natural selection lies in its apparent ability to account for the semblance of design in living organisms in the absence of an intentional design agent. But, unlike organisms, artefacts *do* have their designers. This has led many commentators to argue that the evolution of cultural entities is more Lamarckian than Darwinian in character, in that variations of design are pre-selected in the knowledge of the conditions that are likely to be encountered in putting the artefact to use. However, regardless of whether our theory is Darwinian or Lamarckian, or (which comes to the same thing) of whether the selection involved is consequential or premeditated, it is still assumed that to ask about the forms of objects is, in essence, to pose a question about their design. That is to say, organisms are presumed to have designs, just as artefacts are: at issue is merely the extent to which the designs themselves have been self-consciously authored. Even in its strictly Darwinian guise, selection theory offers an argument from design, in that the manifest form of an organism or artefact is alleged to arise unproblematically from the design that precedes it. The one, it is said, is but an 'expression' of the other. The growth of the organism, or the making of the artefact, merely brings out, materially, what was already there from the outset, whether implanted in the organism with its genes, or in the mind of a maker stocked with its equivalent memes. Just as the basic architecture of the organism is supposed to be established as a genetic 'blueprint' at the very moment of conception, so the artefact is said to exist, fully represented as a virtual object in the mind, before a finger has been lifted in its construction. All the *creative* work, it seems, has been done in advance, whether by natural selection or by human reason. What remains is the simple task of mechanically transcribing the prior design on to raw material.

A relational biology, however, questions the very existence of the genotype as a formal pre-specification of organic design. Adopting such a biology, I have argued that the form of the organism has to be understood as a property of the developmental system from which it emerges. I now want to advance precisely the same argument with regard to artefacts. The final form of the artefact, I contend, is no more prefigured on the side of its maker than is the form of the organism prefigured on the side of its genes. It is neither on the 'inside' nor on the 'outside'; rather, it emerges through the unfolding of a field of relations that *cross-cuts* the interface between the within and without of things. Just as the relations comprising the developmental system cut across the interface between organism and environment, so the relations whose unfolding give rise to the form of the artefact cut across the boundary between the maker and the material with which he or she works. Thus the form of the pot emerges from the movements of the potter's hands, which respond at every moment to the feel of the clay. The resultant artefact is a kind of condensation or sedimentation of that movement: in this sense every constructed object, as G. H. Mead put it, is a 'collapsed act' (Mead 1977 [1938]: 97). This is not to deny that when people set out to make things, they may lay plans and formulate intentions. They may have an idea in mind of what they mean to make; and may even construct models and blueprints. But it is not from such plans and blueprints that the forms of artefacts arise, but from the skilled, sensuous activity of those who make and build them. Where plans or blueprints exist, as they often do in the fields of architecture and engineering, they too are artefacts generated within the same, environmentally situated process from which also emerge the forms they are said to specify. But, as David Turnbull has shown in his brilliant re-analysis of the building of the great cathedral of Chartres (1993), they may not exist at all.

Artefacts, then, have life-histories, just as organisms and persons do. But these histories are not suspended, as the genealogical model would imply, between initial conception and final form, any more than the organic life-history is suspended between genotype and phenotype. To the contrary, both the forms of artefacts, and the conceptions to which they correspond and of which they may be taken to be the realisations, are suspended as moments of their life-histories. Earlier, I referred to the way in which, for certain forest-dwelling peoples, the life-histories of persons are intertwined with those of trees. But what goes for trees could equally well go for artefacts such as buildings. They, too, are formed through a process of development within an environment that critically includes their human builders-cum-inhabitants. And through their presence in the environment they, in turn, condition the development of those who dwell in them. That the life-histories of trees can continue even after they have been felled and incorporated into buildings is beautifully exemplified by John Knight's (1998) ethnography of Japanese upland foresters. They say that trees have two lives. During their first life they are grown and nurtured in the ground. But in their second life, as house timbers, they form a part of the environment of nurture for the human domestic group. In this example, we can see how buildings are no more procreated entities than are trees or persons, but are rather loci of progenerative activity. People grow trees, trees become parts of buildings, buildings grow people. The cycle is never-ending.

In short, the history of an artefact is a history of its involvement in the pro-generative process that is life itself. Conventionally, we say that organisms are 'living things' whereas artefacts are not. But if, as I have suggested, we regard life not as an interior property of things but as the creative potential of a dynamic field of relationships, then artefacts can be *in* life just as much as organisms can. Many non-Western peoples do indeed consider artefacts to be alive in this sense. Such peoples are often branded by us as 'primitive animists'. But in reality, as Nurit Bird-David (1999) has shown, their understandings are perfectly consistent with a relational epistemology. I have already shown that life, as conceived within an epistemology of this kind, does not start or stop, but is continually going on. For the same reason, artefacts, like persons (and indeed organisms in general), are never really complete or finished. Conventionally, we say that an artefact is finished at the point where its form matches an initial con-ception; thus any further changes are said to belong to the phase of 'using' rather than 'making'. From a relational point of view, however, using is not something that *follows on* from making, as dwelling in a house follows on from building it. Rather, as the philosopher Martin Heidegger put it, 'to build is in itself already to dwell' (Heidegger 1971: 146). Thus persons and things are continually coming into being through their mutual implication in certain practices and patterns of use. This coming into being is a process of evolution.

REPLICATION AND REPRODUCTION

It remains for me to tackle the question of how the forms of artefacts, or of cul-tural entities more generally, persist over time. The genealogical model explains such persistence as a consequence of the inter-generational transmission of particles of information, from which are fashioned the models, recipes, or designs which in turn instruct people in their activities of making. Crucially, it is assumed that information is copied, from one mind to another, independ-ently and in advance of the activities in which it is subsequently brought to bear. Likewise, as we have already seen, orthodox evolutionary biology assumes that information specifying the construction of an organism is copied, with the DNA, in advance of its life in an environment. I have argued, to the contrary, that copying is tantamount to the development of the organism in a specific environmental context. I now want to show, along precisely the same lines, that the copying on which the continuity of cultural forms depends is not an automatic transcription of informational content from mind to mind, prior to its application in the world, but rather an aspect of the growth and development of the person, involving repeated tasks and exercises—or what Whitehouse (1996: 113) aptly calls 'the labours of maturation'. It is, in short, a matter of *following, in one's actions, what other people do*. Below, I elaborate on this point.

The conventional idea that cultural information is 'handed down' across generations finds support in traditional theories of social learning. Though differing in detail, these theories hold that novices first acquire a model or schema for a certain operation by observing the movements of already accomplished practitioners, and then go on to imitate these movements by running off exemplars of the operation in question from the schema. Now I do not deny that the learning of practical skills involves both observation and imitation. But the former is no more a matter of forming internal, mental representations of observed behaviour than is the latter a matter of converting these representations into manifest practice. To be sure, novices learn the art of making things by observing other practitioners at work, and by copying what they do. Their observation, however, is not detached from, but grounded in, their own active, perceptual engagement with their surroundings. Faced with certain tasks, in specific situations, they are *shown* what to do and what to watch out for, under the tutelage of more experienced hands. To show something to someone is to cause it to be made present for that person, so that he or she can apprehend it directly. Here the responsibility of the tutor is to set up the conditions in which novices are afforded the possibility of such unmediated experience. Placed in situations of this kind, they are instructed to attend to this or that aspect of what can be seen, touched or heard, and—through successive trials—to bring their own bodily movements into line with those of their attention so as to achieve the kind of rhythmic adjustment of perception and action that lies at the heart of fluent performance. Colloquially, we say that it is a matter of getting the 'feel' of things (Gatewood 1985).

In this process, no information is being handed down independently of the context of its application. To be sure, the tutor may issue verbal instructions, or, in the absence of a tutor, instructions may be read from a recipe book or manual. But, just as in the life of an organism it is impossible to say what any gene is *for* outside a specific environment of development, so, likewise, instructions draw their meanings from their positioning within a field of practice. For example, I can follow the instruction in a recipe for making an omelette, to 'break an egg into a mixing bowl and whisk with a fork', only because it speaks to my own embodied experience of handling the fork, of breaking eggs, and of finding the relevant ingredients and utensils from the various corners of my kitchen. Instructions such as these are like signposts in a landscape: they provide specific directions to practitioners as they make their way through what I have elsewhere called a 'taskscape' (Ingold 2000: 195). What they do not do is *represent* the taskscape. The metaphor of transmission is therefore highly misleading. Nothing, strictly speaking, is being transmitted at all. It would be more appropriate to describe the growth of practical knowledge in the life-history of a person as taking place through *guided rediscovery*. This is not a matter of replicating memes or any other such particles of cultural information. For what each generation contributes to the next are not rules and representations for the production of appropriate behaviour, but rather the specific circumstances under which successors, growing up in a social world, can develop their own bodily skills and dispositions, and their powers of awareness and response. Learning in this sense is tantamount to what James Gibson, the pioneer of ecological psychology, called an 'education of attention' (Gibson 1979: 254).

To conclude, making things—omelettes, clay pots, wooden buildings, or whatever—calls for a precise coordination of perception and action that is learned through copying the movements of experienced practitioners in socially scaffolded contexts. Making, in other words, *is* copying; it is not the realisation of a design that has already been copied. Another way of expressing the same contrast would be in terms of a distinction between *reproduction* and *replication* (Jablonka 2000: 39). To replicate a form means simply to run it off, mechanically, from a template; to reproduce a form means literally to produce it again, through the re-enactment of specific tasks or activities within an environment. A piece of music, for example, is replicated every time it is played from a disc, but is reproduced every time it is performed with an instrument. The genealogical model treats every artefact as a replica, run off from a pre-existing schema. From the point of view of a relational model, however, each time a form is created it is produced anew, as the crystallisation of concrete, situated activity. Every form, then, is an original, not a replica. But by the same token, no form has an origin, in the sense of a 'master' to which all subsequent instances stand as replicas. Precisely the same, of course, applies in the case of organic forms. Here, the 'master' imputed by the genealogical model would be the genotype. But the genotype, as I have shown, does not exist. In each generation, form emerges anew, in the course of ontogenetic development; it is not run off from a pre-existing design specification. And with organisms as with artefacts, with biological entities as with cultural ones, the trans-generational stability of form is due to the dynamics of reproduction, not to the mechanics of replication.

HISTORY AS EVOLUTION

According to the anthropologist Maurice Godelier (1989: 63), history is to be understood as a movement in which human beings 'produce society in order to live'. I would rather say that it is a movement in which, in the course of their social lives, they *grow* one another. Thus, through history, lives fashioned within contexts shaped by the presence and activities of predecessors, in turn affect the conditions of development for successors. Consider, for example, the historical emergence of those capacities that we are accustomed to calling 'cultural', instantiated in everything from commonplace practices of walking, talking, and thinking to the specialised skills of the writer, musician, or scientist. True to the assumptions of the genealogical model, the orthodox account would have it that these capacities are stored in programmes that are handed down across generations through a process of social learning, prior to their expression in the activities of individuals, as a kind of ideational supplement to the corpus of information encoded and transmitted in the genes. Thus, uniquely for humans, it is supposed that two channels for the inter-generational transmission of information operate in parallel: the one genetic, the other cultural (Durham 1991). But in reality, as I have shown, no information is being transmitted, genetic or cultural. Rather, the manifold capacities of human beings undergo continual formation, re-formation and transformation within the contexts of relations between novices and relatively more experienced hands, through practice and training within an environment.

From a relational perspective, in short, it is evident that the formation of so-called cultural capacities is an aspect of the growth of persons within spheres of nurture. This growth is a process of ontogenetic development, and the capacities to which it gives rise are fully properties of the developing organism. In that sense they are as much biological as they are cultural. For while we may grow out of certain ways of doing things, and grow into others, no-one has ever grown out of biology, or grown into culture! Now if evolution is about the changing forms and capacities of organisms, then we must conclude that whatever capacities have emerged in history, and which may be taken to distinguish humans of one tradition from those of another, have themselves evolved. History, it appears, is no more than a continuation, into the field of human relations, of a process that is going on throughout the organic world. The distinction between history and evolution is thus dissolved. Indeed evolution is proceeding around us all the time, in the very historical unfolding of our lives. As the forms of language, for example, emerge through the people's activities of talking to one another, language evolves even as we speak. Likewise the capacity of the feet to carry us over varied terrain, and that of the hands to deliver precise movements, evolve as we walk around and use tools. Neither language, nor bipedality, nor tool-use is given as a fixed attribute of human nature, outside the current of speaking, walking, and tool-using. Perhaps these observations give a new twist to Karl Marx's celebrated but enigmatic remark that 'history itself is a *real* part of *natural* history—of nature developing into man' (Marx 1964: 143, original emphases).

But to dissolve the distinction between evolution and history is also to do away with the notion of human origins. Implied in this notion is the idea that, at some point in the past, nowadays generally identified with the onset of the epoch that archaeologists call the Upper Palaeolithic, ancestral populations appeared that were equipped with the same basic morphology, capacities, and dispositions that are common to all human beings today. Packaged in the genotype, these evolved components of essential humanity are supposed to have been passed down the generations, with very little change, over tens of thousands of years. Yet over this same period, it is argued, culture and civilisation have advanced at an ever-accelerating pace. History, in other words, is conceived to rise upon the baseline of a fully formed and universal 'human nature'. But if human history has thus taken off from a point of origin, what could it mean to have been living close to that point, or even at the crucial moment of transition itself? Were such people semi-cultural, gearing up for history? How can one conceivably distinguish those actions and events that carried forward the movement of human history from those that set it in motion in the first place? To be able to answer these questions one would have to suppose that humans, uniquely among animals, had succeeded in breaking through the boundaries of nature within which the lives of all other creatures are contained. But there are no such boundaries: 'the edge of nature', as Matt Cartmill puts it, 'is a hallucination' (1993: 244). Hence it makes no sense even to ask what it means to breach them.

The argument I have set out in this chapter suggests that the entire project of searching for the genesis of some essential humanity is seriously misguided. We look in vain for the evolutionary origins of human capacities for the simple reason that these capacities are not fixed genetically but continue to evolve, alongside the conditions of their development, in the course of history itself. It is, I believe, a great mistake to populate the past with people like ourselves, equipped with the underlying capacities or potentials to do everything we do today, such that history appears as nothing more than the teleological course of their progressive fulfilment. Indeed the idea of an origin, defined as the point at which these capacities were first established, ready and waiting to be 'filled up' with cultural content, is part of an elaborate ideological justification for the present order of things and, as such, but one aspect of the intense presentism of modern thought. It is time we recognised that our humanity, far from having been set once and for all as an evolutionary legacy from our Palaeolithic past, is something that we have continually to work at and for which we ourselves must bear the responsibility. Humans are beings; what they are is what they do. The process of their 'origination' is none other than life itself, and far from having been completed at some point in the past, it will continue for as long as human life goes on.

REFERENCES

Bird-David, N. (1990), 'The Giving Environment: Another Perspective on the Economic System of Gatherer-Hunters', *Current Anthropology* 31: 189–96.

Bird-David, N. (1999), '"Animism" Revisited: Personhood, Environment and Relational Epistemology', *Current Anthropology* 40 (Supplement): S67–S91.

Cartmill, M. (1993), *A View to a Death in the Morning: Hunting and Nature through History*. Cambridge, MA: Harvard University Press.

Cohen, J. and Stewart, I. (1994), *The Collapse of Chaos: Discovering Simplicity in a Complex World*. Harmondsworth: Viking.

Darwin, C. (1950), *On the Origin of Species by Means of Natural Selection, or, the Preservation of Favoured Races in the Struggle for Life*. London: Watts (reprint of 1st edn of 1859).

Deleuze, G. and Guattari, F. (1988), *A Thousand Plateaus: Capitalism and Schizophrenia*, translated by B. Massumi. London: Athlone Press.

Dunbar, R. I. M. (1996), 'How Not to Do Biology', *Cultural Dynamics* 8: 363–8.

Durham, W. H. (1991), *Coevolution: Genes, Culture and Human Diversity*. Stanford, CA: Stanford University Press.

Gatewood, J. B. (1985), 'Actions Speak Louder than Words', in J. W. Dougherty (ed.), *Directions in Cognitive Anthropology*. Urbana, IL: University of Illinois Press, pp. 199–219.

Gibson, J. J. (1979), *The Ecological Approach to Visual Perception*. Boston, MA: Houghton Mifflin.

Godelier, M. (1989), 'Incest Taboo and the Evolution of Society', in A. Grafen (ed.), *Evolution and its Influence*. Oxford: Clarendon Press, pp. 63–92.

Goodwin, B. C. (1988), 'Organisms and Minds: The Dialectics of the Animal–Human Interface in Biology', in T. Ingold (ed.), *What is an Animal?* London: Unwin Hyman, pp. 100–9.

Griffiths, P. E. and Gray, R. D. (1994), 'Developmental Systems and Evolutionary Explanation', *Journal of Philosophy* 91(6): 277–304.

Harré, R. (1998), *The Singular Self: An Introduction to the Psychology of Personhood*. London: Sage.

Heidegger, M. (1971), *Poetry, Language, Thought*, translated by A. Hofstadter. New York: Harper and Row.

Ingold, T. (1986), *Evolution and Social Life*. Cambridge: Cambridge University Press.

Ingold, T. (1990), 'An Anthropologist Looks at Biology', *Man* (n.s.) 25: 208–29.

Ingold, T. (1998), 'The Evolution of Society', in A. C. Fabian (ed.), *Evolution: Society, Science and the Universe*. Cambridge: Cambridge University Press, pp. 79–99.

Ingold, T. (2000), *The Perception of the Environment: Essays on Livelihood, Dwelling and Skill*. London: Routledge.

Jablonka, E. (2000), 'Lamarckian Inheritance Systems in Biology: A Source of Metaphors and Models in Technological Evolution', in J. Ziman (ed.), *Technological Innovation as an Evolutionary Process*. Cambridge: Cambridge University Press, pp. 27–40.

Kay, L. (1998), 'A Book of Life? How the Genome Became an Information System and DNA a Language', *Perspectives in Biology and Medicine* 41: 504–28.

Knight, J. (1998), 'The Second Life of Trees: Family Forestry in Upland Japan', in L. Rival (ed.), *The Social Life of Trees: Anthropological Perspectives on Tree Symbolism*. Oxford: Berg, pp. 197–218.

Lehrman, D. (1953), 'A Critique of Konrad Lorenz's Theory of Instinctive Behavior', *Quarterly Review of Biology* 28: 337–63.

Marx, K. (1964), *The Economic and Political Manuscripts of 1844*, translated by M. Milligan, edited by D. J. Struik. New York: International Publishers.

Mayr, E. (1982), *The Growth of Biological Thought*. Cambridge, MA: Harvard University Press.

Mead, G. H. (1977), 'The Process of Mind in Nature' [1938], in *George Herbert Mead on Social Psychology*, edited by A. Strauss. Chicago: University of Chicago Press, pp. 85–111.

Monod, J. (1972), *Chance and Necessity*, translated by A. Wainhouse. London: Collins.

Oyama, S. (1985), *The Ontogeny of Information: Developmental Systems and Evolution*. Cambridge: Cambridge University Press.

Oyama, S. (1989), 'Ontogeny and the Central Dogma: Do We Need the Concept of Genetic Programming in Order to Have an Evolutionary Perspective?', in M. Gunnar and E. Thelen (eds), *Systems in development: The Minnesota Symposia on Child Psychology*, Vol. 22. Hillsdale, NJ: Erlbaum, pp. 1–34.

Oyama, S. (1992), 'Ontogeny and Phylogeny: A Case of Metarecapitulation?', in P. Griffiths (ed.), *Trees of Life*. Dordrecht: Kluwer Academic, pp. 211–39.

Oyama, S. (1993), 'Constraints and Development', *Netherlands Journal of Zoology* 43: 6–16.

Rival, L., ed. (1998), *The Social Life of Trees: Anthropological Perspectives on Tree Symbolism*. Oxford: Berg.

Schutz, A. (1962), *The Problem of Social Reality: Collected Papers I*, edited by M. Natanson. The Hague: Nijhoff.

Shotter, J. (1991), 'A Poetics of Relational Forms: The Sociality of Everyday Social Life', *Cultural Dynamics* 4: 379–96.

Thelen, E. (1995), 'Motor Development: A New Synthesis', *American Psychologist* 50: 79–95.

Turnbull, D. (1993), 'The Ad Hoc Collective Work of Building Gothic Cathedrals with Templates, String and Geometry', *Science, Technology and Human Values* 18: 315–40.

Whitehouse, H. (1996), 'Jungles and Computers: Neuronal Group Selection and the Epidemiology of Representations', *Journal of the Royal Anthropological Institute* (n.s.) 2: 99–116.

An Integrating Scaffold: Toward an Autonomy-Theoretic Modelling of Cultural Change

C. A. HOOKER

1. INTRODUCTION

CULTURE AND CULTURAL CHANGE are at least as complex to understand as are flight and other biological features. This paper applies tools newly developed for the dynamical analysis of biological organisation to take some initial steps toward characterising cultural dynamics. While the ideas are complex, length constraints preclude expansiveness, whence the presentation must proceed rather brusquely.

Knowing that genes associated with flight capacity have increased is not the same as providing an explanatory theory *of* flight, which in addition requires at least an aerodynamic account of what flight requires, a physiological account of how it is achieved and exploited, and an ecological account of when it is advantageous and why it can form stable niches. Without all these we cannot explain how and why flight developed (e.g. as opposed to gliding), what limitations it imposes (e.g. on energy budgets, hence food sources), what its range of expression is (cf. albatross versus humming birds), what are its characteristic failure modes (e.g. inappropriate pectoral blood supply for wind regime), etc. And without these understandings we cannot understand how it might change. Further, explanation deeply involves integrated holistic processes that resist modelling as simple bundles of separate units, genetic or otherwise.[1] Respiration, for example, involves sub-cellular biochemical processes supplied through a system of gas exchange in the lungs and delivered to tissue cells by a cardio-vascular system, coordinated by the nervous system. The overall process of respiration is *multi-level*: involving sub-cellular to organism coordination;

---

[1] See for example Ahouse (1998), Auyang (1998), Christensen and Hooker (2000b, 2000c), Depew and Weber (1999), Griffiths (1992), Jablonka and Lamb (1995), Miklos (1993), Raff (1996). Of course, this does not mean that 'top-down' is the only, or even the dominant, approach we should use for investigating such systems; rather, both analytic ('bottom-up') and synthetic methods should be used interactively and opportunistically.

Proceedings of the British Academy, **112**, 67–86, © The British Academy 2002.

multi-dimensional: involving organised interactions among many body para-meters; *multi-modal*: involved in many different bodily modes of operation (motor, cognition, stress, etc.); *multi-plexed*: for example the cardio-vascular system simultaneously transports resources (oxygen etc.), wastes (carbon dioxide etc.), regulatory hormones, and so on; *multi-produced*: producing many different biochemical products; and *multi-phasic* (asynchronous and non-stationary): respiratory processes occur on many different timescales, with local parameters constantly changing functions of temporary activity while more global respiratory parameters are functions of the longer-term developmental and subsequent functional history of the organism. It is, then, the dynamics of complexes of such processes in their organismic, communal, and ecological setting that are needed to understand biological change.

And similarly, I suggest, for understanding cultural change. Consider clothing as a typical human cultural feature:

(1) Clothing serves many functions simultaneously (multi-plexed): body temperature control, injury protection, personal comfort, social role/status indication, individuality creation, aesthetic expression, social conformity/deviance indication, etc. In consequence it is also involved in modulating many different interactions simultaneously, for example interaction with the surrounding light and air (or water), with nearby solid surfaces, and in various aspects of social interaction.

(2) The realisation of clothing functionality is multi-level, requiring peo-ple with appropriate internal attitudes, preferences, and behaviours; influencing performative aspects of every social activity (e.g. perform-ing authoritatively in a business suit); and involving all of the processes that make up the fabrication, fashion, fabric materials pro-duction (including primary production), and recycling industries. Many different interactive processes thus combine in complex ways to constitute an act or tradition of clothing (multi-dimensional), from production, to performing with and evaluating, to recycling.

(3) There is a large variety of clothing products and product attributes (multi-producted), from swimsuits to business suits to space suits, from see-through, breeze-through to imperviousness (to water, radiation, etc.).

(4) Clothing is involved in many different biological and social modes (multi-modal): differentiating work and leisure, dangerous work from safe work (and many forms of work, e.g. priest from pilot), domestic from public leisure (and many forms of leisure, e.g. swimming from sailing). It is also involved in many industrial production and manu-facturing modes, from agriculture to petrochemicals, many different distributional modes, from commercial catwalk fashion to charity, etc.

(5) This complex of interactive processes persists on many different timescales (asynchronous). The overall structure of production, wearing/performing/evaluating, and recycling provides the basic organisational form that persists on multi-generational timescales, through material and social change in its details and products. Clothing infrastructure processes—in transport, production, commercial and domestic infrastructures—also provide important organisational constraints persisting on timescales of one to a few generations. Clothing products—internal socially referenced clothing attitudes and associated social patterns that result at any time, and the correlative material objects—are by comparison ephemeral (timescales largely sub-generational to one-generation) and, while contributing to change in themselves via human responses to them, mostly touch only relatively superficial details of the process and infrastructure organisation. As technology, work role, and lifestyle requirements have changed, various aspects of this complex have radically changed organisation (non-stationary).

In sum: the cultural aspect, clothing, designates a widely diffused but socially integrative, multi-dimensional, multi-modal, multi-plexed, multi-producted, and multi-phasic complex of highly interactive and plastic, highly organised processes and concomitant states. This is the kind of holistic dynamical feature that constitutes culture, just as respiration and other major biological features constitute living systems. Understanding cultural change involves characterising such features as clothing dynamically, placing the interactive complex of these cultural features in their organismic, communal, and ecological settings. The bad news arising from this is that our modelling of cultural dynamics is as embryonic as is our biological modelling generally in these respects. The good news is that culture reveals a fascinatingly complex dynamical reality for study.

2. CULTURAL ROLE IN DYNAMICAL PERSPECTIVE

2.1 What is culture that we may model it? Eliotese culture

According to T. S. Eliot's *Notes Towards the Definition of Culture*, in its broadest sense culture is 'all the characteristic activities and interests of a people'. For the English this is to include both the Henley Regatta and boiled cabbage cut into sections (Eliot 1948: 31). Beyond this broad but superficial characterisation, Eliot argues for three interesting and important pre-conditions for sustaining a culture: first, a growing, developing complex of processes fostering its transmission; second, detailed regional variations that fit it intimately to local conditions; third, its major institutions manifest an internal richness of diversity within unity. The reason for this is Eliot's view that one cannot form a culture out of any old collection of activities and interests; rather, for a group of people to have a culture they must form a coherent unity that is: (a) locally well adapted and self-regenerating; (b) of sufficient stability for its individuals to adapt to it (to become acculturated) and for it to accommodate environmental and internally generated change; (c) of sufficient internal richness and diversity to provide niches for its diverse individuals plus space for creative variation and adaptation to local conditions; (d) of sufficient communal coherence to provide the resources for continued adaptation; and (e) able to show sufficient adaptability and self-organisation to be able to develop more deeply organised complexity. In short, cultured communities are *thereby* made into 'organic unities', they are organism-like.

Eliot's conception strikes me as going to the essence of the place of culture in the life of a species, squarely locating culture as a natural extension of biological capacities (see further below), and I shall adopt it as my starting point here. Culture plays a central role in organising ourselves and our communities into well-functioning wholes, providing organisational capacities for self-regeneration (including culture), adaptation, and learning. In consequence, cultured communities have an adaptive history that, because of finitude and open-ended responsiveness to local contingencies, will in varying degrees display idiosyncratic local histories at various spatio-temporal scales. From this perspective, cultures are much more than 'surface colour' and penetrate more deeply than a collection of social statistics. Cultures characterise the organisational dynamics of our very communal being. It is these Eliotese intuitions that need capturing in any adequate theory of cultural dynamics.

2.2 Shaped/shaping dynamics: the delicate balance

Given Eliot's characterisation of its deep and multiple roles, we cannot expect any simple cultural dynamics. Culture emerges from dynamical interactions among individuals and between individuals and their environment, and yet constitutes an irreducibly holistic dynamical organisation that shapes individuals even as it is shaped by them. Suppose a group of people together build and sail a fishing boat for a livelihood; the boat emerges from their interactive activities, but in sailing it successfully they are equally bound by its laws of thrust and stability and this shapes their roles and behaviours. Indeed, the same was true of the building of it. Similarly, humans construct and navigate their communities through the ecological, social, and spiritual seas of life in their little boats of culture, shaping it to their discovered communal ends even while it shapes them and the courses of their individual lives.[2]

This shaped/shaping two-way interaction, especially when delicately balanced, leads to exquisitely subtle dynamics. Neuronal interconnections can be physically altered by the organised activities of their local neural assembly, even while their own activity contributes to constituting assembly activity. Here we have an interactive interplay between simultaneous 'top-down' collective, and 'bottom-up' individual, dynamical constraints whose delicate balance permits global integration with local individuation. The balanced interplay of top-down and bottom-up constraints is found in many circumstances—for example in physical phase transitions quite generally—and wherever it is found, in the context of suitable driving (amplifying) and damping (stabilising) processes, it yields rich individual and collective dynamics and powerful self-organisation (cf. note 3 and references), the combination grounding multi-faceted adaptiveness. Humans and their cultures are no exception here. The complex and delicately balanced interrelationships between individuals and cultured society leads to very rich adaptive dynamics marked by complex fusions of individuality and acculturated sociality, generating idiosyncratic individual, group, and communal histories each showing frequent, complex, and unpredictable, yet typically manageably coherent, changes. This integrated, delicately balanced process organisation needs to be captured as distinctive of culture.

The interactive balance involved here is an instance of the basic balance between order and disorder that characterises the organisation of life generally. An organised system is one where every component has an ordered, but unique, role to play in contributing to the whole. Gases are unordered and so unorganised. Crystals, with their regularly repeated identical planes, are highly ordered; for this very reason, however, they are only trivially organised because their component behaviour is too uniform. Living systems, we will see, are essentially highly organised in a profound sense (§4.1) but, because of the uniqueness of component dynamics this implies, are not so strongly ordered. They exist in a delicate balance between insufficient, and too much, order. This basic circumstance has many expressions, of which culture is

---

[2] The analogy is borrowed from Neurath (1959) who, borrowing from Aristotle, likened the continual reconstruction of scientific belief to rebuilding a boat while afloat, an apt metaphor for cultural dynamics generally, cf. Vickers (1970) on political management and, more literally, Hutchins (1995) on cognitive change. While the boat has an interior organisation which can be described from 'inside', within the maritime tradition, it is the 'outside' organisation imposed by sailing and fishing dynamics that is the foundation for understanding it and so it is with culture generally; hence I focus here on the dynamics of Eliotese function and leave the roles of interior cultural content—the dominant description of culture in a culture—for later consideration. But it is worth noting that the contrary approach to science, i.e. that it has a purely internally specified 'logic', has fared badly and we are now paying more attention to its institutional dynamics (Hooker 1995).

one—but of a special character that transcends any simple trade-off between the extremes (see §2.4).[3]

Social constructability is necessary for possessing a culturally suitable plasticity, otherwise the global constraining character of culture would lock its members out of shaping it and so lock it in, extinguishing Eliotese culture. But constructability does not ensure suitably shapeable plasticity; termite society is constructed by termites but is not culturally plastic. Culture requires a particular relationship between the responsive, constructive capacities of individuals and the globally binding capacity of the emergent society; too little binding and the society falls apart into a mere aggregate (e.g. a pure capitalist transactional economy?), too much binding and Eliotese culture is squeezed out by merely rigid habits. But our shaping by culture is significantly plastic still; for example 'stone age' people can be taught to fly jet planes, and even to adopt the jet-set social world. And our cultures are equally plastic and locally responsive to us and our environment across various timescales (cf. clothing above). In such Eliotese cultures, powerful adaptive individual–group dynamics characterise all orders of organisation.

Neurones show something more than group reorganisation in their shaped/shaping dynamics. Individual neurones can also be internally altered by the organised activities of their local neural assembly, even while their own activity contributes to constituting assembly activity. Available individual modification in general adds fine structure to top-down/bottom-up group dynamics and individual adaptiveness to its collective adaptiveness. But it also opens up a special form of this dynamics, where individuals are internally tuned to differentiate among group behaviours. This is true of neurones and contributes to the distinctively powerful adaptiveness of brains. Human brains, in particular, make it true of humans, whose resulting distinctive intentional organisation makes it possible to act in far-reaching communally referenced

---

[3] For technical discussion of order and organisation see Collier and Hooker (1999; cf. note 13). At present we are in the challenging if awkward position of having no insightful mathematical way of capturing top-down/bottom-up dynamics, or indeed of organised dynamics generally. Recent large advances in understanding non-linear dynamics (cf. Pines 1988 and other references in Hooker 1995) have tended to focus on the study of emergent dynamical patterns using as a framework dynamical modelling of differential equations (d.e.s) as flows on system phase space (e.g. Smith and Thelen 1993). Though powerfully modelling process energetics, these flows cannot explicitly describe the physical organisation of the system—a chemical clock and a pendulum may be modelled as equivalent dynamical oscillators. Phase spaces specify only global dynamical states and time evolution, not the organised processes that produce them, whence representing cultural process lies beyond them. Nor is there yet any satisfactory way to model self-organisational changes of the dynamical form of phase space, i.e. phase shifts—see, for example, reviews of difficulties in modelling phase changes in liquid Bénard cells (Collier and Banerjee 2000) and slime moulds (Herfel and Hooker 1999)—whence deeper cultural change cannot yet be modelled. Incorporating organisational principles into dynamical models, including cultural models, is a central theoretical challenge.

ways, generating our peculiarly subtle and powerful cultural dynamics. The next two subsections explore this enriched top-down/bottom-up dynamics.

2.3 Shaping culture and the adaptive function of culture

The capacity of individuals to shape culture is essential to its adaptive capacity. Culture is, in the fishing boat metaphor, a major human means for navigating our world through adapting ourselves to environmental requirements and adapting our environment to us. An environment equipped with fishing boats, and ultimately fish farms, imposes its disciplines but is a much friendlier place than one without either—culture in the root sense of agri-culture and aqua-culture.[4] Without shapeable culture we would be as much at a loss to exploit our possibilities as are termites without their mound that structures their social organisation and environmental interaction processes. With culture, like them (but so much more powerfully), we have the collective capacity to marshal coordinated, specialised resources to a task, and to carry ourselves beyond our present horizons.[5] Like the termite mound, culture amplifies collective capacity to modify sources of natural selection and is in that sense a powerful source of niche creation.[6]

Cultural shaping actions vary, from those enacted oblivious to all but the most immediate local effects to those enacted with explicit reference to communal adaptive requirements. Termites stand near the former extreme, as do humans all too often. At its richest and most powerful, however, human culture is moulded by individuals capable of acting intentionally with explicit reference to holistic communal features and in pursuit (if fallibly) of increased communal adaptiveness. The wise judge reforming a constitution and the wise kindergarten teacher forming tomorrow's adults are equally such visionaries. This creates a powerful, and intricately integrating, shaping dynamics for human culture. Indeed, human cultural richness and shapeability now confers even the capacity to modify the very basis of biological

[4] See also Hooker (1994b).

[5] It is thought, for example, that monumental cultures survive because monument building induces in them the kind of organisation that conduces to communal survival: decreased breeding, communal intentional focus, specialised skills in food storage, etc. Culture is then for us the right functional analogy to the termite mound, it differentiates our social roles and holds a holistic collective memory in its structures, as does their mound for them. While the city is the obvious material analogy to draw, we can survive quite well without cities but not without cultures, as termites cannot without their mound. (Whether culture binds a human community into a 'unit of selection' is another matter—see e.g. Brandon [1996]; irrespective, the adaptive value of culture to the participating individual is not removed, only made more or less indirect.)

[6] Cf. Laland et al. (2000). In this sense it provides an external scaffolding for behaviour that has its corresponding internal scaffolding in constructive development of interaction management—see respectively Clark (1997), Bickhard (1992)—the two together constituting a powerful process for niche formation.

adaptation that, like re-designing while rebuilding a boat at sea, tests the limits of our understanding and self-regulatory capacities.[7]

2.4 Shaping individuals and the dual adaptive function of culture

An equally subtle power works in the reverse direction. Our cultural 'glue' penetrates deeply into us, altering our internal organisation and shaping our lives. Halfway through his book, *Why Humans have Cultures*, Carrithers summarises his argument thus far:

> we have evolved these [shaping/shaped] abilities, that I summarized as sociality. These capacities, which include social intelligence, an intense awareness of self-and-other, creativity, and narrative thought, are the common human nature that underlie social and cultural variability.[8]

Focused on managing social interrelations, together they comprise a profound human intersubjectivity, a 'propensity for mutual engagement and mutual responsiveness' (p. 55). Carrithers quotes Bruner, among other psychologists: 'Infants are, in a word, tuned to enter the world of human action' (p. 56). 'The capacities of sociality may be in individuals, but they are completed only between them' (p. 57). Thus the pattern of our social relationships, including our culture, Carrithers concludes, is embedded deeply in us, as we are in it. It is not just something we add on to ourselves (as decoration is to a fishing boat), it shapes us, it is us, as we shape it and express ourselves in it.

While §2.3 focused on the capacity to shape culture to communal ends in the communal environment, here we find the dual perspective: the capacity of culture (and of sociality more broadly) to shape the developing organism, especially the central nervous system, so as to satisfy the individual's need for internal coherence and development—the homo-cultural counterpart to our agri/aqua-culture. This is strikingly demonstrated in the way humans that are socially deprived are also correlatively cognitively deprived, from those rare humans who did not acquire language at all from their environment to those myriads whose multiple cognitive and emotional deficits derive from impoverished or damaging home environments. Humans are large-brained but small-reflexed, as intelligence in a finite, costly and complex world demands.[9] Whence

---

[7] Reminding us that cultures, like any other amplifying feature, can also be maladaptive, as when they reinforce destructive behaviour or illusory beliefs (see e.g. Munz 1989); but this only sounds a warning against simplistic assumptions (and encourages a critical attitude toward all cultures) while serving to highlight its positive adaptive role.

[8] Carrithers (1992: 146). All subsequent page numbers in this paragraph refer to Carrithers' book.

[9] Humans are highly intentional and intelligent and the point of both is to permit survival in, indeed to take positive advantage of, environments variegated in space and/or time. Intelligence provides adaptable problem-solving capacity while intentionality provides the correlative capacity to constantly and appropriately re-orient oneself to changing circumstances. These capacities are

we humans are born with a massive need to structure our highly plastic, developing brains usefully among its unimaginably vast possible organisations, and an equally intense drive to do so through mutual interaction, mutual interrelationship. This makes our sociality central to the construction of our very selves, Piagetian emergent-from-interaction selves.[10]

2.5 Synergistic two-way shaping: constructive cultural dynamics

In thus having (an Eliotese) culture we mutually shape ourselves and our community to adaptive coherence.[11]

And there is here a still more powerfully synergistic individual–communal dynamics than simply the sum of two relationships, social enabling and social binding, since it is through our culture that we intentionally plastic creatures are also enabled to shape it.[12] Dually, we increase the complexity and depth of our cultures as we accumulatively enrich them to scaffold our individual development. Moreover, both ourselves and our cultures become enriched 'more than we could know' through these processes: only a suitably cultured community makes possible the extended development of complex economies and settlements, public institutions, and the sciences and arts, all of which transcend all individual, local horizons. Our cultures, like termite mounds, act as integrated collective memories through which we have access to the collective work of others, but, unlike termite mounds, they also accumulate, differentiate, and self-reflect, they have no natural completed state, permitting us continually to explore new horizons.

We can gain a crude measure of the importance of socialisation to a species by considering the ratio of *usable* individual parametric plasticity between

thus deeply interrelated, not split into abstract problem-solving and language-like reference, as much contemporary cognitive psychology and philosophy assume—see Christensen and Hooker (2000a, 2000c) for further detail.

[10] For Piaget's insightful position see for example Piaget (1972; cf. Hooker 1994a, 1995 for systems exposition; but here see also Vygotsky 1986.) For a recent supportive neuro-science perspective see discussion in Christensen and Hooker (2000a).

[11] Cultural pathology (cf. note 7) can then be categorised in terms of departures from this dual Eliotese condition and its underlying order–organisation balance.

[12] The language of energetics and constraints is a very general one for discussing dynamics, but it is unfortunately common to consider constraints as only placing restrictions. However, and crucially, constraints are both *dis*abling (some dynamical states are thereby rendered dynamically inaccessible) and *en*abling (some dynamical states are thereby rendered dynamically accessible). The human skeleton, for example, places constraints on shape and size plasticity but also enables all the movement that underlies our powerful behavioural adaptabilities; the grammar of language sharply constrains word character and order, but it makes powerful communication accessible. An enabling constraint is a restriction on a system that opens up new capacities for the system. Because of its constructive character for us, culture is perhaps our most profound enabling constraint. But of course the enabling is always on balance, it cannot be purely enabling, as organised despotism demonstrates (and ask the painter or dancer about the limits of linguistic expressiveness).

isolate and communal states. The upshot of the preceding is that we not only gain basic coherence from culture (§2.4), we increase our coherently usable capacities enormously through it. Unless we humans have a sophisticated, high-quality cultural environment in which to develop, there will be vast reaches of our somatic, especially neural, organisational space that we cannot use because it is not accessible to us. The ratio of humanly usable organisational features in isolate and richly cultured states must be large, certainly well above 1.

Creatures of lesser neural capacities and more rigid social organisation, such as the insects, may lie along a negative sloping competitive trade-off curve between the importance and power of individual and of collective capacities and constraints, with the more of one implying the less of the other. But, on balance (see note 12), Eliotese human cultures lie along a positive sloping curve in which individual and communal capacities coupled *constructively*, each enabling the other, largely dominate those coupled competitively. (We can speculatively picture this effect increasing through the mammalian line as brain size, intense socialisation, and intentional action increase together.) This makes all the difference to the power of culture, to its significance in adaptive evolution, and to the intricacy and globalness of its organised dynamics.

2.6 Cultural strength(s)

A culture's features show a wide diversity of dynamical character, from mere surface patterns to strongly shaped/shaping constructive scaffolding. I shall briefly characterise this variety as an antidote to treating all cultural change as dynamically alike. At one extreme lie the 'decorative details' of our lives, like the decoration on the fishing boat, or the crowd that results from individual curiosity about something. These are at best weakly cultural features because, neither binding nor enabling us to any significant degree, they are more by-product patterns of social dynamics than active factors in those dynamics. Thus the widest use of the contested term 'culture', call it culture$_0$, encompasses all the collective features of a community, including these by-product patterns. Then the requirement that a cultural feature serves both to bind individuals into, and enable them within, a community identifies a stronger sense of culture, the culture$_1$ features. Cultural$_1$ features are complexly graded in the extent and penetration of their impacts across a community (cf. clothing with puppetry, between the agriculture and banking sectors, between Indonesia and Australia) along at least six dimensions. They are characterised distributionally in terms of their scaffolding locations: internal organisation within its members (as skills, mores, self-images, etc.), organisation among sub-communal groups (as authority, competition, etc.), and external organisation of environmental features guiding internal response (e.g. anthems) and social behaviour (e.g. roadways and driving processes). And they are characterised organisationally in terms of their organisational order and depth and the degree to which they may be shaped in communally referenced ways.[13]

We can now characterise various further notions of the cultural strength of a particular feature in terms of various profile strengths. A profile showing consistently high values for both organisational depth and communally referenced shapeability, for example, might be considered a strong cultural feature because it expresses a ramified, communally focused feature of us. Call it a $\text{cultural}_{2(A)}$ feature. A feature showing consistently high values for both internal organisation and communally referenced shapeability might be considered a strong cultural feature because it simultaneously expresses deep social penetration of us individually with strong social tuning. Call it a $\text{cultural}_{2(B)}$ feature. And so on. A strong culture, $\text{culture}_{2(A, B \ldots)}$, would then be one which possessed many strong cultural features of various kinds. Still stronger notions of culture, culture_3, may be constructed by requiring that acculturated individuals possess increasing capacities intentionally to shape their strong cultural_2 features. Possibly only humans show cultural_3 features and possibly only primates and humans show any large degree of cultural_2 features. However, even social insects show some cultural_1 features, as termite mounds demonstrate. Birds (cf. their song traditions) and other mammals surely show many complex cultural_1 features, and at least some cultural_2 features.

The delicate balance inherent in shaped/shaping dynamics re-emerges as a tension among ways a culture may be strong. A culture that penetrates and binds strongly, though enabling, will tend to overwhelm its members, reducing individuality and the capacity for innovation. Contrariwise, to the extent that a culture is shapeable by independent individuals, it is open to change, but its coherence and richness will be weakened by large numbers of idiosyncratic, uncoordinated modifications. In short, strong culture_1 is in tension with strong culture_{2+}. The intricate balance struck between these aspects must be expected to vary in exquisitely complex context-sensitive ways across all the dimensions of all the cultural features of a society if that society is to achieve its full Eliotese cultural potential. Whence there will be no simple rules for determining it, no simple models of its dynamical phase changes.

[13] Organisational order measures how many elements are involved in specifying the organisational relationships, whilst organisational depth is a measure of how many nestings of relations within relations are involved (Collier and Hooker 1999). A culturally *deep* feature is characterised by high-order, nested relationships. Pop music, for example, characteristically has shorter repeating note patterns whereas Mozart's compositions also contain much longer, subtler, nested patterns that are essential to their forms (cf. Pressing 1998). A Mozart composition is organisationally deep in a manner similar to Jane Austen's subtle use of word patterns to reveal character (Burrows 1987); but most pop music and novels are not. Besides such cultural products, organisational depth is also applicable to particular institutions, social processes, and whole cultural aspects (like clothing).

3. INTERLUDE: REFLECTION AND PROSPECT

Cultural features turn out to be incredibly dynamically complex: typically, they are widely diffused but socially integrative, multi-dimensional, multi-modal, multi-plexed, multi-produced, and multi-phasic complexes of highly interactive and plastic, highly organised processes and concomitant states shared by many kinds of individuals and institutions. Moreover the dynamics that creates, transmorphs, and dissolves them is one that generates exquisitely complex and subtle patterns: it is the dynamics of a far-from-equilibrium system driven by resource flows (energy, materials, information, and money), amplified by positive feedbacks on each (those of profit, power, persuasion, and prestige) while complexly damped at many levels by the negative feedbacks of biological and social regulation (from individual health impact to legal sanction), conjoined with a delicately balanced shaped/shaping dynamics enhanced by extensive individual intentional and cognitive capacities. The result is continual non-stationary (form-changing) dynamical transitions that often constructively couple dual increases in the complexity and depth of individual and communal capacities in myriad changing ways across its many facets. We have at present only the faintest of idea of how to model such systems, while in key respects, for example their non-stationary transitions, we face serious hurdles to any detailed mathematical modelling.[14] In the face of these complexities I suggest that there is, for once, little hope for the usual scientific gambit of initially opting for simple first-order, local models, such as meme-bundle models, hoping that the complexities can later be captured as higher-order 'bells and whistles'. The higher-order, non-local features are the heart of culture and cultural change.[15]

Though capturing cultural dynamics is thus daunting, its biological roots provide clues for at least beginning. The shaped/shaping dynamics underlying culture are as old as life itself. Every living entity sustains itself through energy and materials transfer across a dynamically adaptive boundary and hence is internally organised so as to match boundary behaviour to those interaction modes with its environment that will deliver needed resources while avoiding injury. Boundary-mediated, inside is shaped to outside, and, invariably, outside is altered by, and often shaped by, inside-directed actions. Adaptive feedback attunes inside with outside across all organisational scales; creatures and environments become reciprocally interdependent

---

[14] Science is increasingly competent at unravelling the details of many of the processes involved, but has scarcely yet begun on understanding the holistic integrative processes through which they are woven together to form living systems (§5 plus note 3).

[15] And of science–technology dynamics in particular—but that is now (under length constraints) another story. See in part Hahlweg and Hooker (1989), Hooker (1995), Herfel and Hooker (1997, 1999), Christensen and Hooker (1999). On the underlying difficulties of gene-bundle models see §5.

through a shaped/shaping dynamics. Equally, creatures internally regulate those tunings in ways their inanimate environment cannot, aiming to render environmental feedback (their experienced environment) uniformly support-ive. Beyond any general naturalist leanings, the deep-seatedness of this com-plex dynamic suggests that we start there when trying to understand cultural change.

Extant approaches to this task, whether modelling evolution of knowledge, economy, technology, or culture more generally, are dominated by dual-stream models in which genes and the social domain stand in some abstract analogy and co-evolve in parallel.[16] This approach is clearly unsatisfactory in the case of knowledge ('evolutionary epistemology')—both because the analogy distorts the nature of knowledge[17] and now because of the strong gene–knowledge interactions occurring—and these criticisms generalise. Instead naturalism, reinforced by the re-emergence of the phenotype and communities thereof in newer models of evolution, recommends beginning with a unified framework in which biological dynamics take place within a matrix of constraints—genetic, developmental, organismic, communal, and ecological—where all constraints may function, in context, as enabling adaptiveness (genes etc. as adaptive resources).[18] In this setting, culture is modelled as one class of com-plex shared integrative features of biological communities, and it is the dynam-ics of these that must be captured.

The integrative cohesion of any feature, like clothing, will vary in degree across its many aspects, perhaps sometimes swamped by strong interactions with particular groups. However, that parts of clothing, such as hats, can be artificially extracted and their changes recorded, no more shows the legiti-macy of disassembling cultural features into bundles of objects and ideas than the study of hearts does in the case of the evolution/development of respiration or flight or, pertinently, the study of species biomass does in relation to shared multi-plexed ecological properties like compartment resilience, or humic soil content. Rather, a cultural feature is the joint com-plex product of many groups acting for many different reasons, while also partially shaping them all. A long modelling task lies ahead. I begin by try-ing to identify some fundamental relationships for the construction of useful

[16] Extant evolution–culture studies tend to emphasise one side of a dual-mode model (see e.g. Laland et al. 2000), either focusing on genetic determination of culture—for example some sociobiology and evolutionary psychology—or conversely on the impact of cultural practices, for example mate selection and tool use, on gene frequencies through their modification of selection pressures. While understanding whatever constraints genetic inheritance places on accessible cul-tural expression, and conversely, are important, if difficult and controversial, studies, each provides only very partial insight into cultural dynamics itself.

[17] See Hooker (1995), Christensen and Hooker (1999). Additional difficulties result if the analogy leads to bundle models (§5).

[18] See references in notes 1, 16.

first models of these properties.[19] There is space only for the barest sketch of a direction.

4. MODELLING ACCULTURATED INTERACTION

4.1 Autonomy: the basic partition

Because living things dissipate ordered energy to live and their low-energy chemical bonds are easily disrupted, their continued existence is explained only by their *autonomy*, their internally organised capacity to acquire ordered free energy from their environment and direct it to replenish dissipated cellular structures, repair or avoid damage, and sustain the very processes that accomplish these tasks. Autonomy is a subtle, complex global requirement on the whole organism, for its constellation of processes must continually so interrelate as to regenerate the whole of itself.[20] Though the details, especially the dynamical boundaries, vary in graded ways, the autonomy requirement picks out all viable individuals, from cells to multi-cellular organisms to various multi-organism communities, including many business firms, cities, and nations.

The significance of this for developing models of social adaptiveness, including culture, is twofold: (1) the basic normative (i.e. identity-defining) constraint on adaptive processes is a global one: they must interrelate in globally organised patterns focused on the autonomy of the system. All of the more specific normative constraints on particular actions (e.g. avoid hunger, bankruptcy) derive from such global constraints. (2) There is a distinctive organisational asymmetry between the autonomous system and its environment. Necessarily for any complex system, the self-regenerating processes are substantially internally regulated; hunting and eating, for example, are initiated by internal signals and component activities (like running or biting) are under neuro-motor regulation. The essence of the asymmetry is then that the *directive organisation*[21] that

---

[19] Initially, I look for those relationships that remain largely invariant under cultural change—but only under cultural change, since hitherto distinct organisms may, for example, fuse in complex ways under various circumstances (e.g. Rayner 1997). And only 'largely', since culturally implicated transmorphs of these kinds may occur in business firms and the like.

[20] Cells, for example, exhibit several thousand simultaneous biochemical interactions and between them these must continuously regenerate the whole cell. On autonomy see further Christensen and Hooker (1998, 2000b) and their references.

[21] Directive order is the system dynamical constraints which shape physical flows, i.e. shape system interactive processes both internally and with the environment. For autonomous systems I shall instead speak of directive organisation, to underline the complex holistic process organisation required to achieve autonomy and the way it expresses active regulation by the system itself. Directive constraints thus ground system–environment regulatory asymmetries. Christensen and Hooker (1998, 2000a, 2000b, 2000c) discuss directedness and its significance for cognition and agency (cf. note 9).

induces the pattern-formation of physical flows from the environment into system-constitutive processes (and the correlative flows of wastes out) is substantially endogenous to the system itself. Birds organise twigs to make nests, but twigs have no tendency to organise nests or nesting unless co-opted by birds.

4.2 Kinds of relations to autonomous systems

The social world is made up of various kinds of autonomous systems and other kinds of objects (dresses, committees, etc.), all interacting in various ways. The beginnings of an autonomy-based analysis of the multi-dimensional space of social relations involved is to distinguish, in relation to any one autonomous system A, and any one relating object R, first, the nature of the directive order involved in R; second, the role played by R's directive order in A's exercise of autonomy; and, third, the adaptive potentials of A and R in the A–R super-system. As a first crude approximation I shall distinguish five broad classes of relations (briefly, where these are familiar).

Scaffolding (S): R scaffolds A when A incorporates interaction with R into its autonomy-achieving directive organisation. Bird nests scaffold bird breeding, ant colonies scaffold foraging behaviour into communally organised patterns with chemical trails, as do humans with lists, signposts, etc. In each case the scaffolded use confers otherwise-foregone, and sometimes essential, adaptiveness on the using autonomous system. The next two relations characterise the opposite extremes of this relation.

Simple interaction (SI): R simply interacts with A when R interacts with A but does not scaffold A. Non-autonomous objects, and autonomous systems in many respects, simply interact. Though kookaburras de-bug my garden, it does not structure their life in the way that wombat burrows do for wombats. Somewhere between the garden and the burrow, Rs cease merely to interact and begin to become adaptively important to As—scaffolding sets in.

Integration (I): R is interactively integrated into A when R-scaffolding has sufficient importance to A's directive organisation that it becomes essential to A's autonomous organisation. Termite mounds do not merely externally scaffold individual termite behaviour, for without them coherently organised colonies could not exist; the mound is as integrated into the colony's autonomous organisation as our skeletons are into us. An artificial heart or kidney is not an external scaffold to an otherwise autonomous human being, however different its composition, but an essential component in assuring closure of that person's core processes.[22]

---

[22] Nor therefore need these components be inside the skin—as also witness how, with ageing, written memory aids may shift from convenient scaffold to indispensable for life maintenance and so essential to continuing autonomy.

Mutualistic symbiosis (MSY): R is mutualistically symbiotic with A when R is also an autonomous system and R and A stand in a relation of mutual scaffold, either *simpliciter* or one of them is integrated with (possibly physically into) the other yet retains its autonomy. Lichens are mutually scaffolded algae/fungus MSY super-systems, and multi-cellular animals are MSY super-systems of their component autonomous cells, as are eukaryote cells (assuming the endosymbiotic origin of mitochondria). Sponge cells, however, simply interact in mutual adherence, that increases adaptive advantage but is too undirected to count as scaffolding.

MSY systems fall along a continuum of increasingly integrated and dominant super-system constraints, from simple cooperation (e.g. lichens) to full super-system autonomous individuality (e.g. eukaryotes). Call the former cooperative, and the latter integrative, MSY super-system autonomy. Multi-cellular animals lie near the integrative extreme. Moving along the continuum is beautifully seen in the slime mould D. *discoidium* whose independent cells, once starved, first cooperatively aggregate to locomote then produce a fruiting body through integrated cellular specialisation (see note 3).

Parasitic symbiosis (PSY): In its most general sense, R (whether or not autonomous) is parasitic on A when R interacts with the directive organisation of A to increase its own reproduction rate and/or degree of autonomy, but at best makes no net positive contribution to A's autonomy. The degree of parasitism depends upon the organisational depth of the directive organisation in A made use of by R, the effect of that use on R, and the degree of damage done to A. Thus mosquitoes and mistletoe are weakly parasitic because they divert resources (respectively blood, sap) from their host but, being autonomous systems themselves, do not otherwise use their host's directive organisation and damage it only slightly. Viruses are more strongly parasitic because they are not autonomous and cannot reproduce without using the host's reproductive sub-system, a deep part of its directive organisation, and often severely damage the host in the process.

4.3 Collective cultural dynamics

Any biological system can be modelled as a set of S, SI, I, MSY, PSY interaction relations among autonomous (sub)systems and other non-autonomous interacting objects.[23] Modelling a system in this way reveals its fundamental dynamical organisation, hence its basic dynamical modelling frame. (Detailed dynamical modelling is a further, massive, and often problematic step.) From this perspective, cultural features typically form inherently organisationally

---

[23] The ecological relations of predation and competition are largely spread across the SI–S spectrum, with occasional M/PSY aspects.

diverse bundles. The earlier clothing example presents us with at least persons, business firms, and government instrumentalities as autonomous components, and products, other social institutions, and all other social interactants as participating objects. Among all these, every kind of relationship can be found: SI between dresses and shoes, but often S between us and a uniform; I between a dress-making firm and its production technologies; MSY between designers, models, and journalists; and PSY between clothing industries, and charity-run second-hand clothing shops and their customers.

To characterise the distinctively cultural we must bring these interaction relationships together with the cultural characteristics and strengths of §2. A characteristically cultural dynamic occurs, for example, when designers, responding to demand, subtly transform social roles through creation of stylish business suits for women, which stimulates new development pathways for women, business organisations, and designers, and entrenches the new designs. Here suit design, at least a cultural$_2$ shaped feature, scaffolds (S) a mutually beneficial (MSY) relationship between designers and business women, that enables new shaping development for both. And of course this illustratively extracts but one of many like dynamics involved here. Generally, characterising a particular species' culture will require specifying its distinctive mutually reinforcing and antagonistic shaped/shaping dynamics, mediated by these interactive relationships, for its multi-plexed communal features (§3).

5. CONCLUSION: THE WAY FORWARD?

The difficulties facing biological modelling generally are acute for modelling culture. The interaction relations (1) exhibit strong non-linearities and self-organisational phase transitions intractable to simple modelling, (2) need enriching with complex interior dynamics (especially for autonomous components), and (3) are dynamically diverse yet together produce and obey the subtle holistic synergies and constraints characterising cultural features. Moreover, we evidently have no clear idea of how to model the dynamics of such shared, multi-plexed properties, in either biology or culture, and, like the fading hopes for a single treatment of analogous shared ecological features (compartment dynamics etc.), their complexity and variety must raise a doubt that there will be any single kind of dynamics characterising them. Nonetheless, the §4 framework scaffolds piece-wise approximate modelling explorations.

Meanwhile, one negative conclusion seems warranted: it will not be adequate to treat culture as a population of unit ideas and behaviours (called 'memes') that are spread by communication according to their 'fitness'. First, there are crucial disparities with the case of genes, where this approach is most plausible: centring on the communal lability and integration of cultural features, these disparities threaten immediately to disable the proposal.[24] Any-way, second, a deeper negative conclusion is now clearly emerging about the parent strategy of modelling evolutionary dynamics solely as fitness-led change of genome-bundled gene frequencies. While the strategy in both cases is to reduce dynamics to just first-order processes and statistics (counting memes/genes), there is now a substantial, growing and generalisable body of literature showing that this provides too impoverished an *organisational* basis for understanding biological dynamics (see notes 2, 19, and texts). Thus, while such reduced gene/meme models suffice for a range of useful statistical pur-poses, they are strictly limited in explanatory scope, first, because they collapse the dynamical complexities of organismic, communal, and ecological pro-cesses to a generalised 'fitness' factor and, second, because neither gene/meme bundles nor 'fitness' indices can capture holistic, integrated constraints like autonomy or shared multi-plexed features.

However, this scarcely settles the issue of whether cultural change is evolu-tionary. Doing that requires deciding whether culture exhibits stable heritable units and, if so, whether their dynamics implements a selected variation process of a biologically relevant kind. At present this non-trivial question lies unresolved in every respect. Optimism is premature. We should not, for exam-ple, rush to evolutionary heritability conclusions just from patterns of sequen-tial repetition with modification; ripples on a shelving beach show these, as will all similar spatially constrained succession, like urban expansion, plus all processes of self-organisational re-assembly, such as rush-hour queues, all processes of biased copying, such as housing design, etc.[25] Pessimism is equally premature. While simple gene-bundle evolutionary models are inadequate, yet there are molecular genes and they do play quite distinctive—if scarcely the once-touted determining—dynamical roles. Whence cultural disanalogies with genes that rule out simple memetics may yet prove compatible with some underlying evolving modularity. We are rapidly improving our understanding

---

[24] For example Wimsatt (1999). Sometimes an epidemiological model is employed in which memes, virus-like, infect human brains; but these are not evolutionary models and the patterns of themselves do not demonstrate heritability (see note 25 and text).

[25] Beach slope and water viscosity are factors in the explanation of ripple succession, but very dif-ferent factors from those generating genuine lineages, let alone from those reproducing generations as combinatorial assemblies. Whence genuine lineage heritability requires Wimsatt's generative entrenchment conditions (Wimsatt 1999) *at least* to be embedded in his assumed context of a reproductive process, and arguably also requires generated autonomy so as to provide a principled sense of within-lineage individuality and of regulatory entrenchment which is genuinely (re)gener-ative. And this is just the beginning of exploring biologically relevant constraints. How much con-straint, for example, can other self-organisation processes apply and a selection process still be claimed to be operating? Some theorists (the range extends from Wimsatt to Pattee 1977) may still hope to show that there are informational units playing gene-like roles inside every social process, but this remains open and ambitious.

of the issues, and may hope for better models to emerge eventually from the marriage of recent work (see notes 1, 18, 25); but, while we remain so far from adequately understanding these properties and processes, a cautious, open-minded approach commends itself.

Note.   Website: www.newcastle.edu.au/department/pl/staff/CliffHooker/Cliff.htm. Certain notions used here, for example biological autonomy, were developed jointly with Drs Wayne Christensen and John Collier, and they deserve equal acknowledgement for that—see references. The paper has also received the benefit of discussions with them, and with Drs Michael Carrithers, Alan Rayner, David Raubenheimer, and Bill Wimsatt; I thank them all, though I remain solely responsible for its direction and other recalcitrant errors.

REFERENCES

Ahouse, J. C. (1998), 'The Tragedy of A Priori Selectionism: Dennett and Gould on Adaptationism', *Biology and Philosophy* 13(3): 359–91.

Auyang, S. (1998), *Foundations of Complex-System Theories*. Cambridge: Cambridge University Press.

Bickhard, M. H. (1992), 'Scaffolding and Self-Scaffolding: Central Aspects of Development', in I. T. Winegar and J. Valsiner (eds), *Children's Development within Social Contexts: Research and Methodology*. Hillsdale, NJ: Lawrence Erlbaum.

Burrows, J. F. (1987), *Computation into Criticism: A Study of Jane Austen's Novels and an Experiment in Method*. Oxford: Clarendon.

Brandon, R. (1996), *Adaptation and Environment*. Princeton, NJ: Princeton University Press.

Carrithers, M. (1992), *Why Humans have Cultures*. Oxford: Oxford University Press.

Christensen, W. D. and Hooker, C. A. (1998), 'From Cell to Scientist: Toward an Organisational Theory of Life and Mind', in J. Bigelow (ed.), *Our Cultural Heritage: Proceedings of the Australian Academy of Humanities*. Australian Academy of Humanities, University House, Canberra.

Christensen, W. D. and Hooker, C. A. (1999), 'The Organisation of Knowledge: Beyond Campbell's Evolutionary Epistemology', *Philosophy of Science* 66: S237–49.

Christensen, W. D. and Hooker, C. A. (2000a), 'An Interactivist-Constructivist Approach to Intelligence: Self-Directed Anticipative Learning', *Philosophical Psychology* 13: 5–45.

Christensen, W. D. and Hooker, C. A. (2000b), 'Organised Interactive Construction: The Nature of Autonomy and the Emergence of Intelligence', in A. Etxeberria, A. Moreno, and J. Umerez (eds), *The Contribution of Artificial Life and the Sciences of Complexity to the Understanding of Autonomous Systems*, Special issue of *Communication and Cognition – Artificial Intelligence* 17(3–4).

Christensen, W. D. and Hooker, C. A. (2000c), 'A General Interactivist-Constructivist Model of Intentionality', in J. MacIntosh (ed.), *Contemporary Naturalist Theories of Evolution and Intentionality*, *Canadian Journal of Philosophy*, Special Supplementary Volume.

Clark, A. (1997), *Being There: Putting Brain, Body, and World Together Again*. Cambridge, MA: Bradford/MIT Press.

Collier, J. D. and Hooker, C. A. (1999), 'Complexly Organised Dynamical Systems', *Open Systems & Information Dynamics* 6: 241–302.

Collier, J. D. and Bannerjee, M. (2000), 'Bénard Cells: A Model Dissipative System', Fourth International Conference on Emergence, Odense, Denmark.

Depew, D. and Weber, B. (1999), *Darwinism Evolving*. Cambridge, MA: MIT Press.

Eliot, T. S. (1948), *Notes Towards the Definition of Culture*. London: Faber.

Griffiths, P. E., ed. (1992), *Trees of Life: Essays in Philosophy of Biology*. Dordrecht: Kluwer.

Hahlweg, K. and Hooker, C. A. (1989), 'Evolutionary Epistemology and Philosophy of Science', in K. Hahlweg and C. A. Hooker (eds), *Issues in Evolutionary Epistemology*. Albany, NY: State University of New York Press.

Herfel, W. E. and Hooker, C. A. (1997), 'Cognitive Dynamics and the Development of Science', in A. Ginev and R. Cohen (eds), *Issues and Images in the Philosophy of Science*. Boston: Kluwer.

Herfel, W. E. and Hooker, C. A. (1999), 'From Formal Machine to Social Colony: Toward a Complex Dynamical Philosophy of Science', in M. Dalla Chiara, R. Giuntini, and F. Laudisa (eds), *Language, Quantum, Music: Select Contributed Papers of the 10th International Congress of Logic, Methodology and Philosophy of Science, Florence, August 1995*. Boston, MA: Kluwer.

Hooker, C. A. (1994a), 'Piagetian Psychology, Biology and Evolutionary Epistemology: A Regulatory Systems Approach', *Biology and Philosophy* 9: 197–244.

Hooker, C. A. (1994b), 'Value and System: Notes Toward the Definition of Agri-Culture', *Journal of Agriculture and Environmental Ethics* 7, Special Supplementary Volume.

Hooker, C. A. (1995), *Reason, Regulation and Realism: Toward a Naturalistic, Regulatory Systems Theory of Reason*. Albany, NY: State University of New York Press.

Hutchins, E. (1995), *Cognition in the Wild*. Cambridge, MA: MIT Press.

Jablonka, E. and Lamb, M. J. (1995), *Epigenetic Inheritance and Evolution: The Lamarckian Dimension*. Oxford: Oxford University Press.

Laland, K. N., Odling-Smee, J., and Feldman, M. W. (2000), 'Niche Construction, Biological Evolution and Cultural Change', *Behavioral and Brain Sciences* 23(1): 131–46.

Miklos, G. (1993), 'Molecules and Cognition: The Latterday Lessons of Levels, Language and *Lac*', *Journal of Neurobiology* 24(6): 842–90.

Munz, P. (1989), 'Taking Darwin Even More Seriously', in K. Hahlweg and C. A. Hooker (eds), *Issues in Evolutionary Epistemology*. Albany, NY: State University of New York Press.

Neurath, O. (1959), 'Protocol Sentences', translated by G. Schick, in A. J. Ayer (ed.), *Logical Positivism*. New York: Free Press.

Pattee, H. H. (1977), 'Dynamic and Linguistic Modes of Complex Systems', *International Journal of General Systems* 3: 259–66.

Piaget, J. (1972), *The Principles of Genetic Epistemology*, translated by W. Mays. London: Routledge and Kegan Paul.

Pines, D. (1988), *Emerging Synthesis in Science*. Redwood City, CA: Addison Wesley Publishing Company.

Pressing, J. (1998), 'Cognitive Complexity and the Structure of Musical Patterns', *Noetica* 3(8).

Raff, R. A. (1996), *The Shape of Life: Genes, Development, and the Evolution of Animal Form*. Chicago: University of Chicago Press.

Rayner, A. D. M. (1997), *Degrees of Freedom: Living in Dynamic Boundaries*. London: Imperial College Press.

Smith, L. V. and Thelen, E., eds (1993), *A Dynamic Systems Approach to Development: Applications*. Cambridge, MA: Bradford/MIT Press.

Vickers, G. (1970), *Freedom in a Rocking Boat*. London: Penguin.

Vygotsky, L. S. (1986), *Thought and Language*. Cambridge, MA: MIT Press.

Wimsatt, W. C. (1999), 'Genes, Memes and Cultural Hereditary', *Biology and Philosophy* 14: 279–310.

Culture

ADAM KUPER

I

IN 1952, TWO OF THE LEADING AMERICAN ANTHROPOLOGISTS of the day, Alfred Kroeber and Clyde Kluckhohn, published a book entitled *Culture: A Critical Review of Concepts and Definitions*, through which generations of graduate students have ploughed (Kroeber and Kluckhohn 1952). In good positivist style, they collated 164 distinctive definitions that had been advanced at various times to specify the nature of culture. These they grouped into two broad categories: the élitist, ethnocentric and outmoded notions of the humanists (of which they did not approve), and the forward-looking, precise, definitions of the scientists.

To be sure, humanist ideas of culture covered a broad spectrum, but a classic notion is perfectly caught by an aphorism of Matthew Arnold: culture is the best that has been thought and said. It is the sum of the greatest spiritual and artistic accomplishments of humanity (which meant the finest flower of the high art of Europe). The acquisition of culture distinguished the elect from the hoi poloi, the civilised from the philistines.

According to an emerging anthropological usage, however, culture did not mark off a small highly educated élite from the undiscriminating masses. Rather, culture was what, apparently, distinguished human beings—all human beings—from other primates. Two years after publication of Arnold's *Culture and Anarchy* in 1869, Darwin published *The Descent of Man* (1871), which asked what, precisely, distinguished all humans from other primates. In the same year, in a book provocatively entitled *Primitive Culture*, the pioneer anthropologist E. B. Tylor answered that it was culture or civilisation that made human beings different (Tylor 1903 [1871]). He insisted that culture included every custom and skill, every accomplishment of human beings that was transmitted by society rather than by biology, by nurture rather than nature. Every people, and every individual in every society, had culture. Human evolution was the story of the progressive development of human culture.

Kroeber and Kluckhohn identified Tylor's formulation as the first approximation to a scientific definition of culture. It had gradually been refined by anthropologists, and was now, at last, poised to sweep away the self-serving conceptions of the humanists and to take its rightful place as one of the great, organising scientific ideas: 'In explanatory importance and in generality of application it is comparable to such categories as gravity in physics, disease in medicine, evolution in biology' (Kroeber and Kluckhohn 1952: 3). It has not worked out like that. Almost fifty years on, the boundaries between humanist and social science ideas about culture seem still to be fuzzy. We now recognise the kinship between Tylor's notion of culture and the formulations of Enlightenment historians. Modern American anthropologists have generally been content to operate with definitions of culture that would have been familiar to Coleridge or to Goethe.

Rather than oppose a humanist and a modern, social science idea of culture, I prefer another grouping of the main ideas about culture into three broad traditions of thought, that have persisted for two centuries, and that have been shared—and disputed—by philosophers, critics, social scientists, and politicians. These traditions are sometimes identified loosely as French, German, and English; or alternatively, and equally loosely, as the Enlightenment, the Romantic, and the Classical conceptions. It is a crude classification, but it will serve to provide an orientation.

In the French tradition, civilisation was represented as a progressive, cumulative human achievement. The progress of civilisation could be measured by the advance of reason in its cosmic battle against raw nature, instinct, and unthinking tradition. This advance was most obvious in science and technology, and in the growing rationality of government. Civilisation had progressed furthest, of course, in France, but it was also enjoyed, if in different degrees, by savages, barbarians, and other Europeans. This was, naturally, a theory that spoke particularly to radicals and to social reformers. In anthropology and in the social sciences generally this tradition was recast in the last decades of the nineteenth century in evolutionary terms.

In the German tradition, the key term was *culture*. Culture was contrasted to civilisation, and it was associated with spiritual rather than material values. Its affinities were with religion, and its most characteristic achievements were to be found in the arts rather than the sciences. But while civilisation was universal, culture divided peoples. Each *Volk* had its own *Geist*, and its specific destiny. Its particular spiritual values were expressed above all in its language and arts. Consequently, this intellectual tradition stimulated the study of folklore, folk arts, customary law, and philology, which were held to express the uncontaminated spirit of a particular people.

The English, as ever, stood somewhat aloof from these Continental arguments, although John Stuart Mill had tried to bring the French and German traditions together, in his famous essay on Bentham and Coleridge. In any case, the English had their own specific preoccupations. As industrialisation transformed England, intellectuals identified a spiritual crisis, a defining struggle between what Shelley called Poetry and Mammon. The technology and materialism of modern civilisation was the enemy. Against it, the liberal intellectuals pitted eternal cultural values, distilled from the great tradition of European art and philosophy. As mentioned earlier, Matthew Arnold defined culture as 'the best that has been known and said', an enduring, cosmopolitan canon. Acquiring culture, we acquaint ourselves with 'the history of the human spirit'.[1] The possession of culture marks the elect off from the unlettered barbarians. But now this humanist legacy was under siege from the armies of industrial civilisation. 'As civilisation advances, poetry almost necessarily declines.'[2] The great historical question of the day was whether the intellectual culture of the educated élite could somehow sustain the spiritual values of society. Perhaps culture would falter, and be overwhelmed by the Gradgrind materialism of hard-faced men who had done well out of the culture wars, men who knew the cost of everything and the value of nothing.

In all these traditions, culture or civilisation stood for ultimate values. It has been suggested that these conceptions spread in the eighteenth century because religion was losing its grip on many intellectuals. They provided an alternative, secular source of meaning (Starobinski 1993). The French idea of civilisation is perhaps most closely related to a Catholic vision of a universal church that will embrace all humanity, while the German notion of Kultur— first advanced by the Lutheran pastor, Herder—has affinities with Protestant ideas about the destiny of an elect. Thomas Mann, after all, suggested that the Reformation had immunised the Germans against the ideas of the French Revolution. There is also a religious inspiration behind much English writing on culture, most evident in the writings of Coleridge, Newman, Arnold, and Eliot: the imperative to treasure the life of the spirit above all else.

While the major discourses on culture were deeply rooted in older ideas, and characteristically associated with particular national arguments, they nevertheless had much in common, as European intellectuals were well aware. More commonly, these conceptions developed in tension with each other, and sometimes they met in fraternal—or fratricidal—debates. In the very shadow of the First World War, the brothers Thomas and Heinrich Mann took opposite sides—the German and the French—in a famous debate about culture and civilisation.

There were also many attempts at synthesis, and exercises in subversion too, as dissident intellectuals turned the accepted judgements on their heads, opting for savagery rather than civilisation, or popular culture rather than the arts of the élite. Baudelaire, for example, could call France 'a truly barbarous country',

[1] 'Culture, the acquainting ourselves with the best that has been known and said in the world, and thus with the history of the human spirit' (Arnold 1900 [1873]: Preface).
[2] Thomas Babington Macaulay, 'Milton' (first published, 1825).

and speculate that perhaps civilisation 'has taken refuge in some tiny, as yet undiscovered tribe'. Finally, each generation modernised the idiom in which the old ideas were cast, usually adapting it to current scientific terminology: evolutionism in the late nineteenth century, organicism in the early twentieth century, relativity in the 1920s, and so on.

II

If culture or civilisation could determine the destinies of nations and even of all humanity, ideas about the nature of culture naturally fed political debates, even dignifying wars. Such debates became particularly intense at times of great political upheaval.

The Great War was fought by one army in the name of Western civilisation, by the other for the sake of German culture. In the aftermath of that war, and in the shadow of a greater Armageddon, a number of leading intellectuals dedicated themselves to the study of ideas of culture and civilisation that were, it seemed, at the heart of the crisis of the age. Consider two such scholars, one French, one German. Rather than taking sides, their aim was to reveal the origins—intellectual but also social and political—of the German and French models; and to insist on the relationship of these conceptions to each other.

In 1930, the French historian, Lucien Febvre, convened a weekend seminar on the subject of '*Civilisation: le mot et l'idée*', to which he contributed the main address, entitled 'Civilisation'. He began by noting that a thesis had recently been presented at the Sorbonne on the 'civilisation' of a South American people, the Tupi-Guarani, and remarked that a previous generation would have considered such people to be savages, devoid of civilisation. '*Mais depuis longtemps la notion d'une civilisation des non-civilisés est courante.*' Yet at the same time intellectuals took it for granted that civilisation progressed, and that the word refers primarily to our own tradition, which is valued above others. How could a language '*reputée claire et logique*' have arrived at two contradictory usages for one word (Febvre 1930: 2–3)?

Febvre's research led him to the conclusion that the term *civilisation*, coined in the 1750s, had become current only at the end of the eighteenth century, when French intellectuals constructed a notion of a progressive human civilisation. Civilisation occupied the highest place on a scale in which savagery led to barbarism, barbarism to civilisation. Their model, he suggested, was the relationship between the species in Lamarck's version of the great chain of being. Febvre showed that this universal and progressive idea of history developed in tension with a more conservative and pessimistic vision, one that appeared to be more realistic in the aftermath of the Revolution and the Terror, and again when France experienced further political setbacks. At such times,

French intellectuals might question the destiny of civilisation, and of France, and flirt with relativist and cyclical ideas of history. The German notion of *Kultur*, he argued, had developed a similar ambiguity, and for the same sort of reasons. In 1930, both conceptions of civilisation were current, and Febvre formulated the intellectual and political challenge represented by these two conflicting conceptions. Is a relativist conception of civilisation compatible, he asked, with universalism and a belief in progress?

A few years after Febvre's seminar, Norbert Elias, a German exile writing on the eve of the Second World War, compared the evolution of the German notion of *Kultur* and the French idea of civilisation. Like Febvre, Elias constructed a genealogy of the idea of culture, from the perspective of the doom-laden 1930s, but he spoke particularly to the German tradition, as Febvre spoke to the French.

In *The Civilizing Process*, Elias argued that the concept of civilisation 'expresses the self-consciousness of the West . . . It sums up everything in which Western society of the last two or three centuries believes itself superior to earlier societies or "more primitive" contemporary ones' (Elias 1978 [1939]: 3–4). For the French and British, this usage reflected a pride in national accomplishment as much as the general progress of the West, or all humanity; and they used the term to refer indiscriminately to political, economic, religious, technical, moral, or social facts. When Germans expressed pride in their achievements, however, they appealed to their *Kultur*. They used the term to refer 'essentially to intellectual, artistic, and religious facts', Elias noted, and he insisted that the Germans typically 'draw a sharp dividing line between facts of this sort, on the one side, and political, economic, and social facts, on the other' (Elias 1978: 4).

Elias identified social purposes behind these different ideas. The concept of a universal and progressive civilisation, for obvious reasons, appealed to the dominant classes in imperial states such as France or Britain, while 'the concept of *Kultur* mirrors the self-consciousness of a nation [like Germany] which had constantly to seek out and constitute its boundaries anew, in a political as well as spiritual sense' (Elias 1978: 5). Moreover, French and British intellectuals identified with the aspirations of the ruling class, while their German counterparts defined themselves in opposition to the aristocracy. The civilisation of the courts was borrowed from France, and it was purely formal and outward. In contrast, the culture of the intellectuals was German, achieved, inward. Their base was the university, which Elias described as 'the middle-class counterweight to the court' (Elias 1978: 24). Later, this opposition was internationalised, and the contrast between *Kultur* and *Zivilisation* came to define the competing values that (in the view of some Germans) divided Germany and France: depth and superficiality, honesty and artifice, true virtue and mere outward politeness.

The first volume of Elias's study offered a social and political history of the ideas of culture and civilisation. It is an exercise in what his mentor, Karl Mannheim, called the sociology of knowledge. The second volume put a particular conception of civilisation to work, to describe a long-term historical change in manners, which he called the civilising process, which meant, in essence, the control of nature. The European princely courts grew powerful by establishing a centralised control over the independent, violent, boorish feudal lords. They subdued them not so much by force as by etiquette. The court taught them to mind their manners, subjecting the body and its functions to a series of cumulative constraints. What Elias termed the 'social constraint towards self-constraint' grew in force, and the 'threshold of embarrassment' was raised. As a central order replaced violent anarchy, so civilisation imposed customary, formal rules to control what had been expressive or instinctual acts. This was also, of course, a theme of Freud, particularly in his almost contemporary *Civilization and Its Discontents* (Freud 1963 [1930]), but Elias linked the civilising process to the extension of control by the state, a thesis that was later developed by Foucault in relation to other realms of practice.

In England, although John Stuart Mill had struggled to bring the French and German traditions together, in his great essays on Bentham and Coleridge, specific English preoccupations persisted. As industrialisation transformed England, intellectuals wondered what might replace the old hierarchical social order; and they identified a spiritual crisis, a defining struggle between Culture and Materialism.

T. S. Eliot may serve as a spokesman for the English tradition at that terrible crisis of European identity, in the 1930s and 1940s, although he presented himself as an opponent of the English orthodoxy, represented quintessentially by Matthew Arnold. For Arnold, the sole barrier against the threatening Philistines was a classical culture that was preserved by a small élite. In his *Notes Towards a Definition of Culture*, Eliot (1948) opposed to Arnold's conception what he termed the anthropological idea of culture (as used for instance by E. B. Tylor in the title of his book *Primitive Culture*). In its fullest sense, in its anthropological sense, Eliot suggested, culture 'includes all the characteristic activities and interests of a people'. It connotes the way of life of a society, and every class makes a necessary and distinctive contribution to it. At its core are the sacred values that could broadly be termed religion.

Eliot offered a catalogue of English cultural traits that was intended to bring out the commonplace nature of cultural institutions, and their distribution across social classes: 'Derby Day, Henley Regatta, Cowes, the twelfth of August, a cup final, the dog races, the pin table, the dart board, Wensleydale cheese, boiled cabbage cut into sections, beetroot in vinegar, nineteenth-century Gothic churches and the music of Elgar' (Eliot 1948: 31). The message was that culture included high and low, élite and popular, sacred and profane. Eliot believed, however, that the essential core of culture was a religion. 'We may go further', he wrote, 'and ask whether what we call the culture, and what we call the religion, of a people are not different aspects of the same thing: the culture being, essentially, the incarnation (so to speak) of the religion of a People' (1948: 28). 'Bishops', he suggested, 'are a part of English culture, and horses and dogs are a part of English religion' (1948: 32).

In the late 1950s, Raymond Williams, like Febvre and Elias before him, published a historical account of a tradition of reflection on culture, in this case a specifically English tradition. When the English critics wrote about culture, their concern was with the spiritual values of a whole society in the face of what Carlyle termed industrialism, the avatar of materialism and positivism. The central issue was whether the intellectual culture of the educated élite could somehow sustain the spiritual values of the society, or whether the Philistines, the bourgeois enemies of a Matthew Arnold, or the masses, whom F. R. Leavis so feared, would overwhelm them.

Williams insisted that Eliot's so-called anthropological approach was not in fact a novelty. On the contrary, 'The emphasis on "a whole way of life" is continuous from Coleridge and Carlyle' (Williams 1983 [1958]: 232–3). Their characteristic ideal was a harmonious but hierarchical community, in which each class contributed appropriately to a complex culture. Culture was therefore the work of all, rather than the special preserve of an educated minority. Raymond Williams welcomed this concern with the positive role of the masses in sustaining a moral order, but he argued that Eliot's was not a realistic vision in the modern, industrial world. For a socialist like Williams, change was urgent, class conflict real: but the people were not the enemies of culture, as Leavis believed. On the contrary, his faith was that the working-class value of collective solidarity would provide the enduring ground for a new and more just social order. There is something specifically English about this discourse, in its preoccupation with the values of different social classes, and its assumption that there were enduring cultural values, that transcended the accidents of time and place. Yet comparable ideas were abroad elsewhere in Europe in the middle decades of the twentieth century. Eliot was himself deeply influenced by the right-wing Catholic philosophy of Maurras. On the left, Gramsci in Italy, and Adorno and Horkheimer in Frankfurt, wrestled with similar issues to those that preoccupied George Orwell, Raymond Williams, or E. P. Thompson in Britain, but with greater desperation, as the working-class succumbed to the cynical propaganda of fascism. For all of these writers, culture had a similar meaning and a comparable historical importance. It was the sphere of ultimate values, purveyed in the educational system, expressed most powerfully in the arts.

What, then, was distinctive about the anthropological discourse on culture? In 1952, Kroeber and Kluckhohn represented it in terms of a gradual evolution from humanist to scientific conceptions, but in fact the ideas about culture that were in play in anthropology were not, on the whole, very different from those that distinguished the intellectual debates more broadly. What made the anthropological discourse distinctive was that it addressed two very specific questions. One concerned the relationship between culture and biology, particularly race. The other had to do with the apparently inevitable transformation of the little traditions of the world by the forces of colonialism and industrialisation.

The most sophisticated statement of these issues is to be found in the long essay that Lévi-Strauss wrote for UNESCO, entitled *Race and History*, and also published in 1952. The immediate political impetus was two-fold: a reflection back on the horrors of the Second World War, and forward to the consequences of decolonisation, immediately after the independence of India, Pakistan and Indonesia.

For much of the way, Lévi-Strauss retraced arguments made familiar by Boas. Racial differences are not age-old or fixed, and they are largely irrelevant to cultural differences, which are much more numerous, and cross-cut racial boundaries. Moreover, distinctive cultures arise through a constant process of borrowing, imitation, and competition. Nevertheless, it was very generally believed that cultural and racial differences were equally fixed and decisive. Few would take a tolerant attitude to the habits of their neighbours. On the contrary, people all over the world tend to regard the customs of the others as monstrous, scandalous, not fully human.

What basis is there for challenging this virtually universal ethnocentrism? First, a relativist perspective must be encouraged. Different peoples have different values, different goals, and therefore there can be no objective measure of progress, or of moral superiority. Second, it must be shown that no culture is closed and self-sustaining. Every culture is multicultural. 'All cultures are the result of a mishmash, borrowings, mixtures that have occurred, though at different rates, ever since the beginning of time' (Lévi-Strauss 1971). A degree of ethnic pride is perhaps necessary to sustain cultural variety. We all depend on difference, for new ideas will usually come from outside. Advances, better adaptations, come about normally through the collaboration of cultures. However, Lévi-Strauss's conclusion was sombre. Since the sixteenth century a Western, industrial, scientific civilisation has spread through the world, imposing, or buying, uniformity. The consequence has been the progressive elimination of variety, and the end result will be stagnation or entropy.

III

I have been tracing the great debates on culture in the middle of the twentieth century, debates that resonated with the world-shattering events of the period. Ideas about culture have also defined the stakes in less bloody but often bitter political battles within the universities. What is at issue is the organisation and control of academic disciplines. (Henry Kissinger remarked that academic battles were so bloody because so little was at stake in them.) The first eruption of academic culture wars was in Germany, at the turn of the century, when the *Kulturwissenschaften* were establishing themselves. Modern American debates about culture have been decisively shaped by developments in the universities. They were stimulated, first, by the institutionalisation of the social sciences in the first decades of the century, when they fed on the very similar debates that had taken place in Germany. Debates about culture revived, with a fresh urgency, in the 1950s and 1960s, when the social sciences, having won their wings in public service during the Second World War, became relatively rich and powerful. Perhaps the most important initiative in the social sciences in America at the time was the establishment by Talcott Parsons of the Department of Social Relations in Harvard in the late 1940s.

Parsons called for a new and more systematic division of labour within the social sciences. All social scientists were trying to explain what he called social action, but they tended to be reductionists. However, social behaviour could not be reduced to biology, or to economic determinants, or to symbols and beliefs. Social action was shaped at once by the biology and the psychology of individuals, by the social and economic institutions of the society, and by ideas and values. These factors constituted distinct systems and should be studied independently, in the first instance at least. Ultimately someone (Parsons perhaps) would put them together again, to show how they combined to determine action.

A more rigorous specialisation was therefore required within the social sciences. In the new dispensation, psychology would deal with the individual. Sociology would concern itself with social relations and the institutionalisation of values. There remained culture, which was the name Parsons gave to the realm of ideas and values. Culture meant for Parsons what it had meant to the German idealists, although he translated their conception into a sociological jargon: 'Cultural objects are . . . ideas or beliefs, expressive symbols or value patterns' (Parsons 1951: 4). A science of culture would focus on 'the culture pattern system as such, and neither on the social system in which it is involved, nor on the personalities as systems' (1951: 553). The nearest thing to a science of culture in the American universities was anthropology, and Parsons proposed that it should be recast as a branch of the social sciences, with its own subject-matter: culture. 'Only by some such definition of its scope can anthropology become an analytical empirical science which is independent both of sociology and of psychology' (1951: 554).

Kroeber and Kluckhohn's *Culture* appeared the year after Parsons published *The Social System*, and it is quite obviously their response, on behalf of anthropology, to his challenge. They criticised Parsons for writing of culture 'in a sense far more restricted than the anthropological usage', although they suggested hopefully that more recently he 'has moved in the anthropological direction'. But their own definition of culture was not in fact very different from his, and they struggled to identify their precise reasons for dissent, until, at last, they came clean and admitted that they were not happy with Parsons's programme because it would require anthropology to redefine itself, and in the process to abandon parts of its empire. Parsons, they complained:

> leaves little place for certain traditional topics of anthropological enquiry: archaeology, historical anthropology in general, diffusion, certain aspects of culture change, and the like. . . . In particular, we are resistant to his absorbing into 'social systems' abstracted elements which we think are better viewed as part of the totality of culture. (Kroeber and Kluckhohn 1952: 136)

But they soon capitulated, and by the early 1960s the Parsonian programme had taken centre stage in American anthropology. Two products of the Department of Human Relations, Clifford Geertz and David Schneider, instituted the famous 'systems course' as the core of graduate education in anthropology at the University of Chicago, introducing the next generation of anthropologists to Parsons's three-pronged approach to action. 'I beat the culture drum', David Schneider recalled. 'Geertz beat the culture drum. We both got it through Parsons from Kroeber and Kluckhohn' (Schneider 1995: 203).

Of course, there was opposition. This took the form of a revival of evolutionism. A familiar idea was dusted down, the idea of a progressive civilisation, essentially technological and scientific in nature. Culture was a machine for controlling nature, and it was progressive, adaptive, and ultimately universal. By the 1960s, then, there were two rival schools of American anthropology, one in the tradition of German idealism, the other in the tradition of French positivism. It was by no means evident which would triumph. Parsons, characteristically, tried to synthesise evolutionism into his functionalist framework. But the future lay elsewhere. Clifford Geertz, the outstanding figure of the new movement, soon moved in a direction that Parsons would have found much less encouraging.

Geertz began as an orthodox Parsonian. 'The Parsonian theory of culture', he declared, 'suitably emended, is one of our most powerful intellectual tools' (Geertz 1973: 254). He also endorsed the characteristic Parsonian strategy. Social scientists were directed 'to distinguish analytically between the cultural and social aspects of human life, and to treat them as independently variable yet mutually interdependent factors' (1973: 144). Writing on Indonesia, he tended to oppose a traditional state of affairs, in which culture and social structure form a single, mutually reinforcing system, and the modern situation, in which old ideas and values become less and less satisfactory as explanations of the world, and as guides to action in it, and are challenged by new ideologies that may, in turn, introduce fresh lines of social conflict. Culture and social structure must be distinguished analytically, but they act together. Anthropology specialised in culture, the realm of ideas, values, and symbols, but within an interdisciplinary social science project, never forgetting that culture and society were 'mutually interdependent factors'.

In the late 1960s, however, Geertz moved away from the Parsonian project. This was the time when the Vietnam War divided the campuses. Parsonian sociology was a specific target of the New Left, and indeed one section of Alvin Gouldner's influential book, *The Coming Crisis of Western Sociology*, which appeared in 1970, was entitled, 'From Plato to Parsons: The Infrastructure of Conservative Social Theory' (Gouldner 1970). The New Left hoped to revive Marxist theory, which was a version of the Enlightenment narrative of technological and political progress. Geertz identified a new intellectual movement as an alternative both to materialism and to Parsonian functionalism. This was, it turned out, a radically relativist form of cultural idealism. In 1973, just at the moment that Parsons was identifying Geertz as the representative Parsonian anthropologist, Geertz himself announced that he discerned 'an enormous increase in interest, not only in anthropology, but in social studies generally, in the role of symbolic forms in human life. Meaning . . . has now come back into the heart of our discipline' (Geertz 1973: 29). Ten years later, in his second collection of essays, *Local Knowledge*, Geertz described and welcomed a new configuration of disciplines. An interpretive, symbolic anthropology would now link up with linguistic philosophy and literary theory. The common subject-matter was culture, but culture now appeared as an object to be deciphered, a text to be translated, rather than as an ideology arising from social processes and constraining them.

In Geertz's later work there is a distinct tendency for culture to appear as high culture, characteristically as art or ritual. As he noted approvingly, 'the analogies are coming more and more from the contrivances of cultural performance . . . from theater, painting, grammar, literature, law, play' (Geertz 1983: 22). An example is his account of the court rituals—court operas, he calls them—which he described as constituting the real centre of Balinese life in the nineteenth century. In the *Negara*, culture was produced by the élite, goods by the peasants: 'culture came from the top down, while power welled up from the bottom' (Geertz 1980: 85). It is a view of culture that would have been agreeable to Matthew Arnold, and it was immediately intelligible to historians and literary scholars, who were delighted to discover that they had been anthropologists all along. Parsons would have been appalled to discover that, under the insurgent leadership of his old student, his bid to reconfigure the social sciences had been replaced by a rival project, which aimed to achieve a fresh configuration of disciplines in the humanities, concerned, one and all, with the interpretation of culture.

IV

To wrench culture apart from its social context leads ineluctably to an idealist theory of history, a history made by ideas and values that are carried by symbols and expressed in rituals and in the arts. Geertz relegated everyday politics and economics to the margins of history, but there was an alternative way of looking at the matter. If culture shaped history, it followed that the most fundamental political conflicts take place in the sphere of culture. Political interests must follow from cultural identities.

During the 1990s, American intellectuals have been embroiled in 'culture wars', and 'cultural politics' have dominated American public discourse. In the wider society, politicians and journalists routinely assume that 'culture' explains problems of crime, poverty, illegitimacy, and industrial competitiveness. Cultural identity is held to legitimate political claims, so it was an urgent question whether there was an American culture, or whether America was a multicultural society, every minority a political constituency, with its own legitimate agenda. Even international relations would now apparently be determined by cultural differences. In 1993, Samuel Huntington published an apocalyptic book, *The Clash of Civilizations and the Remaking of World Order*, in which he suggested that the future of the whole world would be shaped by cultural conflicts rather than economic competition or ideological differences. 'The great divisions among humankind and the dominating source of conflict will be cultural' (Huntington 1996).

Nowhere have these debates been conducted with more virulence than in the universities, for once again the identity of academic disciplines is also at stake. In the 'culture wars' that tear the campus apart, multiculturalists confront cultural conservatives, the patriots of Western Civilisation. The conservatives, of course, invoke Matthew Arnold. Radicals propagate a very different theory of culture. It takes somewhat different forms in different disciplinary traditions, though there is considerable convergence. I shall limit myself here to the version that has been developed within cultural anthropology: as the designated scientists of culture, anthropologists were particularly sensitive to these questions.

In 1986 a new movement announced itself in American anthropology with a book—at once manifesto and conference proceedings—entitled *Writing Culture* (Clifford and Marcus 1986). The target at which all the contributors took aim was the established anthropology of the day, and in particular the interpretive ethnography of their own teachers and their foster-father, Clifford Geertz. The charge was that ethnographers imposed a single reading on what was really a chaotic, discordant babble of voices. They 'essentialised' a people or a way of life, by insisting on a static and homogeneous representation of what, for example, 'the Balinese', think, or believe, or feel, or do; or what

'Balinese culture' amounts to. Using the resources of modern critical theory, the rhetorical tricks of authorship (authorising) could be revealed.

The new ethnographer was called to reinvent the nature and purpose of ethnography. It should represent a variety of discordant voices, contending about culture and identity, and should emphasise that cultural boundaries are provisional and uncertain, identities fragile and fabricated. The methodological critique also implied a political purpose; it was part of a call to arms in a new cultural politics. The author of the old ethnography spoke not only for himself (or, for that matter, herself), but served the interests of a political class that wished to impose its order on colonial subjects abroad or minorities at home. The postmodernist—or postcolonial—ethnographer should take sides in the great cultural struggle of the day, the epic battle between centre and periphery, Imperialism and anti-colonialism, the West and the Rest. The West has encompassed the little worlds of the Rest, but it is now in turn exposed to the jostling presence of immigrants. In the old colonies, the subaltern peoples have begun to answer back. The West is not guaranteed victory in its own terms. The struggle, as one might say, between Civilisation and *Kultur*, is not over yet. 'It is too early to say', according to James Clifford, 'whether these processes of change will result in global homogenization or in a new order of diversity' (Clifford 1988: 272).

In this struggle, the weapon of the weak is culture, and we must take the part of those who are fashioning a cultural defence against the West, by crafting new identities, new cultural configurations. This means celebrating difference —for difference is the only basis for resistance against the hegemony of the West. 'Culture', James Clifford concludes, 'is a deeply compromised idea I cannot yet do without' (1988: 10).

The roots of this discourse lie in German Romanticism, and, like other romantic movements before it, it rejects the Enlightenment notion of a common human destiny, shaped by a common nature and a common rationality, and opposes the increasingly global, dominant technical civilisation that they call Western. It may also be conceived of as 'Capitalism', and George Marcus, for example, has revived the line of cultural critique inaugurated by Raymond Williams. He calls for an anthropology that is part of cultural studies, and that is dedicated to a cultural critique of capitalism.[3]

Yet although the postmodern theorists draw on ideas that are familiar enough, theirs is nevertheless a specifically American discourse, shaped by the Civil Rights movement, by the trauma of Vietnam, and the emergence of identity politics in America, and also by the internal disciplinary politics of American universities. It is very different from the cosmic pessimism of Lévi-Strauss. The optimistic battle-cry, the image of a new, last frontier on which the

[3] See, for example, the introduction to Marcus (1992) and Marcus and Fischer (1986).

Indians may defeat the cowboys, is, I think, in general, very foreign to
Europeans. After two world wars, after the Holocaust, the politics of identity
appear less innocent, less inspiring, the power of primordial attachments less
fictitious, the assertion of a common humanity less banal. Nor does this
American discourse necessarily speak to intellectuals in formerly colonial
countries. Colonial politics of divide and rule exploited cultural differences. In
South Africa, *Apartheid* was premised on theories of cultural identity. These
historical experiences bred scepticism, even hostility to the celebration of
cultural difference.

V

My subject has been the ideas about culture and civilisation that recur in
Western thinking in the twentieth century. I have taken for granted that these
ideas are themselves shaped by social and political forces, and that they have
social and political consequences. It is hardly a novel point, and I have cited
Febvre, Elias, and Williams to the same effect. This mode of analysis of the idea
of culture itself implies a critique of cultural theories. It suggests that a purely
cultural history of the idea of culture would make little sense, for it would leave
out the social and political forces that shape ideas, and that are shaped by them.

I would like to suggest that a more realistic, but radically different,
approach to culture can be sketched if we take as our starting-point not the
native but rather the immigrant. And why not? After all, the authentic and typical modern cultural actor is not the native but rather the trader, the voyager,
the refugee, the hopeful young person moving with light baggage to a land of
opportunity. Even the most determined stay-at-home must rediscover himself
through often troubling encounters with alternative ways of life. Every person
is obliged to consider what it is that distances him from the experiences of his
parents, even if he lives still in their old home.

I favour the image of the ethnographer as an immigrant, learning how to
cope in a new place; and I believe that many ethnographers succeed in that, just
as many immigrants do. The immigrant becomes adept at making situational
choices of norms, idioms, and strategies. Perhaps because I am myself an immigrant, and a grandson of immigrants, I am confident that we immigrants—
and ethnographers—can operate very well, given the chance, in our new
homes, not forgetting our origins, but ever adaptable. The immigrant must also
become a practical theorist of culture. There is no option, for this is the dominant discourse of identity in many parts of the world today. In his fascinating
ethnography of Southall, in West London, Gerd Baumann shows that the
Asian immigrants in this diverse community can and do manipulate, and
deconstruct, and contest several *discourses* on culture (Baumann 1996). My

modest hope is that professional anthropologists will achieve a comparable competence.

The pragmatic empiricism of the immigrant is based on more satisfactory theoretical assumptions than any form of cultural determinism. If the immigrant is the exemplar of the cultural actor, it will not do to essentialise culture, and we must be even more wary of essentialising difference. I confess that I find these conclusions morally attractive, but the underlying argument is nevertheless based firmly on empirical considerations.

The theory also has consequences for the future of anthropology. Like immigrants, ethnographers can indeed hope to understand others. After all, it is obvious that immigrants to our own countries, and also the people we go abroad to study, learn to grasp what we are up to, and what drives us. Natives, immigrants, and ethnographers necessarily make comparisons to help them in this learning process. There is also no reason why anthropologists should shrink from making broader comparisons, drawing on the studies of their colleagues. The argument can be pushed a step further. As citizens of a modern metropolis, as immigrants, as diplomats, as traders, people construct syncretic discourses in which they communicate effectively across cultures. There is no obvious reason why anthropologists cannot do the same, and do it at least as effectively.

Note. The ideas set out here are developed in my book, *Culture: The Anthropologists' Account* (Kuper 1999). An earlier version of this paper was delivered as the Eilert Sundt Lecture at the University of Oslo in 1997, and published in the *Yearbook of Sociology* (University of Oslo) for 1997.

REFERENCES

Arnold, M. (1932 [1869]), *Culture and Anarchy*. Cambridge: Cambridge University Press.

Arnold, M. (1900 [1873]), *Literature and Dogma: An Essay towards a Better Apprehension of the Bible*. London: Smith, Elder and Co.

Baumann, G. (1996), *Contesting Culture*. Cambridge: Cambridge University Press.

Clifford, J. (1988), *The Predicament of Culture: Twentieth-Century Ethnography, Literature and Art*. Cambridge, MA: Harvard University Press.

Clifford, J. and Marcus, G. E. (1986), *Writing Culture: The Poetics and Politics of Ethnography*. Berkeley: University of California Press.

Darwin, C. (1871), *The Descent of Man, and Selection in Relation to Sex*. London: John Murray.

Elias, N. (1978 [first German edn, Basel, 1939]), *The Civilizing Process: The Development of Manners. Changes in the Code of Conduct and Feeling in Early Modern Times*. New York: Urizen Books.

Eliot, T. S. (1948), *Notes Towards the Definition of Culture*. London: Faber and Faber.

Freud, S. (1963 [1930]), *Civilization and Its Discontents*, International Psycho-Analytical Library, no. 17. London: Hogarth and the Institute of Psycho-Analysis.

Febvre, L. (1930), 'Civilisation', in *Civilisation: le mot et l'idée. Exposés par Lucien Febvre, Émile Tonnelat, Marcel Mauss, Alfredo Niceforo et Louis Weber*. Paris: Centre International de Synthèse, La Renaissance du Livre.

Geertz, C. (1973), *The Interpretation of Cultures: Selected Essays*. New York: Basic Books.

Geertz, C. (1980), *Negara: The Theater State in Nineteenth-Century Bali*. Princeton, NJ: Princeton University Press.

Geertz, C. (1983), *Local Knowledge: Further Essays in Interpretive Anthropology*. New York: Basic Books.

Gouldner, A. (1970), *The Coming Crisis of Western Sociology*. New York: Basic Books.

Huntington, S. P. (1996), *The Clash of Civilizations and the Remaking of World Order*. New York: Simon and Schuster.

Kroeber, A. L. and Kluckhohn, C. (1952), *Culture: A Critical Review of Concepts and Definitions*. Cambridge, MA: Papers of the Peabody Museum, Harvard University, Vol. 47.

Kuper, A. (1999), *Culture: The Anthropologists' Account*, Cambridge, MA: Harvard University Press.

Lévi-Strauss, C. (1952), *Race and History*. Paris: UNESCO.

Lévi-Strauss, C. (1971), 'Race and Culture', *Revue Internationale des Sciences Sociales* 23(4): 608–25. Collected in Claude Lévi-Strauss, *The View from Afar*. Oxford: Blackwell, 1985.

Macaulay, T. B. (1843 [1825]), 'Milton', in *Critical and Historical Essays*. London: John Murray.

Marcus, G. E., ed. (1992), *Rereading Cultural Anthropology*, Durham, NC: Duke University Press.

Marcus, G. E. and Fischer, Michael M. J. (1986), *Anthropology as Cultural Critique: An Experimental Moment in the Human Sciences*. Chicago: University of Chicago Press.

Parsons, T. (1951), *The Social System*. New York: Free Press.

Schneider, D. M. (as told to Richard Handler) (1995), *Schneider on Schneider*. Durham, NC: Duke University Press.

Starobinski, J. (1993 [French edn, 1989]), *Blessings in Disguise: Or, The Morality of Evil*. Cambridge, MA: Harvard University Press.

Tylor, E. B. (1903 [1871]), *Primitive Culture: Researches into the Development of Mythology, Philosophy, Religion, Language, Art and Custom*, 4th edn, revised. London: John Murray.

Williams, R. (1983 [1958]), *Culture and Society, 1780–1950*, 2nd edn. New York: Columbia University Press.

Learning from Culture

HENRY PLOTKIN

CULTURE IS A NATURAL PHENOMENON with some very interesting properties. Traditionally falling within the domain of the social sciences, indeed regarded by many as lying at the heart of the social sciences, attempts over the last three or four decades to use biological theory and conceptions to understand better just what culture is, have led to a number of statements on how to capture the essence of the relationship between the social and the natural sciences, and analyses of exactly what is that relationship. Whilst not generally recognised as such, one of the most exquisitely precise of these lies in the last lines of Dawkins's (1976: 215) book: 'We are built as gene machines and cultured as meme machines, but we have the power to turn against our creators. We, alone on earth, can rebel against the tyranny of the selfish replicators.' Understanding that capacity for human 'rebellion' against the causal forces that drive the activities of all other species is one way of increasing our understanding of that relationship. Culture also poses formidable problems for the natural sciences and challenges some of the conventional assumptions in the conceptual toolkit of biology. Acknowledging these problems and challenges does not mean accepting some of the more absurd charges made against biological theory, but it does mean that biologists can learn about shortcomings in their own theory, which, ironically, will strengthen the inevitable naturalising of the social sciences. There are, in turn, lessons to be learned by social scientists from biology. In the end, both sides can and must learn from a naturalised science of culture. In each of the following sections an attempt is made to answer a specific question, by which device some of these problems, shortcomings and challenges, for both social scientists and biologists, will be considered.

IS CULTURE UNIQUE TO HUMANS?

Whiten *et al.* (1999) report on an accumulated 151 years of observation of chimpanzees living under natural conditions. Thirty-nine different behavioural patterns, which included tool usage, grooming, gestures, and courtship behaviours were found to be habitual and widespread in some communities but

Proceedings of the British Academy, **112**, 103–118, © The British Academy 2002.

absent in others. For example, in Tanzania one community gains access to ants by using a short stick to probe an ant-nest and then transferring the insects directly to their mouths, whereas in another community a longer stick is used and the ants are swept off the stick by hand and then transferred from hand to mouth. And in the West African communities, nuts and stones are present in both localities reported on, but whereas west of the Sassandra-N'Zo river nuts are cracked open using blows from a stone, such nutcracking is not present east of the river. Neither genetic nor ecological factors seem adequate explanations of such differences. In some cases the populations were members of the same sub-species, isolated from one another for, in evolutionary time, just short periods, thus reducing the likelihood of explanations based on genetic differences; and nothing is known in behaviour genetics which would suggest genetic coding for such fine detail as 'straight to mouth' versus 'first to hand and then mouth'. Such small behavioural variations also have no foundations in ecological differences, because the identical ecology holds for groups with different customs. The most likely explanation is that these 39 behaviours are shared as a result of the animals learning in some way, not necessarily by imitation, from one another.

Culture is a word which has been defined in many different ways (see Keesing 1974; Kuper 1999). In part this arose through the commitment of different schools of anthropology to differing interpretations of culture. The adaptationist school of thought, for example, considered culture as the means by which an open-ended human nature finds expression within a particular ecological setting, thus allowing survival in the diverse circumstances of human existence. For such anthropologists culture is the pattern of behaviours and material objects which express the technologies and economies which aid survival. From such a perspective, religion, ritual, and other symbols are, as Keesing notes, secondary properties of cultures, or even epiphenomena. How different from the symbolists, for whom meaning shared by social actors is all (e.g. Geertz 1972). And how different again are adherents to the ideational schools for whom culture is knowledge, which is either an expression of human cognition (Goodenough 1990) or of the universal structure of the human mind expressed within a particular historical, social, and physical setting (Lévi-Strauss 1966).

Despite these fairly deep anthropological divisions, outsiders who are not card-carrying members of one or other of these schools of thought can discern obvious links between these different approaches, which are not exclusive of one another. I want here to pursue a different approach, though, because what is clear through the welter of possible meanings of this 'hyper-referential word' (Kuper 1999) is that whether it be technologies, texts and symbols, or knowledge, in each case what distinguishes culture is that it refers to groups of individuals sharing something, a sharing whose proximal cause is not rooted in genetics. The chimpanzees of Whiten *et al.* also share something whose proximal cause is not rooted in genetics. The behaviour of fishing for ants or gaining access to the kernel of a nut is different from building and using a plough, subscribing to a particular metaphysical belief, or belonging to a poetry society, but if the core of culture is sharing through learning, then culture is not unique to humans. The cultural entities of the chimpanzee may be uncomplicated behaviours, but they are cultural entities nonetheless.

A simple and obvious point is being made. If those free-living chimpanzees are granted culture, it is culture in the same sense as humans have culture, by virtue of sharing through learning. That is the core feature of culture. But what is shared, what the cultural entities are, varies both within and between cultures and species. This brings us to the second question.

HOW SHOULD WE THINK ABOUT THESE DIFFERENT KINDS OF CULTURAL ENTITY?

Biologists entering into the social sciences have to learn to deal with degrees of complexity unknown in the natural sciences. Anything that can be culturally transmitted is a cultural entity. These would include methods of doing things, like using tools and preparing food, narratives, moral codes, and even the minutiae of each of our daily lives. As a start to dealing with such complexity we need to be able to make some kind of conceptual sense out of the millions of cultural entities with which human cultures are awash. Rather than attempting an exhaustive survey, separating every kind of cultural entity from all others, I want to explore the functional range of cultural entities.

Like chimpanzees, humans can learn motor acts by observing the behaviour of others, though not necessarily by way of the same psychological mechanism. Actions and methods as cultural entities form a relatively clear-cut grouping. Another comprises our being able to relate to one another the details each of us has stored in episodic memory, including conjectures based on such memories about the behaviours and intentions of others. Trivial though such details may seem, the exchange of such cultural entities may have important social function. Following Dunbar (1996) we can refer to such cultural entities as gossip, which functions as a form of social grooming. Then there are artefacts, the material products of cultures. For clarity, it is probably worth making a distinction here too. Some artefacts are practical, ranging from the stone axes of our ancestors to the products of modern industrial plants like the computer on which this is being written. Other artefacts are products of human aesthetic sense and range from works of literature through music and on to paintings and sculpture. Yet others may have important roles to play in rituals and as symbols.

Actions, methods, gossip, and artefacts are relatively clear-cut groupings of cultural entities which stand apart from one another functionally. They differ also from two other major categories of cultural entities whose role is foundational in the process of enculturation. One of these will be referred to as concepts and schemata and the other as social constructions. Distinguishing between the two is convenient, but the distinction is not absolute. Because of their importance to the way in which we enter into specific cultures, but also because most biological approaches to culture hardly ever mention them, it is worth dwelling upon them a little.

Much of what humans communicate to one another in the course of everyday life is based upon an enormous reservoir of knowledge. When a parent tells a child that they can have a pet provided that the child takes on the responsibility of caring for it, the child needs to know what set of animals make up pets (tigers and elephants are not included), that animals in the confines of a house need to be fed and cleaned, and that pleasure (in this case, the fun of having a pet) must often be paid for (the chores involved in caring for the pet). And when one tells a friend that a shop on the High Street is selling good claret at knock-down prices, the friend needs to know, and share that knowledge with oneself, what shops and High Streets are, what is claret, what is good claret, and what money and good value are. Such background knowledge is the cultural water within which we all swim and it is this that is being referred to by the shorthand of concepts and schemata, though the ungainly phrase 'higher-order knowledge structures' is more appropriate.

Knowledge structures are built cumulatively. The young child learns that Livingstone, the cat next door, is different from Laertes, the cat from across the road, yet that both are cats and in turn different from Max the dog that lives in the corner house; in time the child will abstract the qualities of cats and dogs and the birds in the garden and form the concept of animals; and in further time the sub-set of pets will be formed and plants added to animals to form the over-arching concept of living things. By the time a child requests a pet of its own, it knows that neither tigers nor rose bushes are being considered by the parent. There is much evidence that some non-human animals are also able to form concepts (e.g. Herrnstein *et al.* 1976), but they do not transmit them to others. The process of enculturation by which children come to form the complex network of concepts that characterises their culture is a product of their own cognitive mechanisms for abstracting meaning driven by constant interaction with parents, sibs, peers, and teachers. Enculturation is not a discrete event in the way that gene transmission is a discrete event. It is a gradual, 'smeared-out' process covering a period of years and intimately bound in to social interactions. No aspect of human cognition is untouched by social interaction, of course. But concepts exemplify the messy and fuzzy nature of enculturation into a set of cultural entities, concepts, that are essential background knowledge that we share with others, and by which we communicate knowledge of the world. Many concepts, it might be noted, are culture-specific (some cultures do not have pets).

Contrary to the then prevailing view of memory as a passive and automatic process, Bartlett's (1932) seminal studies of memory were based on the notion that memory is a process of creative reconstruction. Memories change in time as we reinterpret the events in our lives, partly as a result of our wants and needs, but partly also as a result of the effects of unconscious generic knowledge structures which act, to use a metaphor, as mental gravity forces which distort memories. These knowledge structures, which are complex models of the world, he called schemata. Take as an example the schema for a beach. For most people it would include surf, bathers, umbrellas and the like. Horses would be less likely elements of a beach schema whereas rock pools would be more likely elements. Experiments, beginning with Bartlett, show that when recalling a narrative, which might include a beach scene with horses, the latter might be forgotten whereas a rock pool might be added even though one was not present in the original story. Bartlett's ideas did not thrive in the associationist, atomist climate of mid-twentieth-century psychology. However, with the rise of cognitivism, and especially artificial intelligence in the 1970s, the idea of schemata was revived by Minsky (1975), who called them frames, and by Rumelhart (1975) who retained Bartlett's word of schemata. Schank and Abelson's (1977) scripts followed hard on their heels.

Whilst all cultures everywhere have schematas and scripts, the contents of these are, like concepts, culture-specific. The schema for a factory does not exist within the cultures of hunter-gatherers, whilst that for animal tracks is usually absent from the minds of urban dwellers. Like concepts, schemata are core cultural entities that arise from a long period of development within the framework primarily of informal interactions with caretakers and peers, but which also originate in more formal tuition. We cannot function properly within a culture without mastering this type of cultural entity and the forms that characterise that culture.

Animals can be seen and touched and beaches walked on because they exist as material structures in the world. Justice, on the other hand, is not something that we can smell or hold. It is without material substance, yet it has a powerful influence upon our lives. I follow Searle (1995) in calling these entities, which exist by virtue of the members of a social group agreeing upon their existence, social constructions. Like higher-order knowledge structures, social constructions are culture-specific and the product of a long period of enculturation during childhood. The Western construction of justice is based largely upon the notions of ownership, protection of the individual, and fairness. Other cultures have different social constructions of justice based on kinship, service, revenge, or, in some cases, metaphysical systems. In each case the social construction of justice serves to regulate social relations and interactions, but the basis of the construction varies from culture to culture, and may change in time within a culture. Social constructions take myriad forms. Money and marriage are social constructions. So too is patriotism and politics.

Three features of social constructions must be mentioned. The first is that whilst social constructions exist within the minds of the members of a culture, they often find expression in material forms constructed as accessories to the social constructions that gave rise to them. Court houses, prisons, and the curious wigs worn in law courts are all physical embodiments of British justice. These physical expressions become bound in to the social constructions and may powerfully reinforce them. The main criminal law court in London, the Old Bailey, is at once a physical feature of English law and a powerful symbol reinforcing the notion of justice.

The second point is that social constructions have very real causal power. Every major war of the last century, which the International Committee of the Red Cross estimates together resulted in the deaths of at least a 100 million people, was caused by social constructions such as patriotism, ideologies like National Socialism and Marxism, religious differences, and the need to protect economic interests. Furthermore, the causal forces may be persistent, localised, and seemingly immune to outside influence. The United Kingdom has been wracked by the religious divide of Northern Ireland for decades. Unionists (sometimes known also as Loyalists), whose allegiance and loyalty is to the British Crown, are, as this is written, skirmishing with the armed forces of that selfsame Crown. The undisguised distaste of the rest of the population of the United Kingdom for what are widely viewed as anti-Catholic bigots parading in bowler hats to commemorate centuries-old battles is without effect on the rioters and marchers. But then there is nothing unique, of course, about the entrenching effects of social constructions within the culture of Northern Ireland. In similar fashion, ethnic and religious differences divide the peoples of the Balkans and the Middle East. There can be no doubting the causal power of this kind of cultural entity.

The final point relates to the feedback into these causal forces of the effects of the social construction itself. Often, perhaps almost always, social constructions lead to circumstances that reinforce that construction. For half a century, *apartheid* in South Africa deprived the majority of South Africans of their fundamental rights, including an adequate education. *Apartheid* was the material expression of the social construction called *baaskap* (an Afrikaans word without English equivalent, but 'bossedness' will do), which is a doctrine of white supremacy and which had dominated South Africa for centuries prior to the formal political institutions of *apartheid*. Depriving people of schooling that would allow them to function properly in the modern world, *baaskap* and *apartheid* resulted in the majority of South Africans seeming to be inferior to properly educated whites, which, of course, reinforced the belief in white supremacy.

Biologists with an interest in human culture would be hard pressed to find cultural entities that are more pervasive, more powerful, and more puzzling, than the social constructions whose force seems to emanate from group agreement. Of course, they are no more than neural network states within the brains of the individuals making up a culture. But somehow, for reasons that are not yet understood, they drive and dominate human cultures in a way that no other cultural entities do. People do not do violence because of differences in concepts and schemata, or because of diverse ways of preparing food or using tools. They do kill one another driven by social constructions or because of the differences that arise from social constructions. The success of biology in helping us to understand human culture can be measured by the extent to which it can explain social constructions.

Is the distinction between concepts and schemata on the one hand and social constructions on the other justified? There is a strong case that social constructions are a form of schemata, albeit they are social creations in the way that beaches and animals are not. Social constructions, however, do have a force that derives, at least in part, from their emotional impact. It is possible that social constructions tap into certain fundamentals of human biology in a way that higher-order knowledge structures like schemata do not.

Each one of these groupings of cultural entities is shared within cultures by the people comprising that culture. But is there a way of justifying the distinctions drawn above? Here is something that the social sciences can learn from biology. This is the difference between process and mechanism.

IS CULTURE TO BE UNDERSTOOD IN TERMS OF PROCESSES OR MECHANISMS?

A process is a sequence of events governed by a set of rules or procedures that leads from an initial state to an end state. For example, a card game like patience (solitaire) begins with a semi-random array of cards, the initial state, and then by manipulating the cards in accordance with a limited set of rules, the game proceeds to the end state, which is the most orderly array of cards possible given the initial state. Examples of processes in biology include growth, where the initial state is a set of linear arrays of DNA base pairs within the cytoplasmic chemistry of the ovum and the end state is the adult phenotype, and evolution, where the initial state was the first simple organisms of 3.5 billion years ago and the end state is the organic world of the present. What science aims to do, of course, is understand the rules that govern processes.

Everyone knows that Darwin's formulation of the theory of evolution in 1859 was a process account of the transformation of species by individual variation, the presence of consistent selection pressure, and the transmission of successful variations to offspring. He had no knowledge of the mechanisms involved. Over the following hundred years, beginning with the speculations of his friend T. H. Huxley, and those of Darwin himself, the possibility was explored that the process account of the evolution of species could be extended to understand the transformation of other complex biological systems, including individual development, the functioning of the immune system, learning and thought, and how change occurs in science itself (Plotkin 1993). Murdock (1956) was the first, as far as this writer knows, to apply an evolutionary process account to cultural change at large. Dawkins's (1976) notion of the meme was in this tradition of espousing what is sometimes referred to as universal Darwinism.

Process accounts are a powerful and necessary tool in biology. Bohm's (1969) observation, made with regret, that just as physics was moving away from mechanism, 'biology and psychology are moving closer to it' was an accurate reflection of the increase in understanding of, and emphasis on, molecular biology and neuroscience. For Bohm 'all is process'. His was an elegant account. But it denies the necessary and complementary side of biology, which is to describe how specific processes are embodied in causal mechanisms. The description given above of the game of patience as a process is what Dennett (1995) calls a substrate neutral account. These days patience is a game that comes as standard entertainment on many desktop and laptop computers where the mechanisms are partially embodied in the electronics of the computer (only partially since an understanding of the rules must still be coded in the neural networks of the human player—a computer could, of course, be programmed to play the game all by itself). Played by hand with a real pack of cards, the mechanisms of the process of the game are entirely contained in the head of the player. Contrary to what Bohm thought they should be doing, most biologists see it as their job to supply an account of those causal mechanisms if we are to claim a scientific understanding of the game of patience. To take a less trivial example, neural network modelling is providing increasingly powerful simulations and mathematical accounts of various forms of learning. These are substrate neutral accounts of the process of learning. However, there can be few neuroscientists, and few network modellers, who would rest content with learning in just these terms. What real neural networks are being activated, how, where they are in the brain, and what biochemical changes occur in different kinds of learning are absolutely essential to any claim to have a full science of learning.

The same reasoning applies to understanding culture and cultural entities. Despite Murdock's priority in the matter, it was Dawkins (1976) who founded memetics, the substrate neutral process account in which memes are the cultural analogues of genes, both being instances of replicators. Whether memetics can mature into a science of culture remains unclear (see Aunger 2001 for a variety of views). It certainly has strong advocates. But as in the case of learning, no biologist should rest content just with a process account of culture. Understanding of the causal mechanisms of culture contained in the mind/brain of each member of a culture is essential. And not only essential in itself, but essential to a better understanding of the process.

Memetics has not yet grasped the difficulties posed by lumping all cultural entities into some single category and assuming that everything is a meme and all memes are equal. Current favourite songs are memes and viewed in the same light as memes such as political ideals and the beliefs of major world religions. But any account of culture couched in such terms of equality and identity loses an important feature of the dynamics of cultures and is thus disturbing to social scientists. Pursuing the mechanisms of memes is one way of making sense and sorting out different kinds of memes from one another. For example, memes in the form of motor acts acquired by imitation, which is commonplace in humans, will be different from motor act memes acquired by emulation learning in chimpanzees.

This needs a small digression. There is much disagreement amongst primatologists as to whether chimpanzees and other great apes can imitate, if imitation is defined by the classic 'learning to do an act from seeing it done' (Thorndike 1898). Byrne and Russon (1998), for example, argue that the evidence is positive; Tomasello (1999) disputes this. Tomasello claims that what is taken for imitation in the great apes is more likely one animal observing the behaviour of another and learning from the act observed an affordance of objects not known before, and not learning the act in itself. In his own example, a mother rolls over a log and reveals insects beneath it. What her infant learns when seeing this is not how to roll logs but that they may conceal insects. Because the case against chimpanzee imitation rests on a negative, no data is available that absolutely clinches the argument either way, though Tomasello has performed experiments (Nagell *et al.* 1993 for example) that cast strong doubts on the abilities of chimpanzees to imitate.

Thus it is that teasing apart the mechanisms underlying memes for motor acts in humans and those underlying the memes of chimpanzees allows the strong claim that motor act memes as cultural entities in humans are different from motor act memes in chimpanzees. Such cross-species differences will surprise nobody. But now the same procedure and reasoning can be applied within human culture to sort out our within-species cultural entities. Are the psychological and neural mechanisms underlying the learning of how to tie shoe laces by imitation different from those by which that same child learns the concept of animal by a process of cumulative abstraction of features? We know very little of the neurology of either, but they have different developmental trajectories and make different computational demands. Very few psychologists would consider these to be manifestations of the same form of learning. How, then, could they both be instances of the same thing? The generic term *meme* may be useful, but not if it obscures such obvious differences. The same reasoning applies to schemata, social constructions, gossip, and artefacts.

Sorting out cultural entities in terms of the mechanisms that give rise to them begins to introduce some reality to the dynamics of culture. The schema of dentist lasts each of us a lifetime. When we are told that the new dentist in town is very good, that is a more fleeting and insubstantial meme. Dentists come and go. So do bargains in claret or the appearance of a new fashion of dress. We know little as yet as to how a schema relates to a specific token of itself but there is no reason to think that they are identical entities drawing on identical mechanisms. There is also no reason to think it a case of little fleas living on big fleas.

In summary, process accounts of how cultural entities come to be are important. Equally important are accounts of cultural entities in terms of the entitivity of causal mechanisms. The latter provides us with the opportunity to ground cultural entities within current and future psychological and neuroscience theory. Nor is this a reductivist strategy. If ethnography tells us that cultures have dynamics, then anthropology is telling us something important about how to understand culture in terms of psychology. This is building bridges between the sciences, not eliminating one discipline in favour of another.

WHAT IS THE RELATIVE IMPORTANCE OF INDIVIDUAL DEVELOPMENT AND EVOLUTION?

There is a general argument that little in biology, and certainly nothing in psychology, can be understood from outside a developmental perspective which ascribes no primacy of cause either to the environment of development or to the genes that each of us receives at conception (Oyama 2000; Richardson 1998). This is of especial importance to enculturation, which is central to human cognitive development. Cultural psychologists from Vygotsky (1929) to Cole (1996) have noted the inseparable relationship that human cognition bears to the culture within which cognitive abilities develop. Enculturation comes about through cognition, and cognition is shaped to some extent by the developing child's culture. There is little to argue with here. There is, however, the need to position such accounts within the empiricist versus rationalist dispute which weighed so heavily in much of twentieth-century psychology, and behind which, from around 1980 onwards, lurked the issue of how to relate biological evolution to cognition.

There is no quick and easy way to review these matters but one point of immediate entry relevant to the issue of cultural entities lies in studies of cognitive development of the last few decades. Ranging from number discrimination (Xu and Spelke 2000) through understanding of animate objects (Pauen 2000) and on to rule learning (Marcus *et al.* 1999), the general findings are remarkable in showing that infants just a few months old have significant cognitive abilities—far more than was thought twenty or thirty years ago—and that well-mapped development trajectories such as those of language (e.g. Calvin and Bickerton 2000) and theory of mind (Baron-Cohen *et al.* 2000) are strikingly constant. As a result of such findings it is, I think, correct to say that most developmentalists have become increasingly nativist in their thinking in recent years. Fodor (1998: 208) mildly puts it thus: 'If there is a human nature, and it is to some interesting extent genetically determined, it is folly [for humanists] to ignore it.' Significant genetic determination of cognitive development immediately raises the extent to which evolution must be invoked in any account of how humans come to have the kinds of cultural entities that they do. Anthropologists like Boyer (1999) are led to assert that 'Conceptual development is governed by evolved predispositions and governs inferences from cultural input.' After all, if every infant, pathology apart, appears to know so much so soon after birth, and if cognitive development proceeds along the same lines in all children, at least to some extent independently of the environment of development, then whence the causes of this? Can so much reliance be placed upon unconstrained learning in an uncertain and variable environment to give rise to invariant developmental sequences in every child? If the answer is 'no', and if it is not genes that are responsible for the invariance, then what is? And if it is genes, then surely these are genes that are the product of human evolution? These are questions that no social scientist can duck.

There have been, roughly speaking, three kinds of position adopted in relation to these questions. One is to question the extent to which one needs to take a nativist position at all (Elman *et al.* 1996; Paterson *et al.* 1999). The second is epitomised by Fodor (1998) and Chomsky (2000), who embrace what Fodor refers to as the new rationalism, in effect a strong nativism, but remain neutral on the matter of how innate cognitive abilities relate to evolution. The third is to assume that since the genes of each and every one of us are the only links we have with the evolutionary history of our species, that evolution must be seen as having a causal hand in what we cognise about, how we do it, and hence what cultural entities our cognition gives rise to (Pinker 1997; Plotkin 1997). Readers must take their own position on this key issue.

Fodor (1983) presented the highly influential notion, influential whether accepted or rejected, that inputs to the mind/brain are channelled into innately specified and domain-specific modules whose mechanisms are computationally dedicated, informationally encapsulated, and of relatively fixed ontogeny (amongst other features). In his review of cultural psychology, Cole (1996: 199) suggested that there is a strong and a weak version of the modularity hypothesis. The strong version of the hypothesis is that innate constraints are so powerful that the function of these modules, and the cognitive characteristics that they give rise to, are triggered (in Chomsky's 1980 meaning) by environmental events 'and do not really develop at all'. The weaker version, and the one that he prefers, is that while genetic influences are greater than traditional theory recognised:

> these genetically specified characteristics provide the starting point, the initial structure, upon which later cognitive abilities are constructed. They set constraints upon the way the developing organism attends to and hypothesizes about experience, channelling development along species-typical lines. (Cole 1996: 199)

Cole's compromise position is a nice way of reconciling biological and cultural approaches to human cognition. However, an even larger compromise might be needed. This would involve the assumption that there is a dimension ranging from 'triggered' to 'constructed' along which every cognitive domain falls. Some, like language according to the Chomskian view, would be positioned closer to the triggered end of the dimension; and others like theory of mind (e.g. Lillard 1998) and the ability to enter into social constructions, would be closer to the constructed end. Where along that dimension a domain falls is a consequence of the properties of each domain itself. Some properties of the world may be less tolerant of computational flexibility than others.

We simply do not have certain answers to any of these issues. But what is clear to any observer of this corner of science is that how we eventually resolve these matters will crucially determine the way in which the social and biological sciences are brought into fruitful relations with one another. That means that our understanding of cultural entities within a biological perspective hinges on what answers we eventually come up with to these vexed questions of development and evolution.

ARE CULTURE AND CULTURAL ENTITIES ADAPTATIONS?

There is a strong and obvious *prima facie* case that, as anthropologists have emphasised, some cultural entities are adaptive. From clothing and shelters to anaesthetics and antibiotics, many artefacts have clear and beneficial impacts upon human fitness. However, the obvious counter-examples of cars and weapons of mass destruction which have negative effects on fitness make it difficult to maintain the strong position that all cultural entities are adaptations. There are other difficulties for anyone trying to adopt an adaptationist perspective on culture.

For one thing, the capacity to enter into culture is almost certainly not a single trait. This brings us back to the issue of mechanism. Nobody disagrees with the assertion that language is essential for culture, but this, in turn, raises two problems. The first is that language itself is not a single trait but a cluster of already existing psychological mechanisms, like working memory and the ability to discriminate certain patterns of sound which are shared with other primates, and hence must draw on mechanisms that long pre-date the appearance of language in humans (Ramus *et al.* 2000), and the capacity for temporally tagging memories as well as chunking (parsing) streams of sensory input, to which must have been added the special rule-governing mechanism by which protolanguage becomes transformed into true, generative language. Language is a 'supertrait' rather than a single trait in the way that, say, haemoglobin is a trait. This immediately raises the issue of exaptation, which will be returned to below.

The second problem is that language alone is not sufficient to support human culture. For someone to share the social construction of justice with other members of their culture they must be able to bring their own intentional mental states of knowing, thinking, and wanting into some kind of matching relationship with the intentional mental states of others in their culture. In order to do this, all people sharing a culture must have the ability to know that others have intentional mental states. They must, in the parlance of cognitive psychology, have a theory of mind. The experimental evidence strongly indicates that a theory of mind mechanism is a specific organ of mind in the same sense that language is considered an organ of mind. It has a particular developmental sequence, computational requirements, and likely is sited in a specific part or parts of the brain. There is also evidence suggestive of a genetic part-cause, and impairment of theory of mind has catastrophic effects on social cognitive function (Baron-Cohen *et al.* 2000). Tomasello (1999) believes that theory of mind is essential for imitation as well. It may also play a role in the formation of schemata, the latter and other higher-order knowledge structures central to culture being dependent upon yet other cognitive mechanisms. Each of these mechanisms may well be adaptations on their own, but their collective expression as culture and an array of cultural entities cannot be thought of as a single adaptive trait without taking the meaning of a biological adaptation beyond its normal usage. Put another way, culture is a special manifestation of human intelligence and hence difficult to place within the normal conceptual landscape of biology.

Finally, there is the adaptation–exaptation problem. Williams wrote a classic account of the 'onerous' concept of adaptation, which he defined in terms of our ability, onerous indeed, to attribute 'the origin and perfection of [this] design to a long period of selection for effectiveness in this particular role' (1966: 6). Now evolutionists, including Darwin, have long recognised that some features of organisms have some current utility of function, but origins that do not lie in consistent and prolonged selection for that function. *Preadaptations* was the word commonly used to describe traits whose origins were non-adaptive in nature. Gould and Vrba (1982) extended this line of thinking by identifying phenotypic characters, like feathers in birds, which had previously been shaped by natural selection for a specific function, that is, as an adaptation, but which have now been co-opted for a new use. They termed such traits exaptations. Subsequently Gould (1991) argued that the concept of exaptation is a crucial one for evolutionary psychology. The human brain/mind, Gould asserted, is the best available case for the predominance of exaptation.

Reading and writing are the most obvious examples of exaptive function, given that script was invented just a few thousand years ago and widespread literacy is a phenomenon of just the last few centuries. The evolution of reading and writing adaptations could not have occurred. When we read and write we are using previously evolved mechanisms and structures co-opted to new functions. The reach of exaptations is longer than that, however. As noted above, language requires mechanisms like working memory and the ability to discriminate between certain kinds of sounds, both of which pre-date the appearance of language. There are suggestions that mechanisms of hand usage and gesture have been incorporated into the language organ (Corballis 1999; Wilson 1998), and that cognitive mechanisms for dealing with certain aspects of social organisation were necessary precursors of language (Calvin and Bickerton 2000). Only some of these claims need to be correct for language to be classed as an exaptation. If one wants to understand culture within the conceptual framework of adaptationism, and if language is an exaptation, then human culture, for which language is so crucial, is an exaptation of an exaptation. Indeed, there is a strong case to be made that, with the exception of associative learning, most, perhaps all, of primate and human cognition is the end product of repeated exaptations of exaptations.

While the adaptation–exaptation distinction is increasingly widely discussed (Buss *et al.* 1998; Dennett 1995) people remain divided on whether it is a matter of any importance or just a trivial play on words. Dennett (1995) is inclined to the latter view with his dismissive 'no function is eternal'. In one sense he is right. But one of the most important conceptual tools for one school of evolutionary psychology is reverse engineering (Pinker 1997), which attempts to unravel how an attribute has come to be the way it is now by building a picture of past selection pressures. Present traits which are exaptations of exaptations make this, at best, a hazardous task, at worst, an impossible one.

Cultural entities, then, come in different forms. Generically they may all add to the fitness of humans as creatures of culture. Some specific cultural entities militate against individual fitness. And it is a moot point as to whether any cultural entities can ever be considered to be adaptations or products of adaptations. The concept of adaptation is one of the oldest and most important in evolutionary biology, and yet there is a real possibility that biologists must contemplate, which is that it has little or no role to play in a natural science of culture. Now that would be a hard lesson to learn.

REFERENCES

Aunger, R., ed. (2001), *Darwinizing Culture: The Status of Memetics as a Science*. Oxford: Oxford University Press.

Baron-Cohen, S., Tager-Flusber, H., and Cohen, D. J., eds (2000), *Understanding Other Minds*. Oxford: Oxford University Press.

Bartlett, F. C. (1932), *Remembering*. Cambridge: Cambridge University Press.

Bohm, D. (1969), 'Some Remarks on the Notion of Order and Further Remarks on Order', in C. H. Waddington (ed.), *Towards a Theoretical Biology, Vol. 2: Sketches*. Edinburgh: Edinburgh University Press, pp. 18–60.

Boyer, P. (1999), 'Cognitive Tracks of Cultural Inheritance: How Evolved Intuitive Ontology Governs Cultural Transmission', *American Anthropologist* 100: 876–89.

Buss, D. M., Haselton, M. G., Shackelford, T. K., Bleske, A. L., and Wakefield, J. C. (1998), 'Adaptations, Exaptations, and Spandrels', *American Psychologist* 53: 533–58.

Byrne, R. W. and Russon, A. E. (1998), 'Learning by Imitation: A Hierarchical Approach', *The Behavioral and Brain Sciences* 21: 667–721.

Calvin, W. H. and Bickerton, D. (2000), *Lingua ex Machina: Reconciling Darwin and Chomsky with the Human Brain*. Cambridge, MA: MIT Press.

Chomsky, N. (1980), *Rules and Representations*. New York: Columbia University Press.

Chomsky, N. (2000), *New Horizons in the Study of Language and Mind*. Cambridge: Cambridge University Press.

Cole, M. (1996), *Cultural Psychology: A Once and Future Discipline*. Cambridge, MA: Harvard University Press.

Corballis, M. C. (1999),' The Gestural Origins of Language', *American Scientist* 87: 138–45.

Dawkins, R. (1976), *The Selfish Gene*. Oxford: Oxford University Press.

Dennett, D. C. (1995), *Darwin's Dangerous Idea*. London: Penguin Books.

Dunbar, R. I. M. (1996), *Grooming, Gossip and the Evolution of Language*. London: Faber.

Elman, J. L., Bates, E. A., Johnson, M. H., Karmiloff-Smith, A., Parisi, D., and Plunkett, K. (1996), *Rethinking Innateness: A Connectionist Perspective on Development*. Cambridge, MA: MIT Press.

Fodor, J. A. (1983), *The Modularity of Mind*. Cambridge, MA: MIT Press.

Fodor, J. (1998), *In Critical Condition: Polemical Essays on Cognitive Science and the Philosophy of Mind*. Cambridge, MA: MIT Press.

Geertz, C. (1972), 'Deep Play: Notes on the Balinese Cockfight', *Daedalus* 101: 1–37.

Goodenough, W. H. (1990), 'Evolution of the Human Capacity for Beliefs', *American Anthropologist* 92: 597–612.

Gould, S. J. (1991), 'Exaptation: A Crucial Tool for an Evolutionary Psychology', *Journal of Social Issues* 47: 43–65.

Gould, S. J. and Vrba, E. S. (1982), 'Exaptation — A Missing Term in the Science of Form', *Paleobiology* 8: 4–15.

Herrnstein, R. J., Loveland, D. H., and Cable, C. (1976), 'Natural Concepts in Pigeons', *Journal of Experimental Psychology: Animal Behaviour Processes* 2: 285–302.

Keesing, R. M. (1974), 'Theories of Culture', *Annual Review of Anthropology* 3: 73–97.

Kuper, A. (1999), *Culture: The Anthropologists' Account*. Cambridge, MA: Harvard University Press.

Lévi-Strauss, C. (1966), *The Savage Mind*. Chicago: University of Chicago Press.

Lillard, A. (1998) 'Ethnopsychologies: Cultural Variations in Theories of Mind', *Psychological Bulletin* 123: 3–36.

Marcus, G. F., Vijayan, S., Bandi Rao, S., and Vishton, P. M. (1999), 'Rule Learning by Seven-Month-Old Infants', *Science* 283: 77–80.

Minsky, M. L. (1975), 'A Framework for Representing Knowledge', in P. H. Winston (ed.), *The Psychology of Computer Vision*. New York: McGraw Hill, pp. 211–77.

Murdock, G. P. (1956), 'How Culture Changes', in H. L. Shapiro (ed.), *Man, Culture and Society.* Oxford: Oxford University Press, pp. 247–60.

Nagell, K., Olguin, K., and Tomasello, M. (1993), 'Processes of Social Learning in the Tool Use of Chimpanzees (*Pan troglodytes*) and Human Children (*Homo sapiens*)', *Journal of Comparative Psychology* 107: 174–86.

Oyama, S. (2000), *Evolution's Eye: A Systems View of the Biology–Culture Divide.* London: Duke University Press.

Paterson, S. J., Brown, J. H., Gsodl, M. K., Johnson, M. H., and Karmiloff-Smith, A. (1999), 'Cognitive Modularity and Genetic Disorders', *Science* 286: 2355–8.

Pauen, S. (2000), 'Early Differentiation within the Animate Domain: Are Humans Something Special?' *Journal of Experimental Child Psychology* 75: 134–51.

Pinker, S. (1997), *How the Mind Works.* New York: Norton.

Plotkin, H. (1993), *The Nature of Knowledge.* London: Allen Lane, The Penguin Press.

Plotkin, H. (1997), *Evolution in Mind.* London: Allen Lane, The Penguin Press.

Ramus, F., Hauser, M. D., Miller, C., Morris, D., and Mehler, J. (2000), 'Language Discrimination by Human Newborns and by Cotton-Top Tamarin Monkeys', *Science* 288: 349–51.

Richardson, K. (1998), *The Origins of Human Potential: Evolution, Development and Psychology.* London: Routledge.

Rumelhart, D. E. (1975), 'Notes on a Schema for Stories', in D. G. Bobrow and A. Collins (eds), *Representation and Understanding.* New York: Academic Press, pp. 211–36.

Schank, R. C. and Abelson, R. (1977), *Scripts, Plans, Goals and Understanding.* Hillsdale, NJ: Lawrence Erlbaum Associates.

Searle, J. R. (1995), *The Construction of Social Reality.* London: Allen Lane, The Penguin Press.

Thorndike, E. L. (1898), 'Animal Intelligence: An Experimental Study of the Associative Process in Animals', *Psychological Review Monographs* 2: 551–3.

Tomasello, M. (1999), *The Cultural Origins of Human Cognition.* Cambridge, MA: Harvard University Press.

Vygotsky, L. S. (1929), 'The Problem of the Cultural Development of the Child', *Journal of Genetic Psychology* 36: 414–34.

Whiten, A., Goodall, J., McGrew, W. C., Nishida, T., Reynolds, V., Sugiyama, Y., Tutin, C. E. G., Wrangham, R. W., and Boesch, C. (1999), 'Cultures in Chimpanzees', *Nature* 399: 682–5.

Williams, G. C. (1966), *Adaptation and Natural Selection.* Princeton, NJ: Princeton University Press.

Wilson, F. R. (1998), *The Hand: How its Use Shapes the Brain, Language and Human Culture.* New York: Pantheon.

Xu, F. and Spelke, E. S. (2000), 'Large Number Discrimination in 6–Month-Old Infants', *Cognition* 74: 1–11.

Choosing the Selectors

MARY MIDGLEY

WHAT CHANGES THE WORLD?

I LATELY CAME ACROSS A MUG inscribed with this remark, which it attributed to
Margaret Mead—'Never doubt that a small group of thoughtful, committed
citizens can change the world; indeed, it's the only thing that ever does.' It
struck me at once that this was a mug badly at odds with current thinking;
indeed, it cannot lately have been attending to the media as an educated mug
should. These days, the message that we chiefly hear is that changes in the world
are due to something on a much larger scale—perhaps economic causes, perhaps a shift in the gene pool, perhaps cultural evolution—certainly something
far grander than a few people worrying in an attic.

Is the mug therefore wrong? This seems to me rather an important issue. We
always have a choice about the perspective from which we will look at human
affairs—whether we will examine them from the inside, as participants, or
from some more distant perspective, and, if so, which of many distant perspectives we will choose. Or can we combine them? In theory, we know that these
various angles are not really alternatives but parts of a single enquiry. The different accounts supplement one another. Historians have to try to look at all of
them and must spend much of their time travelling between them. Yet it is often
very hard work to fit them together, and many things today make us unwilling
even to try. The ideology of our age strongly encourages us to find, somehow, a
single standpoint which is satisfactory because it is *scientific*—a standpoint so
solid and final that it is self-sufficient and will save us the trouble of attending
to any others. This project—this hope of a single, monolithic gospel—does
not, unfortunately, accord with the true spirit of science itself. Serious science
always knows that it is one-sided and incomplete. The claim to finality is never
itself scientific. Yet the astonishing success of the physical sciences in the last
few centuries does lead us now to expect this finality from them, and a whole
series of bold prophets who have claimed scientific status for their doctrines has
encouraged that hope.

In order to think how we can best use the concept of cultural evolution, I
think it is worthwhile to look briefly at some of these other long perspectives

Proceedings of the British Academy, **112**, 119–133, © The British Academy 2002.

Mary Midgley

which have been offered in recent times as key explanations of historical change and to consider their advantages and drawbacks. The most obvious of these alternative angles is the most recent one, namely the Marxist conception of history. That approach simply told historians to stop getting mired in personal transactions such as the quarrels and marriages of kings and to concentrate instead on large economic factors such as inventions, diseases, changes of crops and climate, land tenure, labour conditions, and expansions or contractions of trade. This was surely a most liberating and illuminating move—a move whose importance we now take for granted, though we may not always thank Marx for it. It had the characteristic advantage of all such distancing moves. It made large-scale tendencies that had been obscured by the distracting human dramas in the foreground visible at last. It showed up non-human background factors that are crucial to the shaping of human life. And since it did all this in the name of Science, it carried a prestige which seemed to set it above other possible kinds of explanation. That special prestige was, however, bought at a heavy price. It imposed a fatal narrowness—an unwarranted exclusiveness which tended to stop people developing the new insights effectively.

IS FATALISM TRUE?

The history of Marxism lights up two misfortunes that are liable to afflict a theory about social development when it claims scientific status. The first and most notorious of these is fatalism. Dialectical materialism extended the determinist assumptions commonly made in the physical sciences to cover human life and especially its own predictions. This makes it obscure why anybody should take the trouble to work inexhaustibly—as Marx and Engels did—on political projects whose outcome was already foredoomed. The remote perspective which was so useful for studying long-term economic trends simply could not be used for examining practical questions about what to do next, nor for moral questions about what to aim at. Marxist propaganda therefore oscillated between demanding the proletarian revolution urgently as a cure for current iniquities and trying to make people accept it by saying that that, in any case, it could not be prevented.

   This is the point where my mug's predictions surely become of interest. On the face of things, what the mug says has undoubtedly happened. We might instance the Invisible College—the group of influential thinkers who met in London in the mid-seventeenth century and whose discussions developed into the Royal Society. This group included several distinguished scientists, but its interests ran far beyond physical science and gave it a much wider influence. As Robert Boyle put it:

The 'Invisible College' consists of persons that endeavour to put narrow-mindedness out of countenance by the practice of so extensive a charity that it reaches unto everything called man, and nothing less than a universal goodwill can content it. And indeed they are so apprehensive of the want of good employ-ment that they take the whole body of mankind as their care. . . . But . . . there is not enough of them. (Boyle 1744: 20)

Or we could think of Wordsworth and Coleridge and the other Romantic poets, whose new thinking shaped our sensibilities through the Romantic Revival in Britain. Or of John Stuart Mill and his colleagues, the sanitary reformers, who insisted, in the face of huge opposition, on putting drains into British cities. Or of the Buddha and the five friends with whom—after much hesitation—he shared the revolutionary view of life that he had reached in meditation. Or indeed of Marx and Engels themselves and the people— including their opponents—who helped them to shape their theories.

When supporters of the long perspective are asked to explain examples like these, they commonly reply that these people made no real difference. The changes that followed would have come about in any case. In a very general sense no doubt there is something in this. In cases such as the drains it may well be mainly right. Cholera epidemics might have left little choice about that in any case. But in most cases the particular form that the change takes can make an enormous difference.

For instance, it may well be true that, even if Newton and Locke and Boyle had never been born, some group of people in a commercial country like Britain would have set about developing the physical sciences in the late seven-teenth century and would have adapted the background beliefs of the time so as to make room for them. But was it inevitable that these people would have developed and propagated the Augustan ideology that shaped the peculiar British version of the Enlightenment—that exact mix of rationalism, empiri-cism, Whiggish politics, Anglican theology, pragmatism, and misogyny that the champions of science in that age devised—the mix that, under the flag of Reason and Newton, proved benign enough to dominate thought in Britain throughout the eighteenth century? (For a most interesting analysis of that mix see Wertheim 1997: chs 5 and 6.)

Again, in a very general way, perhaps it might have been predicted that the narrowness of that ideology would eventually produce some such reaction as took place at the Romantic Revival. A celestial observer might have foreseen the negative side of that reaction. But the positive suggestions about replace-ments for it varied hugely from one country to another and involved real origi-nal thinking. They were not the kind of thing that could ever be considered inevitable. And they have profoundly affected the way in which English-speaking people still live and think. Besides Wordsworth and Coleridge there was Blake—an extraordinary and quite unpredictable person—and his friends, who included Godwin, Tom Paine, and Mary Wollstonecraft. There were also Byron and the Shelleys.

HOPES OF SCIENTIFIC OBJECTIVITY

Along with fatalism, the second and less obvious drawback that can attend such long perspectives is the illusion of impartiality. The findings of the physical sciences are supposed to be objective—that is, free from bias. A social theory that joins them in gaining the status of a science may therefore seem to qualify for exclusive dominion. Approaches that conflict with it can seem to be necessarily *un*scientific—that is, wrong. Though Marx himself seems not to have been specially keen to claim the authority of physical science, Engels did stress that claim, insisting that Marxist doctrine was unique in being a scientific structure in the narrow sense, something solidly founded on the findings of biology and physics. This encouraged Marxism to become a narrow church— an orthodoxy that denounced its critics as fiercely as any earlier religion, instead of listening to them and learning from them.

It is worthwhile to notice how the illusion of impartiality worked here. Marxist thinkers saw themselves as objective physical scientists because their reasoning was materialistic. They dealt always in physical causes such as crops and climate, rather than in ideas. But of course they were selecting these particular causes out of many other equally physical ones in accordance with their own system of thought. That system centred on simple and dramatic ideas about the class war—ideas generated during the failed revolutions of 1848 and confirmed by Engels's experience of conditions in Manchester. It posited a polarisation of humanity in which (as the *Communist Manifesto* put it) the workers of the world would shortly unite, since they had nothing to lose but their chains. It aimed to complete the violent reshaping of human society that had been envisaged in 1848 by simply reversing the class situation that obtained under Western capitalism.

Though this seemed like large-scale thinking, it had, as usual, a local bias. It has been suggested that the class war might have looked very different to Engels if he had studied it in Birmingham, where numerous small workshops were conducted on a much more cooperative basis than the huge, despotically run Manchester cotton-mills. More seriously, the Marxist account entirely ignored factors outside the human species, and indeed most factors outside Europe. Marx was not concerned about the exploitation of natural resources. He thought those resources were infinite—a doctrine which was widely accepted in countries which adopted his views. He saw capitalist imperialism simply as the oppression of one set of humans by another, not as a source of ecological disaster. And of course, even within human affairs, his theory grossly oversimplified the problem. Marx was very astute in diagnosing many of the evils of capitalism, but he was mistaken in supposing that it was about to cure those evils by collapsing.

In rehearsing this familiar story, the point I want to stress is the illusion of impartiality which can result from taking this long perspective. Marxist theory moved from an immensely abstract general principle about causation—that all changes proceed from conflict—to deduce results about a particular conflict in which its founders had already taken sides. The abstractness of the universal principle seemed to guarantee the impersonality that belongs to physical laws, impersonality of a kind that could not be found in the usual run of historical causes. But this impersonality was deceptive because the principle was being understood from the start in a biased way that predetermined its application to that case.

This deception is even more obvious in the Social Darwinist project that has been Marxism's main rival and that seems to have outlived it. Its prophet, Herbert Spencer, derived his views from a single grand and highly abstract Law of Evolution.

> Evolution is an integration of matter and concomitant dissipation of motion; during which the matter passes from an indefinite, incoherent homogeneity to a definite, coherent heterogeneity; and during which the retained motion undergoes a parallel transformation. (Spencer 1884: 396)

Like many of us who have been struck by a promising idea, Spencer then began to see examples of his principle everywhere. As he said: 'Bearing the generalisation in mind, it needed only to turn from this side to that side, and from one class of facts to another, to find everywhere exemplifications' (Spencer 1904: 11). In case anyone might think his law too vague to provide practical guidance, Spencer drew from it at once the simple and satisfactory political conclusion that heterogeneity called for the utmost political freedom and that this meant, above all, free trade. Commercial freedom would ensure (in the disastrously ambiguous phrase which he invented) 'the survival of the fittest'. He named this as the basic principle of 'evolution'—a word whose meaning he was largely responsible for developing and which Darwin carefully avoided. Accordingly (said Spencer), the working of this principle must on no account be disturbed by charitable attempts to help the unfit—that is, the poor:

> The whole effort of nature is to get rid of such, to clear the world of them, and to make room for better. . . . If they are sufficiently complete to live, they *do* live. If they are not sufficiently complete to live, they die, and it is best that they should die. (Spencer 1864: 414–15)

As James Moore explains, Spencer reasoned that:

> All heterogeneity, all individuality, is the inevitable product of natural forces and
> a manifestation of universal progress. Thus, where markets are freely competitive,
> where government is decentralised . . . there, one could be sure, human beings are
> co-operating with the forces that mould their hopeful destiny. And where else
> were these conditions more fully realised than in the United States? Business was
> booming, untrammelled by regulation, and the fittest were proudly surviving in a
> competitive marketplace. (Moore 1979: 168)

What evolution demanded, then, was universal imitation of the current
methods of American capitalism. Whether this conclusion would have been
ranked as 'scientific' if Spencer had not decided that *The Origin of Species*
supported his doctrine is not altogether clear. After making that decision,
however, he always claimed to be an enthusiastic promoter of Darwin's
theory, which he thought was equivalent to his own. It was thus under the
banner of Darwinian science that Spencer reached, and converted to his
views, a large and receptive audience, especially in the United States. That is
why what is really Spencerism received, and still bears, the name Social
Darwinism. It is also one main reason why a different, but large, section of
American opinion still regards Darwinism itself as immoral and science in
general as morally dangerous. Darwin himself actually rejected Spencer's
methods strongly.

> I am not conscious of having profited in my own work from Spencer's writings.
> His deductive manner of treating every subject is wholly opposed to my frame of
> mind. His conclusions never convince me; and over and over again I have said to
> myself, 'Here would be a fine subject for half-a-dozen years' work'. His funda-
> mental generalizations (which have been compared in importance by some per-
> sons with Newton's laws!) . . . are of such a nature that they do not seem to me to
> be of any strictly scientific use. They partake more of the nature of definitions
> than of laws of nature. (Darwin 1974: 64)

The trouble lay, as Darwin saw, in the transit between the vast principles
and the particular cases. If we ask why Spencer and his converts were so sure
that their principle of heterogeneity demanded specially *commercial* freedom
—rather than (say) the freedom of workers to control their working conditions
or of citizens to protect their environment—the principle itself supplies no
answer. That choice actually flowed from economic ideas current in the day and
had its source in Adam Smith's objections to the rather confused excise system
of the late eighteenth century. Again—as with Marxism—a large black box
intervened here between abstract principle and application, a box that hid an
unexamined jumble of local and personal influences. The intervention of this
black box—this arena for self-deception about bias—seems to me to be the
most serious drawback that is liable to dog attempts to view social change 'sci-
entifically' from a long perspective. Spencerism provides a clear example of this

drawback. Others may be found in the supposed 'laws of history' proposed by theorists like Spengler and Arnold Toynbee.

In all these cases, as in Marxism, serious ideals were at work. Important half-truths were being stated; the trouble lay in their being euphorically universalised. All through their history, Marxists have been moved by a genuine indignation about social injustice. And Spencer's insistence on individual freedom was itself an honourable one, part of the Enlightenment's long campaign against oppressive customs stemming from feudalism. There was also something very good about his attempt to view human life and the rest of nature in a single perspective. The trouble is that this is an enormously harder enterprise than Spencer and his followers ever realised. Our culture had deliberately set up strong walls between humanity and other species for many centuries, allowing quite unrealistic ideas to develop about the foreign country outside the species-barrier. The apparatus of thought that needed to be used in order to generalise across it was therefore shaky and misleading. Apparently simple words like *animal*, *natural*, and *selection* turned out to carry an unexamined load of explosive meaning.

This same combination of good ideals and dubious results can be found, too, in the earlier system which lay behind both these ideologies—the first real attempt at universal historical explanation and the source of their shared emphasis on conflict—the Hegelian Dialectic. This was primarily an account of how ideas develop through opposition, each thesis being resisted by its antithesis and a higher synthesis eventually growing which combines the good points of both. This idea has the enormous advantage of undermining bigotry. It forces contenders to accept that they have no monopoly on the truth. Despite the persistent pugnacity of scholars, it has had a lasting good effect in civilising controversy by making people look for truths outside their own camp.

The down side of all this emerges, however—as in the other cases—in the choice of the theses that are supposed to be in conflict. For instance, for a long time in European history many people thought that the only choice about religion lay between Catholicism and Protestantism. Within these camps, too, the choice could seem even narrower, for instance between Calvin and Luther. The Hegelian perspective tends to concentrate attention on these existing duels, rather than on new directions. In this way it can lock people into existing thought-patterns rather than help them to move out of them. This was what Kierkegaard said had happened to Danish society in his day, where people well-satisfied with bourgeois opinions circled round on a Hegelian pattern of re-harmonising them. He wrote his book *Either/Or* to remind them that it is sometimes necessary to make real choices instead.

Similar pros and cons attended the still earlier paradigm of accounting for all puzzling changes as the dispensations of God. This had the obvious drawback that it could easily lead to fatalism. But it also provided the much more useful option of treating the new situation as a challenge—what the Quakers called a Chariot, an opportunity sent by Providence for new and laudable activity. Thus there is always an up and a down side to these projects.

IS EVOLUTIONARY THINKING DIFFERENT?

So much for past paradigms, earlier ways of explaining social change. What about the latest candidate? What are the special advantages and drawbacks of the current evolutionary pattern for explaining it by selectionism? Clearly it has one enormous advantage in that it treats human life as part of nature, not as something mysteriously set apart from it. It celebrates our continuity with the world we spring from rather than trying nervously to disown it. This strikes me as admirable because I take that continuity to be a central fact of life. I have never believed that human dignity calls on us to claim to have been blank paper at birth, pure beings shaped only by a singular abstraction called Society or Culture and able to change their world in any way they please. That distorted idea of human freedom is still powerful in the social sciences, even if slightly less powerful than it used to be. For this reason, the evolutionary model does us a great service by its insistence that culture itself is part of nature and must be seen as somehow continuing its patterns.

But which patterns? It is a good deal easier to say this as a general matter of faith than to work out how, in detail, we should fit together the ways of thinking which we have developed for describing the natural world from the outside —as spectators—and the ways which we use for dealing with our social life from the inside, as participants. In this book, many contributors will be offering gear-mechanisms for harmonising these two approaches. In doing this they will be riding the wave of current fashion even if they also direct it. Evolutionary talk is the flavour of the age and will be with us for a long time yet in any case. My doubts about it—which are closely related to Darwin's—are certainly not going to make it go away. I think, therefore, that I will do best to leave this positive, constructive work to others and simply concentrate here on the special problems that beset the project, which I think have not yet been fully noticed. By mentioning these, I may perhaps help its proponents to clarify it further.

SELECTION OF WHAT BY WHAT?

The central difficulty that I see here is that of getting a forest into a pint pot. The things that we think of as elements in culture are so various in form that it is not easy to see straightaway how we can find a single pattern of change that suits them all without Procrustean distortion. Is there a way of reducing them to a taxonomy, making them in some way parallel to the known elements of biology such as species, individuals, populations, and genes?

What does the evolutionary model actually demand here? John Ziman, introducing his book *Technological Innovation as an Evolutionary Process* (Ziman 2000), writes that he and his fellow-contributors, when they say that artefacts have *evolved*, 'mean more than that they have developed gradually. We are indicating that this development has occurred through genetic variation and natural selection.' He goes on to ask, 'Do *all cultural entities* evolve in this sense—that is, change over time by essentially the *same mechanism*?' In the last chapter of the book, he and his team give their reply to this question; 'We have come to see the evolutionary perspective as an indispensable tool of thought, highlighting a vital aspect of *all historical processes*. Our contributions to this book ... show *the effectiveness of "selectionism" as a unifying paradigm of rationality*' (2000: 3, 313, emphases mine). This is a big claim, going far beyond the technological examples that they actually deal with. It seems to me important to know how is it to be cashed out in practice. In any given case, what kinds of competing entities ought to form the population which is the raw material for this process of selection? *How do we find our units of selection?* We might ask this (for instance) about some of the more prominent items which constantly get mentioned as 'rising' during the history of the Western world in the last two centuries. This seems a reasonable case to take, since what rises may surely be said to evolve, and these are in fact fair examples of the kind of historical process which we often need to explain. Among these 'rising' items historians commonly list such things as—individualism, the middle class, the commercial spirit, the factory system, mechanisation, urbanisation, egalitarianism, imperialism, the standard of living, rapid transport, feminism, literacy, and population, while other things such as feudalism, faith, and skill in handicrafts are said to have correspondingly declined.

What worries me is not just the wide variation among the kinds of things that these words denote but the prior process of deliberate choice that has to go on before such abstractions are ever named in the first place. Words like this are not simple names of given entities, like the names of particular existing animal species which might be seen as competing to survive. They are abstractions—terms arrived at by cutting up the continuum of history in particular ways in order to bring out particular aspects of what has been happening. And these ways are not arbitrary or imposed by natural selection but deliberate. To use such words is already to have taken a position on questions about what is important there. These terms are *selective* in a quite literal sense of involving considered choice. How is this situation to be meshed with metaphorical talk of 'selectionism' involving selection from without by forces in the environment?

Is it indeed true that there is always 'a vital aspect' of such cases which can usefully be seen as a selection—a competition between a set of rival con-tenders, ending in a victory for the 'fittest'? No doubt, if we have a special con-fidence in the value of this pattern, we can often see it in the events we study. But the point I want to stress is that the decision to apply it to a particular social change already involves a particular view about the meaning and importance of that change. For instance, it is certainly possible to view the rise of the 'mid-dle class' simply as a case of the survival of the fittest—the victory of one given, existing set of people over a given range of other sets because it fits better with the given environment. But this is to commit oneself to a static, essentially Marxist view of class conflict. It misses the possibility that what is going on may be better described as a wide change in the ways in which people make their living—a different spread of occupations, producing different customs and different value judgements for everybody.

When a middle class 'rises' noticeably, it receives many recruits both from above and from below, changing its own constitution along with that of its fel-lows. The result is that everybody ends up viewing both themselves and the whole social hierarchy rather differently and the boundaries between classes become less sharp. There is not (apart from outside physical factors) a fixed, neutral 'environment' to which such a fixed, aspiring class has to adapt. It might therefore seem more natural to say that, if anything is evolving, it is really the whole social structure. More boldly still, it might be equally plausible to say that all the 'rising' items I have listed above are merely aspects of a single big historical process—a wider slice of social evolution. But on both these suggestions it gets even harder to view the process as one of 'Darwinian' (or Spencerian) selection among a given set of candidates.

How do we actually pick out from the cultural scene our main units, the entities that we can usefully describe as evolving? This is easiest in the case of artefacts, which are what Ziman and his team mostly discuss. Cathedrals, rail-way carriages, and Samurai swords are definite kinds of item, almost as clearly demarcated as natural species. The purposes for which they are made can be complex and can sometimes change, but are usually relatively limited. Their makers usually assume that these purposes are clear, and those who study them can normally take them for granted. There is often no need to discuss them. And while those purposes remain unchanged, the pattern of selection among various candidates often looks obvious. Even here, however, problems can arise. Should Victorian railway stations and modern skyscrapers be taken as further stages in the evolution of the cathedral? Or are they rather new life-forms that have competed with it and taken its place? Do they occupy the same ecological niche or a different one? In such cases, the change in purpose quickly becomes the central issue. It arises in Gerry Martin's fascinating article on Samurai swords in the collection on technological innovation, when he feels moved to add an apologetic note;

(Good reader, at this point I ask for your sympathy and understanding; we are discussing an object constructed with consummate and loving skill, revered, collected and exhibited in the world's greatest museums, but whose sole purpose is to violently cut up living human beings, I cannot start to reconcile these conflicting attributes.) (Martin 2000: 92)

But if he carried his study further to consider the way in which these swords eventually gave place to later weapons, the change in the roles that these new weapons played in society would seem to make it hard to treat them as simply more efficient adaptations to the same environment. And if he were writing about the development of modern weapons or methods of torture, this kind of question might become central.

It becomes more pressing still if one is writing about explicit abstractions such as individualism or feminism or imperialism rather than weapons. It does not seem to be possible to mention such items without implying value judgements, and these judgements make a chronic difference to how you identify them in the first place and so to what can count as their 'evolution'. People do not usually talk of something as evolving at all unless they are viewing it in some sort of positive light. They do not commonly speak of the evolution of crime, or drunkenness, or careless driving. Yet surely increases in these things too are among the 'historical processes' that Ziman mentions. My question is: is there some reason why they do not qualify as 'evolutions'?

The evaluative element in the word *evolution* was surely what made Darwin avoid it so carefully. This element comes out interestingly in the first example that the *Oxford English Dictionary* gives for the biological sense of the term. In his *Principles of Geology* Charles Lyell wrote, 'The testaceae of the ocean existed first, and some of them by gradual evolution were *improved* into those inhabiting the land' (Lyell 1830, Vol. 2: ch. 11, emphasis mine). When we are discussing social change, this value-laden way of talking does not, of course, commit us to approving of the particular development that we are discussing. But it does mean that we are picking it out as an enterprise, a project that people are somehow trying to promote, rather than as something that just happens to them (as the 'meme' pattern that we will discuss presently implies). We therefore need to interest ourselves in their own notion of what they are doing, not just in the outside forces that may be working on them. It also means that we have some reason for thinking the topic in question important enough to analyse. If, however, one picks out any of the *isms* in my list as a project of this kind, one is saying something about the whole of society, not just about a single element in it. De Tocqueville, when he invented the word *individualism*, was talking about a pervasive change in the entire American social attitude, not a limited element that had happened to prevail over a given set of rivals (De Tocqueville 1835).

'MECHANISMS'?

In trying to understand such large and various changes, I am not persuaded that the best course is to look for a single 'mechanism' which may be supposed to have brought them all about. (This is where Darwin's objection to wide extrapolation from limited examples seems to me quite right.) In discussing large-scale matters we are inevitably talking in terms of large abstractions that we have already formed. The 'mechanism' to be found—which is presumably a common form of development—must therefore work at the level of these abstractions. This means that it already incorporates our previous biases. And we know how quickly those biases change from age to age, constantly altering the language in which we describe social matters. There is, unfortunately, nothing here like the antiseptic, artificially unchanging language of physics. There are no neutral, naturally given units of selection as there are when we talk about the evolution of an animal species.

This does not mean that we cannot deal rationally with these matters. Our one-sidedness is not fatal so long as we are aware of it and make it explicit. All our opinions are, of course, our own opinions, expressing certain views on what is important. But we can articulate those views and offer them openly to others as contributions to the general stock. The trouble only comes in if, instead, we dogmatically universalise our own generalisations and promote them (as Spencer and Marx and Toynbee did) as laws of nature.

To avoid this, it seems to me fairly important to remember that, if we want to find the entity which is actually causing a given social change—aside from the physical background conditions—we have no real alternative but to concentrate on the actual people involved. They are the only unit that is directly given. Our various *isms* are shorthand ways of describing the activities of human beings, not those of abstractions. In order to understand these activities we have to get some idea of what these people had in mind, what they thought they were doing. Of course this may be quite different from what they finally succeeded in doing. But unless we can get some inkling about how they themselves saw the matter, we cannot hope to understand their actions. And if we are discussing some contemporary change, some process which now lands us with the need to choose a way forward, talking as if a set of competing abstractions were the agents in charge of this choice can only land us in fatalism.

MEME TROUBLE

This flight from concrete to abstract entities seems to me to be one of the most misleading features of the 'meme' pattern which is now popular as a proposed explanation of social change. Richard Dawkins, Daniel Dennett, and their followers hope to impose order on the untidy field of human history by inventing a quite new species of metaphysical entity—the meme—as the single causative agent in this area, a 'universal acid' that will replace all other forms of explanation. (I have discussed this suggestion more generally in Midgley 2001: part 1, ch. 6). Seeing that much of the existing confusion in this field is due to the complexity of human motives, they suggest that, rather than even trying to understand those motives, we should simply credit this parasitical entity with the power to override and manipulate them at its own convenience:

> The meme's-eye perspective challenges one of the central axioms of the humanities . . . we tend to overlook the fundamental fact that a cultural trait may have evolved in the way it has simply because it is *advantageous to itself*. . . . Competition is the major selective force in the infosphere and, just as in the biosphere, the challenge has been met with great ingenuity. . . . Like a mindless virus, a meme's prospects depend on its design—not its internal design, whatever that might be, but the design it shows the world, its phenotype, the way in which it affects things in its environment [namely] minds and other memes. (Dennett 1996: 362, 349, author's emphasis; see also Dawkins 1976: ch. 11)

Thus (he explains) memes contrive to infest us even when they are not useful to us at all, for example, 'the meme for faith, which discourages the exercise of the sort of critical judgment that might decide that the idea of faith was, all things considered, a dangerous idea' (1996: 349). It seems, then, that if we have faith in (for instance) the facts given in the telephone book or the pronouncements of scientists, this faith is not to be accounted for by any particular reasons by which we might justify it but by the alien power of the infesting meme.

Memeticists commonly manage to overlook the strangeness of this story by giving examples drawn from opinions that they already disagree with, such as religious ones (see for instance Dawkins's article 'Viruses of the Mind' [1993] where he asks 'Is God a Computer Virus?'). But—as they occasionally notice —if the theory is really meant to be universal, we have to extend it to all thought, including our own. The common deplorable habit of explaining away one's opponents' views as mere symptoms of their folly, rather than trying to understand them, now becomes the only way of explaining any kind of thought anywhere, including (of course) the thought by which we have just drawn this very conclusion. The urgent need that there is, in studying social change, to understand what people thought they were doing—to grasp the real advantage that they saw in acting as they did—vanishes once we see that the only advantage involved was actually a profit accruing to a bizarre metaphysical parasite called a meme. This discovery can certainly save us a lot of trouble in trying to do history. The only drawback is that thought itself becomes, at this point, entirely inexplicable and has to be abandoned.

CONCLUSION

Memetical talk does not seem to me to help us at all. It simply extends, to the point of open absurdity, the typical faults of explanations which try to use the long perspective when looking at something as close to us as the motivation of social changes. But the respect with which this suggestion has been treated shows how strong the bias towards such methods is today. In resisting that bias, I may, of course, just be showing one of those extraordinary blind spots which we find so entertaining when we study the history of thought. I can only repeat that my objection is not at all to the bringing of human affairs into the same perspective as the rest of nature. That is a move which I strongly support. What worries me is the hasty use of certain patterns that have been found useful in biology to explain human affairs where they have only a somewhat artificial application, at the expense of the directly relevant study of human motives, where we have plenty of useful information.

In this context, any attention to these motives tends to get dismissed as only 'folk psychology' and so not scientific. This approach deliberately bypasses the kind of valuable information which we get directly as participants in the social process within our own species, trading it for the more indirect and patchy kind which we have to use when dealing with species that are quite remote from us. It is choosing to look at human life through the wrong end of the telescope, making it appear far less intelligible than it actually is. As I have suggested in this article, memetics shares this fatal fault with a number of ambitious and influential schemes by which past thinkers have tried—and failed—to look at human affairs from the long perspective.

But is there a better way of doing so? The interesting question now is—can the more modest, careful, sophisticated kind of selectionism that Ziman and his colleagues are developing avoid this drawback? Can it give us the advantage of fully accepting our continuity with the rest of nature, without the kind of oversimplification that artificially distances us from ourselves? Can this new attempt to use 'selectionism as a unifying paradigm of rationality' escape the traps into which so many of these bold paradigms have fallen in the past? These questions can only be answered by trying out the method. The experiment is certainly worth making. As I see it, these pioneers' chance of success depends centrally on their being far more aware of their own preconceptions—far less ready to treat their own ideas as necessarily universal—than earlier theorists have been. This is very exhausting work, but it is surely not impossible. I can only wish them luck.

REFERENCES

Boyle, R. (1744), *Works*, Vol.1, edited by T. Birch. London.

Darwin, C. (1974), 'Autobiography', in *Autobiographies of Thomas Henry Huxley and Charles Darwin*. London: Oxford University Press.

Dawkins, R. (1976), *The Selfish Gene*. Oxford: Oxford University Press.

Dawkins, R. (1993), 'Viruses of the Mind', in B. Dahlbom (ed.), *Dennett and his Critics: Demystifying the Mind*. Cambridge, MA: Blackwell.

Dennett, D. (1996), *Darwin's Dangerous Idea*. London: Penguin.

De Tocqueville, A. (1835 [1840]), *Democracy in America*.

Lyell, C. (1830), *Principles of Geology*. London: John Murray, 1878 edn.

Martin, G. (2000) 'Stasis in Complex Artefacts', in J. Ziman (ed.), *Technological Innovations as an Evolutionary Process*. Cambridge: Cambridge University Press, pp. 90–100.

Midgley, M. (2001), *Science and Poetry*. London: Routledge.

Moore, J. R. (1979), *The Post-Darwinian Controversies*. Cambridge: Cambridge University Press.

Spencer, H. (1864), *Social Statics*. New York: D. Appleton and Co.

Spencer, H. (1884), *A System of Synthetic Philosophy*, Vol. 1, 5th edn. London: Williams and Norgate.

Spencer, H. (1904), *Autobiography*, Vol. 2. London: Williams and Norgate.

Wertheim, M. (1997), *Pythagoras' Trousers: God, Physics and the Gender Wars*. London: Fourth Estate.

Ziman, J., ed. (2000), *Technological Innovation as an Evolutionary Process*. Cambridge: Cambridge University Press.

Evolutionary Theorising in Economics

RICHARD R. NELSON

CONSIDER THE CURRICULA FOR DOCTORAL STUDENTS at top-rated economics departments. Browse through the articles in the most prestigious economic journals. Talk with economists generally regarded as the discipline's intellectual leaders about the central concepts of contemporary economic theory. One surely comes away with the strong impression that, today, neoclassical economics is dominant in the discipline; evolutionary conceptions are hardly mentioned, at least not explicitly, much less entertained seriously. And yet, these first impressions are somewhat misleading. There is a long and honourable tradition of evolutionary theorising in economics. Certain variants and extensions of that tradition are alive and well today, at least in particular crannies.

My objective in this essay is to lay out the anatomy of evolutionary theorising in economics. That anatomy in fact is quite complex. There are a variety of different arenas and modes in which evolutionary conceptions and language have resided in economics, some from the beginnings of the modern discipline. There are several different forms of contemporary evolutionary economic theorising. I will organise my survey in four parts. First, I consider two quite different ways in which evolutionary arguments have entered economic discourse. Then I turn to several contemporary strands of evolutionary economic theorising, and consider where they are similar and where they are different. Next, I describe in a bit more detail the kind of economic evolutionary theorising that I have been working on. Finally, I suggest how that brand of evolutionary economic theory fits with other bodies of evolutionary thought that are coming into the social sciences, and in particular how it fits with evolutionary epistemology.

TWO TRADITIONAL STRANDS OF EVOLUTIONARY THEORISING

There is a long tradition in economics of understanding economic processes as dynamic, developmental, and historical. This certainly is much of the perspective contained in Adam Smith's *The Wealth of Nations* (1937 [1776]). Reflect on Smith's famous pin-making example. His analysis of technological advance

Proceedings of the British Academy, **112**, 135–143, © The British Academy 2002.

and the progressive division of labor, both driven by the expanding 'extent of the market', without much strain can be interpreted as an 'evolutionary' account. There is no hint that these developments are well foreseen by the actors involved; rather it would seem as if they occurred gradually and in a piecemeal fashion. While Smith does not say this explicitly, it would seem apparent that there were a variety of different actions taken by different actors to cope with or exploit the changing context, and the economic environment seems to have 'selected' certain paths of development, reinforcing these while turning back others.

From this point of view, Karl Marx (1932 [1852]) was an evolutionary economic theorist. While Alfred Marshall generally is considered as one of the fathers of neoclassical economics, much of his description of economic process is evolutionary (Marshall 1948 [1890]). Joseph Schumpeter also clearly was an evolutionary theorist; consider his articulation of the concept of 'creative destruction' (Schumpeter 1942). Frederich Hayek clearly espoused an evolutionary theory of the development of contemporary economic institutions (Hayek 1967).

Looking at the current scene, much of contemporary writing in economic history is evolutionary in spirit. The empirical writings of industrial organisation economists concerned with such subjects as how IBM gained and lost dominance in mainframe computers, and the rise of the PC computer industry, is evolutionary (see the chapters on these and other dynamic industries in Mowery and Nelson 1999). Much of the 'new institutional' economics has an evolutionary flavour.

As my reference to Adam Smith indicates, this kind of analysis in economics goes back to before Darwin. It cannot be understood, therefore, as a series of attempts to take Darwinian biological conceptions and apply them to economics. Rather, I would argue that evolutionary notions, at least in the broad sense I articulated above—human actors doing a variety of different things in attempts to cope with or exploit the economic environments in which they find themselves, with some classes of action doing better than others and therefore defining the path taken in economic development—is a compelling way to interpret much of observed economic development. Economists studying economic development have long been drawn to it.

In the days following Darwin, the analogies between this way of theorising about economic dynamics, and evolutionary theory in biology, of course became evident. As this happened, one can witness various economists arguing that the connections ought to be closer. Veblen's famous question 'Why is economics not an evolutionary science?' is an obvious case in point. So too Marshall's remark that 'The Mecca of economics lies in economic biology' (1948 [1890]). These statements certainly reflect a belief that economic dynamic processes had a lot in common with evolutionary processes in biology, and an appreciation that Darwin's theory of biological evolution might help to clarify some aspects of economic dynamics. However, I do not think they should be regarded as a wish to bring biological evolutionary theory in unwashed form to economics. As I will discuss shortly, this point of view has, in recent years, led to the development of formal economic evolutionary theories which, while they have a number of things in common with biological theories, are tailored to illuminating economic not biological change.

On the other hand, there are a number of economists who have argued, and who actually may believe, that at the root, modern neoclassical economics and evolutionary theory in biology are basically the same thing. Or, at least, they yield the same predictions, and for the same kinds of reasons. Thus, Milton Friedman's famous defence of the proposition that 'firms maximise profits' was that, although they do not go through such calculations, the force of competition winnows out all firms that do not somehow arrive at the policies that do maximise profits (Friedman 1953). It probably is true that a number of economists today believe that biological evolutionary theory proposes that only 'the optimal' will survive, and thus is basically equivalent to neoclassical economic theory. This sense of kinship between neoclassical economic theory and evolutionary theory in biology is shared by a number of biologists, particularly those who have proposed that evolution 'optimises'.

This strand of evolutionary conceptualisation in economics, of course, raises some serious questions that were posed sharply by Tjalling Koopmans in his commentary on Friedman's proposition (Koopmans 1957). If economists really believed the implications of neoclassical theory not because they believed that firms went through the actual process of optimising, but because of evolutionary competitive forces, shouldn't their theory be explicitly evolutionary? And shouldn't the proposition that evolutionary forces lead to 'neoclassical' outcomes be a theorem, not an assertion?

Note two things. First, the two contexts I have described in which economists have taken on board evolutionary concepts are very different, and the conceptions of what evolutionary theory is all about are different. Second, economists whose focus is on one or the other of these two contexts are likely to come up with different explicit approaches to evolutionary theory.

RECENT APPROACHES TO FORMAL EVOLUTIONARY THEORY

The last quarter-century has seen attempts to develop more formal evolutionary theories in economics. I would like to identify here three different brands.

One brand, with which I have been most associated, has roots in both strands of traditional evolutionary argument in economics. Some of the early conceptualisation which has led to this class of theorising was motivated by

Koopmans' proposition that economists needed an explicit evolutionary formulation to explore the conditions under which economic evolutionary processes generated outcomes that resembled those predicted by neoclassical theory. This was very much the motivation behind Sidney Winter's first exploration of formal evolutionary economic theorising; an exploration that illuminated that the conditions under which an economically plausible evolutionary process yielded a neoclassical equilibrium as a steady state were rather stringent (Winter 1964).

However, the principal motivation for this line of work has been to develop a way of modelling the kinds of dynamic economic processes which have interested economists since the days of Adam Smith. Many of the economists writing in this camp have been centrally interested in technological advance, and competition in which technological innovation is central. I will call this group of evolutionary models 'post-Schumpeterian', and will discuss this class of evolutionary theory in more detail in the following section.

The interests and predispositions of the second camp I want to mention here—evolutionary game theorists—tend to be very different from those of the post-Schumpeterians (Weibull 1995). For one thing, the source of their interest in 'evolutionary' processes is different. Generally the motivation is not to learn to model economic dynamic processes in a way that fits what is known empirically, but rather concerns about the fact that many dynamic games have multiple equilibria. Therefore, initial conditions, and 'out of equilibrium' behaviour of the players, can affect which equilibrium, if any, ultimately is arrived at. The 'out of equilibrium' behaviour of the collection of actors is, in this tradition, seen as being moulded by some sort of an evolutionary process. One way to regard this body of theorising is as an attempt to prove the Friedman proposition, but in a context more complicated that Friedman had in mind, since there might be multiple competitive equilibria. In any case, the orientation is not to explain empirical phenomena. When one reads in the evolutionary game theory literature, one sees few empirical cases discussed, and where they are discussed, they are brought up mainly as 'examples'.

Still another modern evolutionary economics modelling camp is populated by what might be called the 'Santa Fe Gang' (Anderson *et al.* 1988) The guiding conception here is that economic systems, like weather systems, and some physical chemical processes, need to be understood and modelled as 'complex dynamic systems'. I think it is fair to say that, while the interest in dynamic systems among natural scientists often is closely connected with interest in, and understanding of, complex empirical phenomena, for many of the economists involved in this adventure the spirit is 'have analytic tool—will apply'. Of course, this is not fair to some economists working in this arena, who have got into it because of a long-standing interest in empirical phenomena like the consequences of dynamic increasing returns, or network externalities, and the like

(Arthur 1994). Where the latter is the case, there is considerable overlap of interest, and some interaction with the post-Schumpeterian economic evolutionary theorists.

EVOLUTIONARY MODELLING OF ECONOMIC CHANGE: THE POST-SCHUMPETERIAN TRADITION

In the remainder of this essay, I will focus on what I have called the post-Schumpeterian orientation to evolutionary theorising in economics. Those of us who have been involved in this tradition take the position that most of the interesting phenomena that are in the domain of economic analysis involve processes of change, or need to be understood in terms of the dynamic processes that have generated them, and that evolutionary concepts (in a broad sense at least) and evolutionary language (at least since Darwin) are the natural vehicles for analysing economic dynamics. Indeed, I would like to propose that, when not in a context where theoretical rigour is of central consideration, many economists, not just those of us who are self-professed evolutionary theorists, make heavy use of evolutionary concepts and language. As I noted earlier, descriptions and analyses of the rise and transformation of the biotechnology industry and the computer industry in the United States are full of evolutionary talk (Mowery and Nelson 1999). Verbal analyses of the effect of sharp changes in input prices, say an increase in the cost of labor, will tend to stress the problem-solving activities of firms set in train by those changes, and posit that many firms will not be successful in these endeavours, and will decline and die. While the argument here is Lamarckian, rather than Darwinian, the economic theorising is clearly evolutionary, in the broad sense of that term.

On the other hand, when in a situation where the form and rigour of the theorising is at a premium, most economists will fall back on neoclassical theory, and the analysis will lose touch with the verbal explanations. We evolutionary economists see this as analytic schizophrenia and as a significant epistemological problem.

Some time ago, Sidney Winter and I proposed that theorising in economics (and I would propose social science more generally) proceeds at several different levels of abstraction (Nelson and Winter 1982). What we called 'appreciative' theory is relatively informal, and closely tied to the empirical phenomena under investigation, but clearly is 'theory' in that it involves abstraction, and specification of the key causal mechanisms proposed to explain the empirical phenomena in question. What we called 'formal' theory is farther away from the empirical substance, but more abstract, more 'rigorous', and much more capable of being worked through logically. We proposed that when the intellectual enterprise is going well, appreciative and formal theory are in synch, as it were, with the formal theory being an abstracted version of the appreciative theory.

But what I am arguing above is that much of appreciative theory in economics is 'evolutionary'. Most of the formal theory is 'neoclassical'. And these conceptions actually are at odds.

Much of my own work over the last twenty years has been concerned with trying to develop formal evolutionary theory in economics, much of that work in collaboration with Sidney Winter, and more recently with several of our ex-students (see for example Malerba *et al.* 1999). There are several key elements in our theoretical formulation.

First, the economic actors (in many of our models these are business firms) are boundedly rational, in the sense of Herbert Simon (Simon 1955). They are often skilful, and possess conceptions of what are appropriate actions, at least under familiar circumstances. However, their knowledge is limited relative to the complexity of circumstances with which they must cope, at least from time to time. Thus, their attempts to cope are somewhat 'blind', to use the language of Donald Campbell.

In general, the actors (firms) will be doing somewhat different things (using somewhat different production processes and having somewhat different product designs; working through different broad conceptions of what is important strategically, that guide their investment decisions; having different policies and practices regarding such matters as recruitment and advancement decisions, etc.). How an actor (firm) does in terms of various measures of performance, like profit in the case of firms, depends on what other firms are doing, and the nature of the environment, which may include the preferences and buying procedures of customers, the laws and practices of regulatory authorities, etc. Relatively successful firms tend to grow. Relatively unsuccessful ones tend to decline, or to change their practices. And successful firms also may change their practices, through 'innovation'.

The above discussion enables me to highlight one fundamental way in which evolutionary economic theory (of the brand I am describing) differs from biological evolutionary economic theory. In a manner of speaking, the practices and policies embodied in firms are like 'genotypes'. They mould the behaviour of firms, given the environmental context within which they find themselves. The firms or other organisations that have the practices and policies under consideration are like 'phenotypes'. However, firms are not locked into prevailing practices and policies (which Winter and I call routines). They can abandon the ones they have and take on others as a result of various learning experiences (doing badly in competition) and processes (research and development). They can learn by observing what other firms are doing and radically change their policies.

This loose coupling of routines and organisations means that there are several different perspectives on what is evolving. From one point of view, the subject of interest is the routines, say technologies or basic business practices, that are used by an industry. At any time particular (sets of) firms may be the carriers of these routines, and particular firms may be the sources of new ones. But the analytic focus is on the history of the broad technology. From another point of view, the focus is on the dynamic competition among firms, and the Schumpeterian process of 'creative destruction'. Here the identity and fate of particular firms may be of central interest, and the industry structure that evolves as a result of the competitive process (for example—is there a tendency towards monopoly?).

As I will sketch in the following section, the second of these perspectives links evolutionary economic theory with a body of empirical and theoretical work done by business historians and scholars of business organisation and strategy, as well as with the developing literature in sociology concerned with industry dynamics. The first of these perspectives links evolutionary economic theory with the body of scholarship that has been viewing technological advance as an evolutionary process, and with evolutionary epistemology more generally.

Many of our models take the form of a Markov process in a rather complex state space. We have used simulation as a mechanism for exploring how those models work, although in a number of cases we have been able to derive certain analytic results. However, as my discussion above indicates, for most economists working within this tradition of evolutionary theorising, the models are viewed mainly as vehicles for exploring the logic of the appreciative theory that has been developed in the course of studies aimed at explaining various bodies of empirical phenomena. Thus several of us have built a formal evolutionary model of the development of the computer industry designed to explore the logic used in various verbal accounts explaining the rise to dominance of a single firm—IBM—in the production of mainframes, but the inability of that company to dominate new market segments when they opened (Malerba *et al*. 1999).

To what extent have our attempts at formal evolutionary theorising caught on among our colleagues in economics? Well, for some time there have been several lively overlapping networks of evolutionary economists in Europe, and a new Association for Evolutionary Economics was started a few years ago in Japan. However, as a noted at the start of this essay, economists who work within this tradition certainly are in the minority, and especially so in the United States. I think it fair to say that evolutionary theory has had its best reception among economists studying technological change, and the broader economic growth processes that are driven by technological change. As I noted, economists studying the development of economic institutions increasingly are coming aboard. But ours clearly is a minority position.

EVOLUTIONARY THEORY AS A COMMON PERSPECTIVE ON PROCESSES OF ECONOMIC, SOCIAL, AND CULTURAL CHANGE

On the other hand, evolutionary economics is finding a warm reception among scholars outside of economics who have been developing evolutionary theories of processes of change in their own fields.

Above I noted the connections between evolutionary economic theory and the work of business historians and scholars of business organisation and strategy (Chandler 1990). Increasingly the latter are recognising evolutionary theory as a useful characterisation of the competitive process that the firms they are studying are involved with. There is also a dialogue between evolutionary economic theorists and sociologists studying the dynamics of industrial organisation. One important reason why communication is possible here between economists and sociologists is that the view of firm and organisational behaviour in evolutionary economics, which stresses the bounds on rationality, is consistent with the theory of firm behaviour outside economics, where neoclassical theory is not. More generally, I believe that evolutionary economic analysis has a chance of closing some of the large epistemological gaps that have come to exist across the separate social sciences.

The developing linkages between evolutionary economics and the writings by economists on institutions, an area of economic analysis, which, like evolutionary economics, is experiencing a renaissance, is a good example (North 1990). Geoffrey Hodgson in particular has described the growing connections (Hodgson 1993).

In the same spirit, evolutionary economic theories (at least our kind) seem to be merging with the more recent articulations in cognitive science, and with developments in evolutionary epistemology, regarding the nature of 'human knowing' and 'learning'. I am struck, for example, by the consonance of my views on these matters with those of Merlin Donald in his *Origins of the Modern Mind* (1991), with Walter Vincenti's in his *What Engineers Know and How They Know It* (1990), or with those of Philip Kitcher in his *The Advancement of Science* (1993). It perhaps is not surprising that evolutionary economics and scholarship from other disciplines concerned with technological advance should match up so well. After all, as I noted, many of the economists who have developed and used evolutionary theory did so because of an interest in and empirical knowledge about technological advance. But it surely is noteworthy to find this commonality of theorising across the range of scholarship in evolutionary epistemology.

The fact that different groups of scholars, working from very different starting points, and initially at least considering quite different kinds of questions, seem to be converging on an evolutionary theory is very encouraging. This is a central reason why I think that evolutionary economics has a bright future.

REFERENCES

Anderson, P., Arrow, K., and Pines, D. (1988), *The Economy as an Evolving Complex System*. Redwood City, CA: Addison-Wesley Publishing Co., for Santa Fe Institute.

Arthur, B. (1994), *Increasing Returns and Path Dependence in the Economy*. Ann Arbor: University of Michigan Press.

Chandler, A. (1990), *Scale and Scope: The Dynamics of Industrial Capitalism*. Cambridge, MA: Harvard University Press.

Donald, M. (1991), *The Origins of the Modern Mind*. Cambridge, MA: Harvard University Press.

Friedman, M. (1953), 'The Methodology of Positive Economics', in *Essays in Positive Economics*. Chicago: University of Chicago Press.

Hayek, F. (1967), *Studies in Philosophy, Politics, and Economics*. London: Routledge and Kegan Paul.

Hodgson, G. (1993), *Economics and Evolution: Bringing Life Back into Economics*. Cambridge: Polity Press.

Kitcher, P. (1993), *The Advancement of Science*. Oxford: Oxford University Press.

Koopmans, T. (1957), *Three Essays on the State of Economic Science*. New York: McGraw Hill.

Malerba, F., Nelson, R., Orsenigo, L., and Winter, S. (1999), 'History-Friendly Models of Industry Evolution: The Computer Industry', *Industrial and Corporate Change* 8: 3–40.

Marshall, A. (1948 [1890]), *Principles of Economics*. New York: Macmillan.

Marx, K. (1932 [1852]), *Capital*. New York: Modern Library.

Mowery, D. and Nelson, R. (1999), *The Sources of Industrial Leadership*. Cambridge: Cambridge University Press.

Nelson, R. R. and Winter, S. G. (1982), *An Evolutionary Theory of Economic Change*. Cambridge, MA: Harvard University Press.

North, D. (1990), *Institutions, Institutional Change, and Economic Performance*. Cambridge: Cambridge University Press.

Schumpeter, J. (1942), *Capitalism, Socialism, and Democracy*. New York: Harper and Row.

Simon, H. (1955), 'A Behavioral Model of Rational Choice', *Quarterly Journal of Economics* 69–118.

Smith, A. (1937 [1776]), *The Wealth of Nations*. New York: Modern Library.

Weibull, J. (1995), *Evolutionary Game Theory*. Cambridge, MA: MIT Press.

Vincenti, W. (1990), *What Engineers Know and How They Know It*. Baltimore, MD: Johns Hopkins University Press.

Winter, S. (1964), 'Economic "Natural Selection" and the Theory of the Firm', *Yale Economic Essays* 4: 225–72.

The Evolution of Technological Knowledge: Reflections on *Technological Innovation as an Evolutionary Process*

BRIAN J. LOASBY

THE PROCESS WHICH RESULTED in the book edited by John Ziman on *Technological Innovation as an Evolutionary Process* 'started out with a simple question: could the obvious analogy between technical innovation and biological evolution be developed from a "metaphor" into a "model"?' (Ziman 2000a: 312). This question was explored in a series of meetings by an interdisciplinary group of scholars brought together for the purpose by John Ziman, and the results of this exploration have been organised into a 'provisional reply' (Ziman 2000a: xv). The book concludes with 'An End-Word' by all contributors, of only four and a half pages; both its title and its brevity may indicate a laudable desire to avoid foreclosing any aspect of an enquiry into the relationship between evolutionary processes in technology and in biological organisms, but as a consequence the details of the reply are largely implicit as well as provisional. If this encourages a thorough reading of the volume, so much the better, for, as so often when thoughtful writers are drawing on their specific expertise, the value of these chapters extends far beyond their responses to the organising theme. I shall not attempt a detailed appraisal but present an alternative approach to the analysis of technological innovation, with the aim of contributing to the evolution of thought about this remarkable feature of human history.

I wholeheartedly agree with the consensual endorsement (Ziman 2000a: 313) of 'the explanatory power of "evolutionary reasoning" in a very wide variety of contexts'. However, the quotation marks in the original suggest a wide variety of interpretations of 'evolutionary reasoning' across these contexts, supporting the inference, explicitly stated by Joel Mokyr (Ziman 2000a: 58), that biological evolution is just one context and that the methods which are appropriate there have no valid claim to privilege in others. That inference I readily accept; there are enough similarities between biological and technological development to justify a generic label and an overarching concept, but enough differences to require separate treatment. Technological innovation and biological evolution have in common the generation of variety and

Proceedings of the British Academy, **112**, 145–159, © The British Academy 2002.

selection from this variety; and the cumulative effect of both processes typically (though not invariably) is an increasing differentiation of function matched by a closer integration between functions. But there are also major differences in the ways in which variety is generated and selected and in the content of differentiation and integration. In addition, ex-ante as well as ex-post selection is an essential feature of technological innovation, and the processes of variety generation and selection, far from being sharply differentiated, are deeply entwined (Pavitt 2001): the incubation of a new artefact or method of production typically involves rejection of candidate variants leading directly to new design, and users are shapers as well as selectors. Furthermore, selection criteria in technological innovation, and in the knowledge (both theoretical and practical) that supports it, include emotional and aesthetic as well as 'rational' elements; even the rationality is often of a kind that fails to meet the (emotional and aesthetic) criteria of orthodox modern economists. (The complexities of selection criteria in economic systems are indicated in Loasby 2001: 265–73.)

What perhaps most distinguishes technological from biological evolution is that it rests on the organisation of knowledge, which is itself supported by the organisation of the process of generating, testing, and modifying knowledge. Underpinning all these activities, of course, are the biologically evolved capabilities and motivations of human beings, and it seems to me that an understanding of these capabilities and motivations, rather than transferable models, is the prime contribution that evolutionary biology can make to the study of technological innovation. The relevance of this biological basis will not be examined in this chapter (for examples of such an examination see Loasby 1999; Rizzello 1999); instead I will present an evolutionary argument for the growth of knowledge, which has significant differences from neo-Darwinism, and seek to demonstrate that this argument has more substantial foundations than is generally appreciated.

EVOLUTION, RATIONALITY, AND KNOWLEDGE

Keith Pavitt (1998) recently published an article on technological progress to which he gave the sub-title 'What Adam Smith Tells Us and Joseph Schumpeter Doesn't'; I was tempted to give this chapter the title 'What Adam Smith Tells Us and Charles Darwin Doesn't', but that would be unfair to Darwin, who was less prescriptive than neo-Darwinians about the sources of variety, and also recognised the significance of Smith's work. In fact, Smith gives us more fundamental principles of technological evolution than have been incorporated into biological theory.

Since the evocation of Smith suggests that I shall be taking an economic perspective, it is essential to emphasise that my perspective is not that of mainstream economics, fairly broadly construed. This differentiation between ways of thinking among economists, both over time and at a particular time, has important similarities (not examined here) to the processes of thinking that guide the evolution of technology; but it is appropriate to focus briefly on mainstream economics, because that allows us to identify a fundamental issue in conceptualising evolution, whatever the context.

Several of the contributors remind us of the neo-Darwinian claim that the only alternative to the Darwinian explanation of life-forms is the now-discredited explanation by design. However, explanation by design, in the form of equilibria of rational choosers, is the foundational principle of standard economics (though not, as relatively few economists recognise, of Smith's economics), and it is deemed sufficient for standard economic analyses of technical change, although it does not satisfy the economists who have contributed to this book. An evolutionary process within the economics profession, including directed variation, internal as well as external selection, and tribal behaviour, has led by incremental adaptation to a style of modelling that relies on what outsiders may consider to be an extreme—and even irrational—form of rationality: all agents base their choices on the correct model of the economy, which includes (usually by implication) the correct model of every other agent's behaviour.

This analytical system assumes that selection is highly efficient, and, as in neo-Darwinian theory, it is determined by consequences; but since these consequences are known in advance, if only as probability distributions, selection takes place before the event; there is thus no room for any kind of process that might reasonably be called 'evolutionary'—or indeed anything that might be called a process in the usual sense of the word. (Many economists explicitly refuse to consider modelling anything but equilibria, even when claiming to explain growth and change.) Time is incorporated into models as an additional dimension of goods and information sets, to the exclusion of any analysis of an economy which develops in time. Any deficiencies in the outcomes of economic activity in relation to the best possible allocation of the resources available, are therefore attributable only to inappropriate incentives, which themselves are typically the result of elements of monopoly, missing markets (e.g. for public goods), or asymmetric information which permits opportunistic gains at the expense of others; and it is therefore not surprising that 'today economists can define their field more broadly, as the analysis of incentives in all social institutions' (Myerson 1999: 1068).

Non-economists might be amazed by the phrase 'more broadly', but Myerson is so impressed by the expansion of economic analysis into non-market applications that he fails to register the restriction of analytical content to the effects of incentives, which are themselves narrowly construed, resting on an extremely 'thin' theory of motivation. This is a splendid illustration of the principle that problems are defined by differences, and consequently not recognised if differences are not perceived. It also suggests how problem-generating perceptions which might lead to new knowledge may be crowded out (a phenomenon which is not unknown in the history of technology). In an analytical system which relies on the equilibria of optimising agents, and is constrained by the demands of internal coherence, the information on which choices are based is problematic only when access to this information is costly, and even then it is optimally selected, essentially by choosing the basis and fineness of its partitioning. Thus the set of innovative opportunities is known, though perhaps in somewhat coarse partitions; innovation is a problem of incentives, and perverse incentives may justify public funding of some kinds of innovation. Explanation by design is at the core of economics, which might therefore be considered in direct conflict with biological principles.

However, matters are not so simple. Some economists have suggested that models of rational choice equilibria may be regarded simply as convenient instruments for prediction, and that we may have considerable confidence in their predictive value because even a complete absence of rationality, in a market setting, will result in convergence on outcomes which are similar to those of well-informed optimisation. Ex-ante and ex-post selection, it is claimed, are close to being observationally equivalent; evolutionary processes in market systems are so effective that economists have no need to study them but can rely on models of ex-ante selection, which is both easier and more elegant (one should not overlook the aesthetics of rationality). Thus the economics of technological innovation becomes essentially a race to attain a technology that is known to exist.

The most thoughtful version of this argument, by Alchian (1950), made no claims for the optimality of ex-post market selection operating on non-rational behaviour, but simply for an average response in the appropriate direction to any change in circumstances, which was as much as Alchian thought could reasonably be hoped for. (Endogenous change was not considered.) Other economists have been less cautious in asserting that market selection can duplicate the results of rationality—in striking parallel to the claims, once widely thought to be both irrefutable and significant, that central planning and perfect competition (under appropriate conditions) deliver identical outcomes. It is noteworthy that some neo-Darwinians are similarly inclined to consider the outcomes of biological evolution to be structures and behaviour which are very close to optimality, and may even argue that they have better grounds than economists for this claim because biological selection has had much longer to produce such outcomes (Maynard Smith 1996: 291). Thus it is not surprising to find game-theoretic equilibria being invoked as a short-cut to the terminal points of evolutionary biological processes.

Paul Krugman (1999) warned members of the European Association for

Evolutionary Political Economy in 1996 that evolutionary biologists were increasingly attracted to equilibrium modelling, implying that a distinctively 'evolutionary' economics was a chimera, and even that biologists might be looking to modifications of standard economics for their own models. The contributors to this symposium seem to feel no attraction to equilibrium modelling, even in explaining the reliance on human power in historical Japan (Ziman 2000a: ch. 7) and the absence of change 'in form, function and manufacturing process for over 700 years' of the Japanese sword (Ziman 2000a: ch. 8), where I would have thought that the foundational idea of equilibrium—as the result, sometimes self-destroying, of an emergent balance of forces—would be highly appropriate. Game theory is mentioned twice (Ziman 2000a: 50, 120) but never used; and there are fewer claims to optimality of any kind than warnings of the difficulty of deciding how optimality might be appropriately defined in each context—the most striking examples being found in Constant's chapter on war, where determining what is to count as success and failure turns out to be much less straightforward than one might assume.

There is no doubt that these two conceptions, of natural selection from random mutations, and of optimal choice from known opportunity sets, both facilitate the construction of closed and (apparently) completely specified models which meet fashionable criteria of 'rigour', although, as Ziman (2000a: 42) points out, randomness, like more complex probability distributions, assumes a careful—and correct (but how do we know?)—definition of the relevant search space. Their popularity may therefore be explained by a combination of ex-ante and ex-post selection by and of practitioners. Unfortunately, however, neither is a good match to the problems of human activity, of which technological innovation is a prominent example. The fundamental difficulty with rational choice theory is its untenable assumption about human knowledge (Knight 1921); and the fundamental difficulty about neo-Darwinian explanations of human activity (Penrose 1952) is that it ignores human purpose. Human action is often the result of human design; but human design is inherently fallible, however secure its logic, since it is based on knowledge that is usually incomplete or erroneous. This has long been recognised. 'Purposes mistook, fall'n on the inventors' heads' is the stuff of tragedy—and of comedy too; on the other hand, many of the desirable features of society, though the consequences of human action, were not consciously intended by anyone. Technical change, like most human activities, lies in the interval between optimal choice and chance variation, and by opting for either, or both, of these models (which we might think of as corner solutions in the space of theoretical principles) we exclude at the outset the possibility of understanding what is happening, and not least—though this topic will not be directly addressed in this chapter—of understanding the selection processes within academic disciplines.

Evolutionary processes in human societies do not exclude rationality in the broad sense of acting for good reasons. What is essential is uncertainty: the absence of any procedure for decision-making that is known to be correct (Knight 1921), which often extends to the absence of any means of ensuring that all possibilities have been identified (Shackle 1972). In the presence of uncertainty, the generation of alternative hypotheses (some of which may be embodied in artefacts) and selection among them, which may lead to the generation of further hypotheses, is likely to be an effective means of progress (though not always of improvement in terms of human welfare). Uncertainty seems to be pervasive enough to justify an evolutionary approach to the growth of academic, technological, and everyday knowledge, but an approach which is significantly different from the biological model.

Neo-Darwinian evolution requires stability in both the selection environment and in the genotypes which are subject to selection; it also requires genetic mutation to provide new variants from which to select. This dual genetic requirement can be satisfied only if the chances of a defective copy are extremely small but not zero, and that in turn requires neo-Darwinian evolution to be not only incremental but extremely slow, when measured on a human timescale. This doesn't look like a good model for technological change, though it does encourage us to postulate stable genetic characteristics in the human population over periods which are, by comparison, extremely brief. What it does have in common with technological innovation is the importance of a reliable baseline; without this neither ex-ante nor ex-post selection can be significant.

A more promising hypothesis is Schumpeter's (1934) proposition that purposeful innovation depends on the baseline for decision-making that is provided by a stable economic environment, which major innovations are certain to destroy; his theme, developed at substantial length (especially in Schumpeter 1939), that technological innovation generates real business cycles, has attracted little attention among mainstream economists or even contemporary Schumpeterians. The general principle that I would emphasise is that theories of innovation should explain what does not change as well as what does, and the effect of this balance on particular processes; this requirement is certainly met in the accounts of change in the book which inspired this chapter, but its importance is nowhere made explicit.

One of the features of the book is that the authors fail to reach agreement on a basic neo-Darwinian principle—that in any evolutionary process there should be only one 'unit of selection'. I do not accept this principle for the analysis of evolution in complex systems: techniques, artefacts, and firms are all relevant, and so too are institutions, organisational arrangements, and bodies of knowledge, including know-that, know-why, know-how, and know-who. The essential requirement is to distinguish, at each stage of analysis, between the elements and connections that remain stable and the elements and connections that change. This combination varies according to time and circumstance; and there is no simple hierarchy. Sometimes established elements are assembled into a novel architecture; sometimes a modular architecture facilitates quasi-independent innovation. Stability in the direction of technological change (Pavitt 2001) is likely to encourage variation within that trajectory and also variation in the combination of techniques to produce artefacts. Decomposition and recombination are important principles in technological innovation and in other kinds of knowledge.

THE EVOLUTION OF IDEAS AND CAPABILITIES

David Hume demonstrated that there was no way of proving the truth of any general empirical proposition, either by deduction—for there was no way of ensuring the truth of the premises—or by induction—for there was no way of proving that instances not observed would correspond to those that had been observed. Hume's response had been to turn to the manageable question of how people came to accept certain empirical propositions as true; and in his earliest surviving major work Adam Smith followed Hume's example by producing a psychological theory of the emergence and development of science, illustrating it by the history of astronomy (Smith 1980 [1795]).

The first element in Smith's theory is the motivation for generating new ideas. The evolution of human knowledge, both theoretical and practical, though unpredictable in any detail, is driven by purpose, and this is often an emotional rather than a rational force. Smith argues that people are disturbed by the unexpected, dismayed by the inexplicable, and delighted by schemes of thought that resolve the inexplicable into plausible generalisations. In the absence of any assured procedure for attaining correct knowledge, these are the motives which 'lead and direct philosophical enquiries'. They are a long way from the incentives that economists seek to model, but perhaps not so far from some of the incentives that shape the behaviour of technologists, and of economists also.

The second element is the sequence that is inspired by this complex motivation: the generation of novelty and the ex-ante selection processes which guide its adoption or rejection. People try to invent 'connecting principles' which will afford a basis for collecting phenomena into categories and link each category with an explanation which is credible enough to 'soothe the imagination'. The 'equalizing circle' in Ptolemaic geometry and the rule that 'when one body revolved round another it described equal areas in equal times' in Kepler's system are examples that Smith (1980 [1795]: 61, 90) uses of the resolution of difficulties, by appealing to general principles of motion that conform to prevailing notions of good order; similarly, rational choices based on rational expectations are comfortable principles for explaining economic phenomena.

The third element, already implicit in 'notions of good order', is Smith's attention to the role of aesthetic criteria both in guiding conjectures, for example in the ideas of Copernicus and Kepler, and in encouraging their acceptance (Smith 1983: 146). The importance of aesthetic influences in the natural sciences and in economics (signalled earlier by the reference to the elegance of rational choice equilibria) is occasionally recognised but rarely explored (see Schlicht 2000); aesthetic influences on the design of artefacts are an unacknowledged theme of this book. In cathedral building aesthetic appeal is a major objective, duly reflected in the templates to which Turnbull draws attention; but of particular interest in an exploration of evolutionary processes is the extent to which aesthetic criteria are also surrogates for effective performance; bridges and aircraft are obvious examples, although the flawed design of the Millennium footbridge in London is a current illustration that surrogacy should not be assumed.

The fourth element is Smith's argument that connecting principles which seem to work well are widely diffused, because of the human readiness to look for guidance from others who seem to know better, and because of our desire to act, and indeed think, in ways that merit the approval of others. This is a foundational principle of Smith's (1976a [1759]) *Theory of Moral Sentiments*, which is itself an essential element in Smith's complex account of social organisation, and applicable to technological evolution. (For an excellent discussion of the impact of social approval and disapproval on technological development, effectively linking general principles to detailed histories, see Pool [1997].)

However, because by Hume's argument, invented principles, however widely accepted, are not proven truth (even, Smith notes, when these principles have been invented by Newton), they are liable eventually to be confronted with unexpected phenomena which they cannot be adapted to explain. This disjunction between evidence and established means of explanation defines a pressing problem; when satisfactory adaptation is despaired of, a new search for connecting principles begins. This renewal of the evolutionary process is the fifth element.

The sixth element is the evolution of the evolutionary process itself as this basic human activity generates first an increasingly distinct category of knowledge which comes to be called 'scientific', and subsequently a progressive differentiation between sciences that we might now label speciation. The consequent differences, both of focus and of selection criteria, generate a greater variety of more precisely defined problems and consequently accelerate the growth of science. The division of labour is subsequently presented in the *Wealth of Nations*, not as the best way to make the most of differentiated skills —which was a very old idea—but as the chief instrument of the growth of productive knowledge (Smith 1976b [1776]). This seventh element is easily the most important idea in economics; the coordination problem which normally receives priority among economists would be trivial without the continuous generation of new knowledge and new artefacts.

Smith's prime 'connecting principle' of the division of labour was applied to physiology in 1827 (Milne-Edwards 1827), and this application in turn contributed to Darwin's vision that a Malthusian struggle to survive would result in the differentiation of species (Raffaelli 2001: 208). The other elements in Smith's account of the development of knowledge by motivated trial, error, amendment, and diffusion understandably did not. Meanwhile, in France, Prony was inspired by his reading of Smith to manufacture logarithmic tables like pins, and in turn inspired Babbage to study the division of intellectual labour (Raffaelli 2001: 209). From the point of view of technological innovation, therefore, we may suggest that Smith encompasses Darwin; hence the temptation to give this chapter a different title.

The differentiation of knowledge is a condition of progress in human society. However, it has its opportunity costs, of which two are especially important in understanding technological innovation. One is that differences in the structure of understanding, and in the criteria for good theory and good practice, may create substantial obstacles to the integration of knowledge across disciplines, within organisations, or between technological fields, as well as obstacles to the integration of technological and non-technological perceptions of the value of any particular innovation, which is the primary focus of Pool's book. A special, but not uncommon, case of such differences in perceptual structure is that between sensory perception and scientific categorisation:

> events which to our senses may appear to be of the same kind may have to be treated as different in the physical order, while events which physically may be of the same or at least of a similar kind may appear as altogether different to our senses. (Hayek 1952: 4)

Theoretical developments may not map readily on to recursive practice, and know-how may resist usable codification. The desire to assuage the discomfort of this apparent contradiction led Hayek to construct an evolutionary account of the development of problem-focused sensory perceptions.

The other opportunity cost of the differentiation of knowledge is the neglect of potentially crucial interdependencies.

> When the compass of potential knowledge as a whole has been split up into superficially convenient sectors, there is no knowing whether each sector has a natural self-sufficiency. . . . Whatever theory is then devised will exist by sufferance of the things that it has excluded. (Shackle 1972: 353–4)

Unanticipated technological disasters are frequently traceable to unjustified assumptions (usually unconscious, but not always so) about the sufferance of something excluded from the processes of design, testing, or operator training. The Millennium footbridge already mentioned is an exemplary demonstration.

IMPLICATIONS OF UNCERTAINTY FOR COGNITION AND THE GROWTH OF KNOWLEDGE

The double-edged character of uncertainty is the focus of Frank Knight's *Risk, Uncertainty and Profit* (1921), and of much of Shackle's work. Knight restricted the concept of risk to situations in which both the set of possibilities and the probability distribution over this set are known, either by argument a priori, as in calculating the expected results of throwing dice, or by statistical analysis of appropriate evidence. Choices under risk may therefore be made by a standard procedure which can be demonstrated to be optimal, and cannot be a source of sustainable profit. For conditions of uncertainty, however, no demonstrably optimal procedure can be devised; we must act in the space between optimality and randomness.

But if uncertainty creates difficulties, it also creates opportunities for imagination—as in Smith's psychological theory: indeed, Knight argues that it is a necessary condition for entrepreneurship and profit—and also for the firm, which provides shelter for those who are unwilling to cope with uncertainty in person and prefer the conditional security offered by entrepreneurs. The opportunities perceived by Knight are to be found both within the economic system and in the corpus of economic theory, where it is appropriate to cite the (very different) ideas that economic interaction might be formally analysed as a game between hyper-rational players or that a firm might be conceived, not as a production function or a nexus of contracts but as a pool of resources, of uncertain applicability, within an administrative framework (Penrose 1959).

Most economists assimilate Knight's category of uncertainty to risk by the invocation of subjective probability, sacrificing the opportunities in Knight's analysis for theoretical development 'in order to preserve the coherence of the ideas of the imagination' (Smith 1980 [1795]: 77). Smith would have understood this response very well, even though it is unlikely that he would have approved; and this desire for coherence may help to explain the difficulties noted by Pavitt (1998, 2001) in adapting organisational practices and power relationships to technological requirements. Knight observes that, in a world without uncertainty, 'it is doubtful whether intelligence itself would exist' (Knight 1921: 268): this locates the role of intelligence squarely in the space between optimal choice or optimal design and random activity, and in doing so warns us not to identify intelligence with logical operations. Niels Bohr's rebuke was more blunt: 'You are not thinking; you are merely being logical' (Frisch 1979: 95). Ziman (2000b: 328) points out that the epistemology of science is based on uncertainty; logic is essential but, as Hume insisted, cannot produce new ideas. This dissociation of intelligence from logic underlies Knight's (1921: 241) observation that '[m]en differ in their capacity by perception and inference to *form correct judgements* as to the future course of events in the environment. This capacity, moreover, is far from homogeneous'; moreover, individuals differ in their capacity to change, and learning takes time (Knight 1921: 243). Knight is talking about the effect of the division of labour on the development of differentiated intelligence, though without reference to Adam Smith.

Knight (1921: 206) is also unconsciously close to Smith in arguing that 'in order to live intelligently in our world . . . we must use the principle that things similar in some respects will behave similarly in certain other respects even when they are very different in still other respects': in other words, we rely on 'connecting principles' of association and causation—together with 'the sufferance of the things that [they have] excluded'—in developing our own ideas and in adapting other people's. He also observed that planning is required only because of the differences between past and future, and possible only because of the similarities between them (Knight 1921: 313). What similarities we emphasise and what differences we ignore depend both on our perception of problems and our own evolved connecting principles, or those of our discipline, profession, or organisation. That is how the division of labour leads to differentiated knowledge.

In the book, Fleck (Ziman 2000a: 255) complains that a 'focus purely upon knowledge . . . makes the evolutionary problem very tough. It is difficult to put boundaries around an idea.' Why, indeed, should we assume that, within the categories that we invent, the similarities dominate the differences, while between these invented categories the reverse applies? However, ambiguity, like uncertainty of which it is a special case, is both a problem and an opportunity for the generation of ideas by making new combinations (a principle enunciated by both Smith and Schumpeter); thus the difficulty of putting boundaries around an idea is a major enabler of innovation. The difficulty of putting boundaries around the capabilities of any individual or organisation, and the consequent ambiguity of their range of application, is a prominent theme in Nelson and Winter's (1982) theory, and underlies Penrose's (1959) emphasis on the need to perceive how resources may be directed towards productive opportunities. Ziman (2000b: 297) similarly draws attention to the permeable boundary between science and 'life-world knowledge'.

Ambiguities of both capabilities and 'knowledge that' also explain why diffusion, typically across different contexts of similarity, as my former colleague Frank Bradbury frequently reminded us, is often both unexpectedly difficult and also a major contributor to the content of innovation. The use of metaphor, which has played no small role both in technological innovation and in the attempt to understand it, illustrates the point; abstract thought relies on language which originated in metaphor—indeed the terms 'abstract' and 'metaphor' originate in Latin and Greek metaphors. The Smith–Knight principle of sufficient similarity is fundamental both to making sense and to making artefacts. In Shackle's (1979: 26) beautiful phrase, innovation begins with 'the imagined, deemed possible'; and what is deemed possible, and—even more— what is deemed capable of being made possible, depends upon judgements of the applicability of both theoretical and practical knowledge to novel contexts.

Category-based judgements of possibility guide the innovation process; but because they are possibilities, not specific predictions—and because the judgements are themselves subject to error—they cannot, as some writers on corporate strategy assert, allow us to deduce a successful course of action from the specification of a desired final state. Reverse engineering may allow us to reconstruct the process of manufacturing an existing artefact; but a succesful artefact is a resolved ambiguity (or cluster of ambiguities), and we have the evidence of its resolution to guide our reconstruction. As Perkins (Ziman 2000a: 160) somewhat hesitantly reports, it may also be possible to simulate the path to an achieved scientific discovery, for there is always retrospectively a pathway to current knowledge; but such success does not provide a procedure for deducing fresh knowledge, because there are many divergent pathways from established ideas and many ways of linking ideas, and which path seems worth following depends on conjectured contexts of similarity. Connections have to be invented. (On the significance of the treatment of connections in the analysis of systems, see Potts [2000]). The development of science may be presented to students as a logical progression; but the logic is typically available only in retrospect. There is no better example of this than the centuries-old search for a proof of Fermat's last theorem (Singh 1997).

As Nightingale (2000: 352) observes, Bradshaw's paradox, that we 'need to know the biological results before we can decide on the appropriate space to represent our compounds' (Nightingale 2000: 337) applies to the whole innovation process; indeed the optimal decomposition of any complex problem can be discovered only by solving the problem (Marengo 2000). Knight's principle of supposedly relevant similarities, exemplified by scientific and social scientific theories, design trajectories, recognised good practice (as explained in the chapters by Constant [2000] and Stankiewicz [2000] on recursive knowledge and design spaces), and many other institutional aids to cognition, enable us to do far better (most of the time) than random speculation; but all these forms of ex-ante selection need to be reinforced, modified, and sometimes superseded by ex-post selection in order to achieve successful outcomes.

Problems are defined by differences, but the search for solutions is guided —sometimes in wrong directions—by the perception of similarities with existing solutions. The significance of recent advances in medical knowledge, as Nightingale (2000: 337) emphasises, is that they have created new 'contexts of similarity', which have enabled pharmaceutical companies to refine their search for new compounds and to reduce the costs of search. However, there is no prospect of deducing the specification of a safe and effective drug from a definition of desired effects, and so it is not surprising that reliance on these contexts has not reduced the number of candidate compounds that it is thought necessary to screen, and 'there is little evidence that this is translating into improved performance' (Nightingale 2000: 351). Moreover, we should remember Knight's warning that if there were to be a standard procedure for attaining optimal outcomes, no one could expect to make a sustainable profit from its use. Detailed agreement on the best way to organise research is more likely to reduce than enhance the profits of pharmaceutical businesses, unless they can also erect barriers against rivals. Diversity remains a general condition both for profit and the growth of knowledge; and the effect of system diversity on development is a basic evolutionary theme (Pavitt 1998: 439).

Diversity, especially when based on different ways of connecting perceptions, phenomena, and ideas, entails significant problems of coordination between individuals and between groups; these problems are not ignored by Ziman and his fellow-authors, but they are underplayed. Alfred Marshall (1920: 138–9) offers some helpful advice:

> Organisation aids knowledge; it has many forms, e.g. that of a single business, that of various businesses in the same trade, that of various trades relatively to each other, and that of the State providing security for all and help for many.

Different forms are required in order to accommodate diverse combinations of similar and complementary capabilities (Richardson 1972), each providing a context of similarity which permits some variety within each combination as a consequence of differences in temperament, associations, and experience which define manageable problems (Marshall 1920: 355), and allows people to draw on vicarious experience both to evaluate and to modify their ideas. Moreover, the most effective forms, both of internal structure and external relationships, change over time, largely as a consequence of their own effects; this theme was most forcefully expounded by Allyn Young (1928).

Knowledge itself is organisation, produced by trial and error, and always subject to challenge, including changes in its form and relationships to other bodies of knowledge. As many examples in this book illustrate, an artefact is a social construction, and so is any particular piece of knowledge; in general, both might have been somewhat different from what actually exists. That does not mean that we can construct any *reliable knowledge* (Ziman 1978) or reliable artefacts that we like, for of all the artefacts and knowledge structures that are conceivable, only a very small proportion will actually work. Organisation aids knowledge by guiding us towards this small proportion, though it can also lead us astray. That is why we need appropriate organisation, procedures, motivation and imagination both for selection and the continued generation of variety.

Note. An earlier version of this paper appeared on the website *Evolutionary Theories in the Social Sciences* (*http://letss.net*).

REFERENCES

Alchian, Armen A. (1950), 'Uncertainty, Evolution and Economic Theory', *Journal of Political Economy* 58: 211–21.

Constant, E. (2000) 'Recursive Practice and the Evolution of Technical Knowledge', in J. Ziman (ed.), *Technological Innovation as an Evolutionary Process*. Cambridge: Cambridge University Press.

Frisch, O. (1979), *What Little I Remember*. Cambridge: Cambridge University Press.

Hayek, F. A. (1952), *The Sensory Order*. Chicago: University of Chicago Press.

Knight, F. H. (1921), *Risk, Uncertainty and Profit*. Boston, MA: Houghton Mifflin.

Krugman, P. (1999), 'What Economists Can Learn from Evolutionary Theory — and Vice Versa', in J. Groenewegen and J. Vromen (eds), *Institutions and the Evolution of Capitalism: Implications of Evolutionary Economics*. Cheltenham and Northampton, MA: Edward Elgar, pp. 17–29.

Loasby, B. J. (1999), *Knowledge, Institutions and Evolution in Economics*. London and New York: Routledge.

Loasby, B. J. (2001), 'Selection Processes in Economics', in K. Dopfer (ed.), *Evolutionary Economics: Program and Scope*. Boston, Dordrecht, and London: Kluwer Academic Publishers, pp. 253–76.

Marengo, L. (2000), 'Decentralisation and Market Mechanisms in Problem Solving', paper presented to DRUID Conference, Rebild, Denmark 15–17 June.

Marshall, A. (1920), *Principles of Economics*, 8th edn. London: Macmillan.

Maynard Smith, J. (1996), 'Conclusion', in W. G. Runciman, J. Maynard Smith, and R. I. M. Dunbar (eds), *The Evolution of Social Behaviour Patterns in Primates and Man*. Oxford: Oxford University Press for the British Academy, pp. 291–7.

Milne-Edwards, H. (1827), 'Nerf', in M. Bory de Saint-Vincent (ed.), *Dictionnaire classique de l'histoire naturelle*. Paris: Rey et Gravier.

Myerson, R. B. (1999), 'Nash Equilibrium and the History of Economic Theory', *Journal of Economic Literature* 37: 1067–82.

Nelson, R. R. and Winter, S. G. (1982), *An Evolutionary Theory of Economic Change*. Cambridge, MA: Belknap Press.

Nightingale, P. (2000), 'Economies of Scale in Experimentation: Knowledge and Technology in Pharmaceutical R&D', *Industrial and Corporate Change* 9: 315–59.

Pavitt, Keith (1998), 'Technologies, Products and Organization in the Innovating Firm: What Adam Smith Tells Us and Joseph Schumpeter Doesn't', *Industrial and Corporate Change* 7: 433–52.

Pavitt, K. (2001) Review of Ziman (2000a), *Journal of Evolutionary Economics* 11: 267–70.

Penrose, E. T. (1952), 'Biological Analogies in the Theory of the Firm', *American Economic Review* 42: 804–19.

Penrose, E. T. (1959), *The Theory of the Growth of the Firm*. Oxford: Basil Blackwell.

Pool, R. (1997), *Beyond Engineering: How Society Shapes Technology*. New York and Oxford: Oxford University Press.

Potts, J. (2000) *The New Evolutionary Microeconomics: Complexity, Competence and Adaptive Behaviour*. Cheltenham and Northampton, MA: Edward Elgar.

Raffaelli, T. (2001), 'Marshall on Mind and Society: Neurophysiological Models Applied to Industrial and Business Organization', *Journal of the History of Economic Thought* 8(2): 208–29.

Richardson, G. B. (1972), 'The Organisation of Industry', *Economic Journal* 82: 883–96.

Rizzello, S. (1999), *The Economics of the Mind*. Cheltenham and Northampton, MA: Edward Elgar.

Schlicht, E. (2000), 'Aestheticism in the Theory of Custom', *Journal des Économistes et des Études Humaines* 10(1): 33–51.

Schumpeter, J. A. (1934), *The Theory of Economic Development*. Cambridge, MA: Harvard University Press.

Schumpeter, J. A. (1939), *Business Cycles*. New York and London: McGraw Hill.

Shackle, G. L. S. (1972), *Epistemics and Economics*. Cambridge: Cambridge University Press.

Shackle, G. L. S. (1979) *Imagination and the Nature of Choice*. Edinburgh: Edinburgh University Press.

Singh, S. (1997), *Fermat's Last Theorem*. London: Fourth Estate.

Smith, A. (1976a [1759]), *The Theory of Moral Sentiments*, edited by David D. Raphael and Alec L. Macfie. Oxford: Oxford University Press.

Smith, A. (1976b [1776]) *An Inquiry into the Nature and Causes of the Wealth of Nations*, edited by Roy H. Campbell, Andrew S. Skinner, and W. B. Todd. Oxford: Oxford University Press.

Smith, A. (1980 [1795]) 'The Principles which Lead and Direct Philosophical Enquiries: Illustrated by the History of Astronomy', in *Essays on Philosophical Subjects*, edited by W. P. D. Wightman. Oxford: Oxford University Press, pp. 33–109.

Smith, A. (1983) *Lectures on Rhetoric and Belles Lettres*, edited by J. C. Bryce. Oxford: Oxford University Press.

Stankiewicz, R. (2000) 'The Concept of "Design Space"', in J. Ziman (ed.), *Technological Innovation as an Evolutionary Process*. Cambridge: Cambridge University Press.

Young, A. (1928), 'Increasing Returns and Economic Progress', *Economic Journal* 38: 527–42.

Ziman, J. (1978), *Reliable Knowledge*. Cambridge: Cambridge University Press.

Ziman, J., ed. (2000a), *Technological Innovation as an Evolutionary Process*. Cambridge: Cambridge University Press.

Ziman, J. (2000b), *Real Science*. Cambridge: Cambridge University Press.

Idiosyncratic Production Regimes: Co-evolution of Economic and Legal Institutions in the Varieties of Capitalism

GUNTHER TEUBNER

ANOMALIES

WHY HAS THE AMERICAN TORT REVOLUTION, which led to such a drastic rise of liability that it catalysed an insurance crisis in the United States, not occurred in Europe? Why has judicial control over standard contracts not been exercised in the USA as intensively as it has been in Germany? Why do European 'general clauses' on consumer protection which are customarily used with little difficulty in France, Italy, Germany, run dry in Great Britain? Why is the legal implementation of just-in-time distribution networks, a Japanese export, different on the continent than it is in the USA and in Great Britain?[1]

Such findings challenge both political attempts at European harmonisation as well as the academic discipline of comparative law. They upset their basic tenets—the convergence of economic institutions in advanced societies and the functional equivalence of legal constructs (Bogdan 1994: 60; Zweigert and Kötz 1992: 33ff.; for a critique see Frankenberg 1985; Legrand 1997). They give rise to the question whether European harmonisation produces new divergences instead of legal unity and institutional security (on this debate, see Teubner 1998).

Such findings also challenge institutional theories in economics. Most of them predict that, at the end of an evolutionary process, those economic institutions which are the most efficient will tend to prevail. They identify quite different mechanisms for selection. Transaction costs theory provides that rational actors select a legal arrangement for their transactions which minimises costs, such as information, negotiation, and implementation costs (Williamson 1985, 1991, 1993). Evolutionary economics mistrusts the rationality of actors, identifying instead a mechanism for selection in markets which

---

[1] For the empirical background of these questions, see Casper (1995, 1996, 1998), Collins (1998), Teubner (1998).

allows only the economically efficient to survive, operating in accordance with a routine which has been devised with bounded rationality (Nelson 1995; Nelson and Winter 1982; Winter 1995). Law and economics makes the continuous pressure of 're-litigation' responsible for the selection of efficient rules (Cooter and Kornhauser 1980; Priest 1977; Rubin 1977). Regulatory competition identifies the federal and global coexistence of legal systems as a competitive mechanism which selects the most efficient regimes (Bratton and McCahery 1995).

Theories of institutions are challenged because those anomalies put into question the direction of evolution toward efficiency. Recent empirical results of comparative political economics have come as a surprise. Contrary to all expectations, the globalisation of markets and the computerisation of the economy have not led to a worldwide convergence of economic institutions. Despite all undeniable tendencies to minimise transaction costs, selective mechanisms of the market, processes of re-litigation, and regulatory competition, institutional differences have not been wiped out (Albert 1993; Crouch and Streeck 1995; Porter 1990). On the contrary, globalisation and indeed European harmonisation have produced new institutional divergences. One of the most remarkable developments of the last thirty years is that divergences between economic institutions—corporate finance, corporate governance, industrial relations, education and training, inter-company relations, contracting networks, standard setting, and dispute resolution—have increased in advanced societies and not decreased, despite the liberalisation of the world markets and the establishment of a common market in Europe (Soskice 1997).

How is one to treat such idiosyncrasies of institutions in an adequate manner? Two ambitious theories attempt to explain systematically the institutional varieties of capitalism. The theory of production regimes observes interlocking systems of economic institutions whose elements are self-stabilising (Hall and Soskice 2001; Soskice 1997). The theory of institutional co-selection (Nelson 1995; Nelson and Winter 1982) explains the deviation from the efficiency path by the accumulation of selectors: institutional evolution is not only driven by market efficiency but also dictated by political, technological, and cultural selection criteria.

What response does a theory of self-organising social systems provide? Despite its sympathies to internal dynamics and multiple evolution, it distances itself from both theories. In short, its critique of the theories of production regimes and co-selection is:

(1)   A production regime is not a system.
(2)   Co-evolution cannot be understood as a mere addition of selectors.

If there is no system and no co-selection at work, what then makes institutions differ?

EVOLUTION AND SOCIAL SELF-ORGANISATION

By introducing the ideas self-organisation and self-reproduction, the theory of autopoietic social systems tries to give new answers to old problems of legal evolution in the Darwinian tradition: what are the self-preserving units in law's evolution? Texts, rules, institutions, juridical memes, or *l'esprit des lois*? Social groups, populations, nations, or selfish genes? How to identify in law sources of selective variation: are they external or internal to the law? What are the criteria according to which legal rules are selected: adaptability to law's environment, survival of the fittest rule, mere viability?

Like other post-Darwinian theories, systems theory criticises the dominant evolution-toward-efficiency paradigm which is obviously close to classical Darwinian ideas of natural selection. The four main assumptions of the dominant paradigm are:

(1) The change of legal institutions takes place within one unitary process of bio-social evolution.
(2) The evolving unit is the social group, which gains an evolutionary advantage by adopting successful legal institutions.
(3) The selection mechanism is external to the law as a quasi-natural selection through competitive market pressures.
(4) The selection criterion and overall result of legal evolution is economic efficiency.

The first blow to the dominant paradigm came from path dependency.[2] Evolutionary mechanisms do not work in a historical vacuum but apply recursively to specific historical situations resulting in multiple evolutionary paths of legal institutions. Today's 'varieties of capitalism' have created in different regions on the globe a bewildering multitude of various legal institutions. In the best case, they are different but equivalent in their efficiency. In the normal case they show inefficiencies which they do not remedy because it would be too costly. And in the worst case they are 'locked in' in a situation of inefficiency which, as a result of path dependency (lack of information, political factors), they will not change.

Further blows came from chaos theory that stressed the importance of the initial, often accidental conditions. Indeed, it could be shown that legal institutions tend to be extremely sensitive to these initial conditions, and that twists and turns lead to results far from those originally expected. Furthermore, the idea of punctuated equilibrium made it plausible how legal institutions are propelled to the top of a local evolutionary mountain but, in the absence of cataclysmic change, will remain stuck there and be unaware of the higher summit across the valley.[3]

---

[2] For a discussion in a corporate law perspective, see Roe (1995).
[3] Again, with a view to corporate law, see Roe (1995).

Path dependency, chaos theory and punctuated equilibrium attacked successfully the efficiency criterion in legal evolution, but they left the other three
fundamental assumptions intact. The big blow to the whole edifice came from
theories of self-organisation that were developed in social and legal theory in
close contact with the discussion in biology.[4] The ideas of self-organisation,
autopoiesis, recursiveness, operational closure, and structural coupling have
been incorporated into a theory of legal evolution that totally reversed the
assumptions of the law and economics model.[5] Ironically, the same ideas of
self-organisation which at least partially originated in biological theory, when
applied to law as a hermeneutic process, were compelled to move further and
further away from a biological understanding of social evolution. Law appears
now as the result of autonomous social evolution, of the inner dynamics of
hermeneutic processes. The results of such a reformulation of classical
assumptions will be summarised in the following eight points before aspects of
co-evolution in production regimes are scrutinised more in depth.

(1)   The evolving unit is neither a text nor is it a group but a self-organising
social system. A social system is a rather esoteric species—nothing tangible, no
flesh no blood, invisible like an angel, but at the same time not fictitious, not
transcendent, instead the immanent hard-core reality of a chain of operations,
transformations of differences that drive toward self-continuation.[6] This
excludes from the outset sociobiology, which reduces social phenomena
(behaviour, rules, laws) to their function of maintaining biological units,
whether individuals, species, groups, or genes. Legal institutions do not appear
as properties of a biological unit, which are selected by its survival imperatives,
but instead as the result of an autonomous evolutionary process within self-
organising social systems. Social systems should not be identified with groups
of individual actors nor with a social collective, rather they are constituted by
elementary operations of meaning. Meaning (*Sinn*) is understood here as a specific mode of processing information. To make a long story short, systems of
meaning are characterised by four properties (1) recursive operations, (2) a special relation of actualisation/potentialisation, (3) contextualisation by specific
reference structures, (4) closure, self-reference, and circularity (Luhmann 1995:
ch. 2). Due to fundamental differences between the evolution of life and the
evolution of meaning, the idea of a unitary bio-social evolution needs to be
abandoned and to be replaced by a more complex concept of co-evolution of

[4]   On the impact of self-organisation on evolution, see Atlan (1987), Glasersfeld and Cobb (1983),
Jantsch (1979), Leydesdorff (1994), Luhmann (1982a, 1982c, 1992b, 1995: ch. 9, VIII, 1997:
431ff.), Maturana and Varela (1988), Roth and Schwegler (1990).
[5]   On legal evolution in this perspective, see Ladeur (1987), Luhmann (1985: ch. 3), Teubner (1987,
1993: 47ff.), Willke (1992).
[6]   For a systematic analysis of autopoietic social systems in general, see Luhmann (1995); on the
legal system, see Luhmann (1992a, 1992b).

life and meaning. Autonomous social systems evolve independently from the evolution of living systems, but they are selectively interrelated via co-evolutionary processes.

(2)   The law does not evolve via psychic cognitions of individual minds. Law is a phenomenon of social meaning based on communicative operations which are distinct from psychic operations of the human mind but occur parallel to them.[7] It is exclusively communicative operations that form the basic elements of self-organising social systems. Here we find the self-preserving process that drives legal institutions. This is the reason why the evolving unit in social evolution cannot be the group or the population consisting of human individuals—not to speak of the selfish gene—that needs to be preserved. But also the selfish meme—promising as it might look as a building block for the law—cannot represent the evolutionary unit, because it is designed as a psychic phenomenon combined with a rather reductive social dimension—imitation (*sic!*)—which never will have the necessary copying fidelity.[8] Law's evolutionary dynamic does not take place in a stream of psychic cognitions, but instead, in a stream of communications, that is, a dynamic information process creating its own stable eigenvalues independently of what individual lawyers might think about it. Driven by the imperative of self-continuation, legal communications (judicial decisions, legislative acts, contracts) which are recursively applied to prior legal communications transform the hermeneutics of law (rules, principles, doctrines, institutions).

(3)   The structures that evolve in law and society are not behaviour in the sense of statistical regularities. Nor are they expectations of action, whether of a cognitive or a normative nature. Rather it is law as 'textuality' that constitutes the changing structures (Luhmann 1993: 253ff.). It is the problematic space between written texts and their interpretation by legal actors, the circularity of legal hermeneutics, where the evolutionary dynamics of law takes place. Legal texts (political constitutions, legislative statutes, judicial precedents, private contracts and wills, organisational charters) constitute the 'medium' into which various and controversial 'forms' of interpretation are inscribed. Legal evolution, thus, is not a simple change of behaviour or of rules, but rather an institutionalised process of legal controversies in the courts and legislative chambers, and a conflictual relation between dominant opinions of legal authorities and deviant theories.

(4)   So far, one still would arrive at a 'natural selection' concept of legal evolution. It would be understood as the willingness of an informationally open system to respond to the demands made upon it by the environment.

---

[7] For this important distinction as basis for a theory of social systems, see Luhmann (1995: chs 6 and 7).

[8] For this concept, see Blackmore (1999), Dawkins (1976), Dennett (1995).

Driven by society-wide forces of selection, among them especially markets with their pressures toward efficiency, law's internal institutions would adapt to their external social environment. This is, to be sure, a widespread concept in legal sociology and legal economics. However, it does not take into account one crucial development that has taken place in modern societies—the radical closure of the legal system. Modern legal institutions have de-coupled themselves from society-wide evolution by developing evolutionary mechanisms—variation, selection, retention—of their own.[9] The crucial transformation takes place when, in court litigation, legislation, and contracting, legal argumentation begins to refer to past legal materials (precedents, rules, principles) in a very specific way. It is the exclusion of arguments *ad hoc* and *ad hominem* which makes the legal process independent from direct social influences, especially from clientelism, kinship, politics (Luhmann 1993: 263). 'The artificial reason of law' which Sir Coke invoked against the political interventions of the King makes it autonomous vis-à-vis moral arguments, economic considerations, political expediency, and common sense

(5)   In autonomous law, variations occur in the constitution of specific legal 'cases' (a court suit, a legislative proposal, a contractual offer) which have—as we all know from sad experiences—only very little to do with the underlying social conflict. Social conflicts are not only translated into legal language, they are reconstructed anew as claims of validity, as conflicts between technical legal rules which are, in their legalistic artificiality, rather meaningless for the social participants and their real conflict.

(6)   As against ideas of natural selection, in autonomous law the selection process is internalised. Rules are selected in highly specific evolutionary dynamics; they are not exposed to an efficiency-driven market but to a complex interaction between clients, lawyers, judges, and legal scholars, which makes the legal validity of a rule dependent upon whether the innovation fits with existing normative structures and is compatible with the legal code. The law, like other autonomous social systems, has its own 'hidden hand' which guides the evolution of rules in a different direction than a competitive market would.[10]

(7)   Modern law has institutionalised its own re-stabilisation—legal doctrine—an elaborate structure of legal concepts and precedents, rules and principles in which selected variations are incorporated only if they pass the test of temporal and conceptual consistency.

(8)   Thus, the autonomy of legal evolution leads law to a developmental path of its own, in which rules are selected not according to their efficiency but according to their structural fit with vast and accumulating legal materials. To

---

[9] For some details, see Teubner (1993: 55ff.).
[10] Ziman (1999) makes a similar case for the 'hidden hand' in technology.

be sure, this does not rule out economic influences, but they are effectively mediated and substantially transformed via their selective reconstruction on the internal screens of law. The straightforward idea of law's evolution toward efficiency needs to be replaced—this is the main thesis of this article—by the more complex construct of a co-evolution of autonomous legal and economic institutions.

HYBRID CONFIGURATIONS

A closer look at production regime theory may show its strengths and weaknesses. Production regimes are the institutional environment of economic action. They organise the production of goods and services through markets and market-related institutions and determine the framework of incentives and constraints. Production regimes are the 'rules of the game' which govern economic action (Aoki 1994; Hollingsworth 1993). Their idiosyncrasies, which equally perturb legal harmonisers and evolutionary economists, are explained by the fact that single institutions are not isolated from each other but interact as interdependent elements of a stable system. Financial arrangements and corporate governance are strongly influenced by industrial relations, education and training, contracting networks, inter-company relations, standard setting, and dispute resolution and vice versa. They constitute an interlocking system which tends to be self-perpetuating. Fed by strategies of rational collective actors, economic institutions interact with each other and produce specific stable configurations which in their turn enable institutional advantages to be formed in the international competition of production regimes (Porter 1990). 'Varieties of capitalism' are thereby explained by the intra-systemic dynamics of production regimes (Hall 1997).

Regimes differ widely from economy to economy, even within the European context. As can be expected, the strongest divide exists between continental European production regimes (Austria, Benelux, Germany, Norway, Sweden, Switzerland) on the one hand and their Anglo-Saxon counterparts (Australia, Canada, Great Britain, Ireland, New Zealand, the USA) on the other. Each production regime reacts against external influences as an interlocking system. Thus they develop a considerable stability in relation to efficiency-driven evolutionary pressures, a remarkable resilience towards changing demands of various markets, a continual resistance against institutional transfers, in short: a considerable historical continuity in their independent development, and all this during the age of levelling globalisation (Hall and Soskice 2001; Soskice 1997).

In effect, this theory gives an impressive account of the idiosyncrasies of production regimes. However, systems theory, which usually sees systems at

work everywhere, would object that production regimes cannot be characterised as systems and their main idiosyncrasies cannot be attributed to
internal dynamics. If one applies a strict definition and does not identify
every social order with a system, then it becomes clear that the actual existing production regimes do not have elements, structures, boundaries of their
own which would make them into autonomous social systems.[11] Rather, they
constitute something completely non-systemic. Production regimes are
structural links between autonomous social systems—between the economy,
law and politics—but do not themselves evolve into autonomous systems
with their own elements, structures, and boundaries. As forms of structural
coupling (Maturana and Varela 1988: ch. 5), production regimes are mere
configurations of quite heterogeneous components, hybrids in the gap which
exists between the economy and society. As a matter of empirical observation it can be shown that production regimes do not constitute elementary
operations of their own—'regime acts' as it were—which could, comparable
to economic transactions, legal acts, and political decisions, interlock into
self-reproductive social systems. As such, production regimes are neither
functional systems nor formal organisations, nor interactions in the technical sense of systems theory but are merely linkage institutions between
them.[12]

Production regimes are indeed a specific structural ensemble of economic
institutions. This, however, does not make them a subsystem of the economy.
Rather, as institutions they link the economy to other autonomous social systems. If one wants to understand their evolutionary dynamics then their character as linkage institutions bridging the economy, the law, politics, and
education, must be taken into account.

To be sure, the majority of economists and lawyers view this differently, and
regard economic institutions as unitary phenomena, either as bundles of rules
or as incentive systems, and reduce the difference between their legal and economic aspects to a matter of definition by diverse scientific disciplines. In a systems perspective, however, economic institutions appear as fundamentally
different from legal institutions. Economic 'rules of the game' are not identical
with legal rules. This does not only refer to the much cited distinction between
Is and Ought. Economic property rights are factual opportunities to act on the
market with relative distance from legal entitlements to ownership, which as
ensembles of legally valid rules structure the resolution of conflicts and cannot
be identified with mere opportunities to act. An economic transaction must
be clearly distinguished from a legal contract, even if both regularly though
not necessarily occur at the same time. Legal personality as the benchmark

[11] *Locus classicus,* Luhmann (1995).
[12] For these distinctions, see Luhmann (1982b, 1987).

for binding legal acts, subjective rights, and duties is not identical with an economic enterprise as a self-reproducing social system. To give a shorthand definition of the difference: economic institutions are constraints and incentives that influence cost–benefit calculations of economic actors, while legal institutions are ensembles of legally valid rules that structure the resolution of conflicts. While being in a relation of tight structural coupling—which creates the wrong impression of their identity—economic and legal institutions are not only analytically but empirically distinct from each other (see Teubner 1992).

But even the tightest structural coupling between the law and the economy does not create a new identity, that is to say, a production regime as a social system, but rather binds both participating legal and economic institutions so closely together that they become almost indistinguishable. Paradoxically, the coupling occurs with the help of a distinction, namely, the distinction of the systemic codes which separate law from the economy. This does not establish a new unity of law and society or common socio-legal structures. While their events (may) occur simultaneously, they remain distinct parts of their specific discourse, with a different past and a different future. The only condition for their synchronisation is this: they need to be compatible with each other. They are and remain social hybrids which arise out of the coupling of legal and economic operations.

This structural coupling—and not their role as a social system—is the cause of their idiosyncrasies and their resistance against efficiency-driven impulses. Their resistance to change should not—as the production regime theory provides—be traced to interdependencies of individual economic institutions effected by strategies of self-interested collective actors. Production regimes are not unified, self-perpetuating economic institutions made up of economic transactions and strategies of actors. Their resistance to change has to do with their hybrid character. Their inertia is not determined primarily through internal interdependencies of individual institutions but through external dynamics, namely, through their connectedness to other social systems.

If the legal rules of hybrid institutions are changed through a legal act, the compatibility with its economic aspects can no longer be presupposed; it would have to be recreated in the new context, which is a difficult and time-consuming process which in turn alters both interlocking structures. This involves a double transformation, that is to say, a change on both sides of the distinction of the institution, not only a recontextualisation of its legal side but also a recontextualisation of the economic constraints and incentives. The contrary equally applies. Efficient adaptation to changing markets is subverted by their legal structures, which are subject to a different form of logic of change. Adaptation is not necessarily blocked but moves in other directions.

ULTRA-CYCLES

Systems theory defines institutions like contract and property as bilateral structural couplings between the economy and the law (Luhmann 1993: 446ff., 1997: 783ff.). However, production regimes are more complex than that. They are not merely regimes of contract and property, but also encompass, *inter alia*, institutions of education and training and technical standardisation. They establish not only bilateral but trilateral—if not multilateral—relations between social systems. Production regimes do not merely foster relations of the economy with the law but also foster relations with politics, with science, and with education. Thus, production regimes are characterised by multi-polarity and not by bipolarity, by cyclicity and not by reciprocity.

Cyclicity, however, does not mean that production regimes should now be defined as autopoietic social systems. If economic demands for change in industrial education are taken up by politics, and new legal rules concerning examination and qualifications are implemented which give rise to innovations in education, which for their part have an effect on the economy, then this circulation of information does not take the form of operations which couple themselves as a continuation of self-reproduction but remain political decisions, economic transactions, legal acts, educational interactions. They remain operations in the systems concerned.[13] The cyclicity works not via operations within one closed system but via perturbations between several autonomous systems.

Chinese whispers—the child's game—catches the logic involved. Autonomous systems do not understand each other but nevertheless connect with one another and produce something novel in this chain of misunderstanding. To this extent, the concept of the ultra-cycle as defined by Ernst von Weizsäcker is suitable to production regimes (Ballmer and Weizsäcker 1974). As opposed to a hyper-cycle which connects cyclical processes within a system (Eigen and Schuster 1979), an ultra-cycle extends beyond the boundaries of a system and connects cyclical processes of several systems. To be sure, in an ultra-cycle the participating systems do not merge into a new super-system with common elements. Their explicit characteristic is the added value which arises whenever the sparks of perturbation explode on the boundaries between participating systems. An ultra-cycle does not eliminate their autonomy, establishing a recursion of operations. Instead it utilises their autonomy in a recursion of perturbations.

---

[13] This does not exclude the possibility that new social systems evolve within production regimes. Systems of negotiation or circles of conversation may emerge as specific formal organisations or more informal interactions. These are indeed systems in the technical sense; they are not, however, identical with the production regime itself but are merely its components. See Hutter (1989), Willke (1995: 109ff.).

Consider technical standards. Scientific knowledge in the definition of technical standards cannot be transformed directly into law but can only work as a legal irritant (perturbing factor). It forces law to reconstruct the technical standard as a new legal rule. On the scientific side of the production regime, correlations between growth and risk have been produced. On the other side of the production regime, the law cannot map correlations into binding rules. It can only misunderstand them as though, at a particular point on a sliding scale, they defined behaviour as illegal. This threshold value of legal/illegal represents then the new legal standard, which can be recontextualised in the network of legal distinctions. When the legal standard in its turn is incorporated in economic transactions, rational economic actors do not perceive it as a valid norm of conduct but as a cost factor which is dependent on the probability of discovery and the intensity of sanctions. But when the cost increases are perceived as too burdensome for the economy, lobby groups begin to perturb the political system, pressing for a political reformulation of the standards. Under pressure, the politicians will harass the technicians until they come up with a novel formulation of the original standards. The Chinese whisper of technical standards produces a cyclical dynamic of continuous change which only stabilises when the participating systems develop their own standard values in such a way that they are compatible with one another.

Not every coupling between economy and society, however, constitutes a production regime. A myriad of 'wild' relations between systems exist in which the economy perturbs other social systems and vice versa. A production regime in the technical sense emerges once the perturbation channels are formed in such a way that the impulses for change are not only occasional, punctual, and one-sided, but merge either into a reciprocal perturbation, as in the bilateral case, or into a perturbation circulation, as in the multilateral case. Only then is a production regime established in its own right. It stabilises itself as an ultra-cycle of social institutions characterising the 'economic culture' of a whole region.

Just as in the game of Chinese whispers, the differential structures of the circulation explain the different outcomes. One only needs to alter the direction of the circulation of the whispers while keeping the other conditions constant, in particular the informational input, and one obtains different results. The mere difference of circulation and counter-circulation explains some empirical results which are indicative of the differences between technical standards within Europe. They can be traced back to the differences between technical standardisation in the German, French, and new European regimes. Particularly important is the point in time at which public authorities are talked to in the European whisper between technicians, managers, accountants, and lawyers (Hancke and Casper 1996).

CO-SELECTION OR CO-EVOLUTION?

If these are the synchronics, what would the diachronics of a production regime look like? Richard Nelson (1995) constructs a model of co-evolution. Economic institutions are not converging on a global basis because they co-evolve with regional technological progress, industrial structures, political programmes, and political institutions. The emerging specific national constellations of industry structure are responsible for institutional advantages in global competition.

This is remarkable for a version of evolutionary economics because it goes beyond mere efficiency as a selection criterion and explicitly involves the context of science, politics, and law as selective environmental pressures (Bijker *et al.* 1989). From the standpoint of systems theory, however, this would appear not as a fully fledged co-evolution of autonomous evolving systems but only as a co-selection in the same evolutionary process, as a mere enrichment of the criteria for selection concerning market efficiency by further criteria which operate in the environment of the institutions. This version of evolutionary economics models social evolution according to a classic pattern of natural selection in which various institutions co-evolve in a narrow sense, so that they constitute selective environments for one another.

One does, however, pay a price which is too high for overcoming an exclusively economic view of evolution, which in itself is to be welcomed (the market as the exclusive selective environment of the firm). What gets lost is the idea of an autonomous evolution of the economic system which, particularly for a multiplication of the perspectives, should not be relinquished. The result is a de-differentiated model of social evolution in which the diffuse selector of 'society' exerts diffuse environmental pressures on the adaptive economic institutions. One still can weight the various effects of these pressures of environmental selectors differently (for enterprises, primarily the market with secondary influences of politics etc). Taking this to a logical conclusion, however, such a process leads to a general de-differentiation of institutions, given that there is no space for autonomous evolving institutions in such a diffuse co-selection model.

The history of production regimes displays itself as a co-evolution in its strict sense. This means—contrary to a unified social evolution in which there is diffuse environmental pressure of various selectors on social institutions—that several autonomous systems are exposed to their very specific evolutionary mechanisms. Each of them has different patterns of variation, selection, and retention. The result is a multitude of autonomous evolutionary processes which in their turn influence each other via mechanisms of co-evolution. There is no unified trajectory within one production regime which would arise from the social environment by virtue of natural selection. Rather, a variety of diverging evolutionary dynamics are going on simultaneously within one regime. Independent evolutionary mechanisms in the autopoietic systems of the economy, politics, law, science, education force their institutions within the production regime to take an idiosyncratic evolutionary path. And the production regime in its turn provides for its specific mechanisms of co-evolution which regulate how these evolutionary paths influence each other.

CHANNELS OF CO-EVOLUTION

Autopoiesis theory has transcribed the dynamics of co-evolution as a 'structural drift' with indicators for analogue or digital forms (Luhmann 1997: 777; Maturana and Varela 1988: ch. 5). However, if one wishes to understand the independence of the production regime, one must not look merely at the individual evolutionary paths of participating systems but must analyse more specifically whether and how mechanisms of the reciprocal influences have been developed within the process of co-evolution itself. This is the second source of the varieties of capitalism. The first source can be found within the individual subsystems. Economic institutions have always been shaped by specific legal, political, scientific, educational developments in their region. They display cultural particularities, the history of which can only be explained in relation to the special histories of other systems. The other source of capitalist variety can be found on the border between cultural provinces, within the production regime itself, where particular co-evolutionary relations within its partial institutions emerge.

The hypothesis provides that the relevant differences between production regimes are traceable to the regional political and legal histories as well as to their peculiar mechanisms for co-evolution. These are interpreted as various structural links between autonomous subsystems which perturb each other. The various institutional traits of production regimes appear to be dependent on how co-evolution is arranged in two different dimensions. One concerns the quality of the co-evolutionary influences, the other concerns the density of coordination.

(1) As regards their quality, the mutual influences of the institutions are either

(a) *perturbation*: external factors and forces stemming from one institution affect the internal variety mechanisms of the other institutions, or

(b) *simulation*: the mechanism for selection of one institution reconstructs internally the selection criteria of the other institution, or

(c) *endogenous symbiosis*: the external results of selection of one institution are incorporated into the restabilisation mechanism of the other.

(2)   As regards the density of their coordination, the co-evolutionary con-
      tacts can be typified according to the following differences:
      (a)   spontaneous vs. organised
      (b)   simultaneous vs. sequential
      (c)   fragmented vs. integrated
      (d)   antagonistic vs. coordinated

The hypothesis will be sketched in by drawing from the experience of *just-
in-time* contracts in the USA and in Germany. Where traditional comparative
law merely sees similarities, convergence, or chances for legal harmonisation,
and where institutional theories presuppose a pressure of selection towards
efficiency, our approach identifies drastic differences in legal rules as well as
institutional advantages of production regimes, and traces them back to the
peculiar mechanisms of institutional co-evolution.

CO-EVOLUTION OF JUST-IN-TIME

Just-in-time arrangements are contracts between automobile-assemblers and
their suppliers. As against the traditional market contract where the supplier is an
independent market actor, just-in-time contracts integrate the supplier almost
totally into the production arrangements of the assembler. As a satellite firm, the
supplier is supposed to comply to the general business plan of the assembler as
well as to specific orders, and to deliver the customised parts, 'just in time'.

At first sight the similarities of the development are indeed astounding.
Originating in Japan, just-in-time contracts have found their place in commercial practice in both the USA and in Germany, and have been assimilated by the
law of both countries as exchange contracts with elements of cooperation
(Oechsler 1997: 473ff.; Rohe 1998). Usually formulated as standard contracts,
they are subject in both the USA and in Germany to judicial control via legal
concepts, policies, and principles which are considerably alike. Both legal
systems have recognised standard contracts which are stipulated by collective
actors for a particular number of transactions as being legally enforceable.[14]
Both legal systems make their validity dependent on certain conditions, which
are clearly different from individual contracts, and make them subject to
special judicial review according to general principles (good faith, fairness,
unconscionability).[15] Interim score: 1 : 0 for convergence.

---

[14] Chirelstein (1992: 56, 68), Dawson *et al.* (1993: 508ff.), Kessler *et al.* (1986: 2ff., 583ff.), Ulmer *et al.* (1997: Einl. Rz. 1ff., 80), Westphalen (1998), Wolf *et al.* (1994: Einl. Rz. 4ff.).
[15] Which includes the exceptional feature of open control of content in Germany; compare the decisions of the Federal Court of Justice or *ENTSCHEIDUNGEN DES BUNDESGERICHT-SHOFES IN ZIVILSACHEN (BGHZ)* 22, 90, 97ff.; Ulmer *et al.* (1997: Einl. Rz. 80); as regards

A score of 2 : 0 does not appear to be too far away if one regards the quality of co-evolutionary contacts. By accepting just-in-time standard contracts, both legal systems favour leaving the development of the new forms of contracts to the whims of coincidental irritations (Model 1a, see p. 173). Economic innovations perturb the legal system as 'cases' for isolated court decisions, which rule on the validity of individual contracts. In addition, both use a mixture of simulation and endogenous symbiosis (Models 1b and 1c). They reconstruct economic criteria in the judicial review decisions and they assimilate results of economic selection in their doctrine.

Divergence, however, manages to score a point. The mixture of Models 1b and 1c is decisive. And here the legal systems differ. Germany favours simulation (Model 1b), America favours endogenous symbiosis (Model 1c). In Germany, an extraordinarily high degree of judicial control exists, using mainly legal criteria and incorporating some economic criteria (Model 1b). American practice, however, incorporates directly the results of economic evolution of just-in-time *per se* (Model 1c), which it only rarely corrects through recourse to its own legal control mechanisms.

The key to this different practice lies in the endogenous symbiosis of economy and law, that is to say, the way in which law integrates selections of its economic processes (Casper 1998). It is arranged differently in both countries and establishes different requirements for the informational capacities of the courts (Schwartz 1992).

In the USA, it is individual firms that secure their contractual domination in the market through the aid of local legal expertise. This decentralised mode of private governance leads to a plethora of standard contracts—indeed, there are so many that it is difficult to gain an overview of individual sectors of industry, which transcends the detailed control of the informational capacity of the courts. This is the reason why judicial controls in the USA are relatively underdeveloped, despite the similarity of the legal instruments. In Germany, however, it is not individual firms but business associations which, with the aid of considerable legal expertise, formulate rather centralised contractual regimes which, in principle, apply throughout the entire industrial sector. This phenomenon of private regulation in entire sectors of industry through business associations is much less common in the USA (Casper 1998).

Moreover, in Germany, contractual regimes which are specific to a particular branch of industry are frequently scrutinised by public bodies. The Federal Cartel Office or *Bundeskartellamt* is often called upon to assess contractual aspects as well as anti-trust issues. As a result, German courts have a relatively good overview of the universals in this sector, such as the distribution of

the USA, compare Kessler *et al.* (1986: 586), which refers to the practice of the courts that rely on the 'due process of law' and the principle of 'unconscionability'.

economic risks, transparency, the political aspects, and legal justification behind rules. In contrast to the USA, the judicial review of contractual regimes is frequent and highly detailed. Subsequent to the relatively recent AGB-Code of 1976[16] there have been thousands of judicial decisions. Thus, we have a score of 1 : 1 in the match between Convergence and Divergence.

Divergence finally leads with 2 : 1 when the density of co-evolutionary contacts comes into play. In the USA, contacts between standard contracts are hardly coordinated even within one industry sector. Just-in-time regimes are implemented by individual firms and the other market side often reacts with its own standard contracts; relative market power decides whether or not one of the colliding forms of contract prevails. American courts, which, as has been said already, exercise relatively weak control in their review of standard contracts, react *post hoc* when unacceptable risks have materialised. But then they do not review standard contracts, they apply tort law. This explains *inter alia* why one speaks of the tort revolution in the USA on the one hand and the death of contract on the other (Gilmore 1995). The dominant economic control exercised by courts in the USA is exercised through tortuous duties of conduct and not through detailed review of the distribution of risks inherent to standard contracts. At the same time, the enactment of the Uniform Consumer Credit Code 1974 and the activities of the Federal Trade Commission (FTC) enhances the power of legislative intervention, particularly as regards the regulation of individual questions concerning the completion of contracts (Kessler *et al.* 1986: 586f., 592ff.). A similar fragmentation of institutional decision-making is illustrated by the intervention of the regulatory agencies and the legislative interventions of the legislature of individual states. (Kessler *et al.* 1986: 593). To conclude, in the USA, the picture of a market-oriented fragmented-sequential co-evolution is displayed. There is a plethora of just-in-time regimes where judicial intervention is markedly limited.

This is in direct contrast to the density of coordination in Germany. Whilst the position is not akin to the position in Austria, which is characterised by a centrally organised and integrated co-evolution of production regimes, the German case is characterised by coordinated interactive co-evolution. Considerable cooperation already exists in the economic sector. Standard contracts are produced by the majority of business associations whose peak organisations are often involved.[17] Sometimes, agreements on standard contracts are

---

[16] *Bundesgesetzblatt (BGBl.)* I 3317.

[17] Within the framework of the legislative process of the statute on standard contracts, the associations were not successful in pushing their demand for the enactment of a procedure for the nomination and creation of privileges of specimen conditions, whilst a corresponding practice within the legal framework provided by §§ 2, 38, subsection 2 S.3 GWB (Act against the Restriction of Competition) was developed under the supervision and control of the Federal Cartel Office, cf. Ulmer *et al.* (1997: Rz. 21).

reached with the opposite market. At the same time, agreements with third markets are reached, especially concerning insurance as regards risks of liability (Casper 1996: 7ff.). Administrative and political bodies, in particular the Federal Cartel Office, are activated at a relatively early period, together with other supervisory bodies, in relation to the agreement. Relatively few just-in-time regimes exist; those that do exist, however, are highly coordinated.

A comparative economic politics study (Casper 1998) has contrasted the USA and Germany in their density of coordination:

(1)   Germany: high regulatory capacities of business associations.
      USA: not associations but decentralised regulatory capacities of firms.
(2)   Germany: intensive horizontal regulatory coordination between associations.
      USA: limited coordination.
(3)   Germany: intensive vertical coordination between firms, associations, public supervisory authorities and courts.
      USA: not state control, but sporadic judicial control.

The same author comes to the following conclusion: 'The advantage of the German associational governance system is that the "para-public" links between the Courts, Kartellamt and firms through trade associations are more likely to produce new legal frameworks customized to the precise needs of firms' (Casper 1996: 28). And the German courts intervene. In the renowned 'Pizza-Salami' case, the Federal Court of Justice (*Bundesgerichtshof*) held that it was impermissible to exclude via standard contract the duty to inspect goods upon delivery contained in the commercial code (*Handelsgesetzbuch*).[18] The reason for this is to protect the supplier from claims for guarantees which are more difficult to prove later on, and to enable him at the same time to protect himself against further damage.

This is totally incomprehensible from the Anglo-American standpoint—a clear case of Eurosclerosis. A judicial dictate of this nature appears as highly traditional. It is bound to the old supplier model, relying on a strict distinction between the boundaries of the firms. It does not sufficiently avail itself of new forms of hybrid or symbiotic contracts. Second, it is paternalistic. This type of judicial review not only seeks protection of consumers but also corrects the transfer of risks in the professional business sphere. Third, this raises the issue

---

[18] *BGH NEUE JURISTISCHE WOCHENSCHRIFT (NJW)* 1991, 2633; *BGH NJW* 1991, 2631 concerns the unenforceability of an AGB-agreement according to which the party to a contract is denied the possibility for alteration and reduction but who nonetheless retains the right to withdraw from the contract. See Westphalen (1998: Rz. 21); cf. Wolf *et al.* (1994: Einl 69 m.w.N., Rz. Z 106); see also Schmidt (1991: 141, 150). As regards the decision of the Federal Court of Justice: Lehmann (1990: 1849, 1851ff.).

of transaction costs. Assemblers must, by law, retain their control over receipts. This entails an unreasonable duplication of quality controls in view of the initial control of the suppliers and the control of receipts of the assemblers. Fourth, the judicial dictate is hostile to innovation. With its harmonised regulation it inhibits innovative contractual regimes which attain an efficiency advantage as they render the rigid boundaries of enterprises more permeable.

The decision of the Federal Court of Justice makes sense, however, if one takes into account the varieties of capitalism. After everything that has been said about the special path of German production regimes, it is consistent and reasonable for the courts to intervene. The actual criterion as regards just-in-time contracts appears to be whether or not the contractual regime represents an authentic innovation. The suggestion is to distinguish between authentic innovations which increase the efficiency of the organisation and spurious innovations, that is, mere price strategies, which are made possible only through the transfer of risks to suppliers (Casper 1998). Thus, the policy principle for the judicial intervention is not to protect medium-sized companies nor to treat the interests of suppliers preferentially. Rather, the courts support technological cooperation between firms through protection of autonomy and facilitation of cooperation. Accordingly, the judicial review produces incentives for two different types of just-in-time contracts:

(1) either the contract respects the organisational boundary of supplier and assembler—it retains the inspection duties but also separates the risks;

(2) or it transfers the inspection duties of the assemblers to the suppliers so that the boundaries between the firms are blurred and a hybrid organisation between exchange and cooperation is formed. In this case, however, the risks are borne collectively.

The result is as follows: it is not possible to strike out the commercial law provision unless the assembler offers a fair distribution of damages, so that the risk of liability as regards initial controls is also borne by the assembler. The old-fashioned commercial duty of inspection, when it is applied to just-in-time contracts, works as a lever in order to create—aided by the cooperation of business associations and the Federal Cartel Office—a contractual model for just-in-time supplier contracts which is tailored to the regional production regime.

Note. This article was translated from the German by Miriam Aziz. I would like to thank Peer Zumbansen for his constructive and critical contribution.

REFERENCES

Albert, M. (1993), *Capitalism against Capitalism*. London: Whurr.

Aoki, M. (1994), 'The Japanese Firm as a System of Attributes: A Survey and Research Agenda', in M. Aoki and R. Dore (eds), *The Japanese Firm: Sources of Competitive Strength*. Oxford: Clarendon.

Atlan, H. (1987), 'Self-Creation of Meaning', *Physica Scripta* 36: 563–76.

Ballmer, T. T. and Weizsäcker, E. von (1974), 'Biogenese und Selbstorganisation', in E. von Weizsäcker (ed.), *Offene Systeme I: Beiträge zur Zeitstruktur von Information, Entropie und Evolution*. Stuttgart: Klett, pp. 219–64.

Bijker, W., Hughes, T. and Pinch, T. (1989), *The Social Construction of Technology Systems*. Cambridge, MA: Harvard University Press.

Blackmore, S. (1999), *The Meme Machine*. Oxford: Oxford University Press.

Bogdan, M. (1994), *Comparative Law*. Deventer: Kluwer.

Bratton, W. and McCahery, J. (1995), 'Regulatory Competition, Regulatory Capture, and Corporate Self-Regulation', *North Carolina Law Review* 73: 1861–948.

Casper, S. (1995), 'How Public Law Influences Decentralized Supplier Network Organization: The Case of BMW and Audi', WZB-Discussion Paper FS I 95–314. Berlin: Wissenschaftszentrum.

Casper, S. (1996), 'German Industrial Associations and the Diffusion of Innovative Economic Organisation', WZB-Discussion Paper FS I 96–306. Berlin: Wissenschaftszentrum.

Casper, S. (1998), 'The Legal Framework for Corporate Governance: Explaining the Development of Contract Law in Germany and the United States', WZB-Discussion Paper FS I 98–303. Berlin: Wissenschaftszentrum.

Chirelstein, M. A. (1992), *Concepts and Case Analysis in the Law of Contracts*, 2nd edn. Westbury: Foundation Press.

Collins, H. (1998), 'Transnational Private Law Regulation of Markets', *Europa e diritto privato* 4: 968–91.

Cooter, R. and Kornhauser, L. (1980), 'Can Litigation Improve the Law without the Help of Judges?', *Journal of Legal Studies* 9: 139–63.

Crouch, C. and Streeck, W. (1995), *Modern Capitalism or Modern Capitalisms?* London: Pinter.

Dawkins, R. (1976), *The Selfish Gene*. Oxford: Oxford University Press.

Dawson, J. P., Burnett Harvey, W. and Henderson, S. D. (1993), *Contracts: Cases and Materials*, 6th edn. Westbury: Foundation Press.

Dennett, D. (1995), *Darwin's Dangerous Idea*. London: Penguin.

Eigen, M. and Schuster, P. (1979), *The Hypercycle: A Principle of Natural Self-Organisation*. Berlin: Springer.

Frankenberg, G. (1985), 'Critical Comparisons: Re-thinking Comparative Law', *Harvard International Law Journal* 26: 411–55.

Gilmore, G. (1995), *The Death of Contract*, reprint (orig. 1975). New Haven, CT: Yale University Press.

Glasersfeld, E. von and Cobb, P. (1983), 'Knowledge as Environmental Fit', *Man–Environment Systems* 13: 216–24.

Hall, P. A. (1997), 'The Political Economy of Europe in an Area of Interdependence', in H. Kitschelt, P. Lange, G. Marks, and J. D. Stephens (eds), *Continuity and Change in Contemporary Capitalism*. Cambridge: Cambridge University Press.

Hall, P. and Soskice, D. (2001), *Varieties of Capitalism: The Institutional Foundations of Comparative Advantage*. Oxford: Oxford University Press.

Hancke, R. and Casper, S. (1996), 'ISO 9000 in the French and German Car Industry: How Quality Standards Support Varieties of Capitalism', WZB-Discussion Paper FS I 96–313. Berlin: Wissenschaftszentrum.

Hollingsworth, J. R., ed. (1993), *Comparing Capitalist Economies*. Oxford: Oxford University Press.

Hutter, M. (1989), *Die Produktion von Recht: Eine selbstreferentielle Theorie der Wirtschaft angewandt auf den Fall des Arzneimittelpatentrechts*. Tübingen: Mohr and Siebeck.

Jantsch, E. (1976), 'Evolution: Self-Realization through Self-Transcendence', in E. Jantsch and C. H. Waddington (eds), *Evolution and Consciousness: Human Systems in Transition*. Reading, MA: Addison-Wesley, pp. 37–70.

Kessler, F., Gilmore, G., and Kronman, A. T. (1986), *Contracts: Cases and Materials*, 3rd edn. Boston, MA: Little Brown.

Ladeur, K.-H. (1987), 'Perspectives on a Post-Modern Theory of Law', in G. Teubner (ed.), *Autopoietic Law: A New Approach to Law and Society*. Berlin: de Gruyter, pp. 242–82.

Legrand, P. (1997), 'Against a European Civil Code', *Modern Law Review* 60: 60–77.

Lehmann, M. (1990), 'Just in Time: Handels- und AGB-rechtliche Probleme', *Betriebsberater* 45: 1849–55.

Leydesdorff, L. (1994), 'The Evolution of Communication Systems', *International Journal of Systems Research and Information Science* 6: 219–30.

Luhmann, N. (1982a), 'The Evolution of Meaning Systems: An Interview with Niklas Luhmann', *Theory, Culture & Society* 1: 33–48.

Luhmann, N. (1982b), 'Interaction, Organization, and Society', in N. Luhmann, *The Differentiation of Society*. New York: Columbia University Press, pp. 69–89.

Luhmann, N. (1982c), 'Systems Theory, Evolutionary Theory, and Communication Theory', in N. Luhmann, *The Differentiation of Society*. New York: Columbia University Press, pp. 255–70, 394–5.

Luhmann, N. (1985), *A Sociological Theory of Law*. London: Routledge.

Luhmann, N. (1987), 'The Evolutionary Difference between Society and Interaction', in J. Alexander, B. Giesen, R. Münch, and N. J. Smelser (eds) *The Micro–Macro Link*. Berkeley: University of California Press, pp. 112–31.

Luhmann, N. (1992a), 'The Coding of the Legal System', in A. Febbrajo and G. Teubner (eds), *State, Law, and Economy as Autopoietic Systems: Regulation and Autonomy in a New Perspective*. Milano: Giuffrè, pp. 145–85.

Luhmann, N. (1992b), 'The Direction of Evolution', in H. Haferkamp and N. J. Smelser (ed.), *Social Change and Modernity*. Berkeley: University of California Press, pp. 279–93.

Luhmann, N. (1993), *Das Recht der Gesellschaft*. Frankfurt: Suhrkamp.

Luhmann, N. (1995), *Social Systems*. Palo Alto, CA: Stanford University Press.

Luhmann, N. (1997), *Die Gesellschaft der Gesellschaft*. Frankfurt: Suhrkamp.

Maturana, H. R. and Varela, F. J. (1988), *The Tree of Knowledge: Biological Roots of Human Understanding*. Boston, MA: Shambhala.

Nelson, R. R. (1995), 'Co-Evolution of Industry Structure, Technology and Supporting Institutions, and the Making of Comparative Advantage', *International Journal of the Economics of Business* 2: 171–85.

Nelson, R. R. and Winter, S. G. (1982), *An Evolutionary Theory of Economic Change*. Cambridge, MA: Harvard University Press.

Oechsler, J. (1997), 'Die Anwendung des Konzernrechts auf Austauschverträge mit organisations-rechtlichem Bezug', *Zeitschrift für Unternehmens- und Gesellschaftsrecht* 26: 465–92.

Porter, M. E. (1990), *The Competitive Advantage of Nations*. London: Macmillan.

Priest, G. L. (1977), 'The Common Law Process and the Selection of Efficient Rules', *Journal of Legal Studies* 6: 65–83.

Roe, M. (1995), 'Chaos and Evolution in Law and Economics', *Harvard Law Review* 109: 1–29.

Rohe, M. (1998), *Netzverträge*. Tübingen: Mohr Siebeck.

Roth, G. and Schwegler, H. (1990), 'Self-Organization, Emergent Properties and the Unity of the World', in W. Krohn, G. Küppers, and H. Nowotny (eds), *Self-organization: Portrait of a Scientific Revolution*. Dordrecht: Kluwer, pp. 36–50.

Rubin, P. H. (1977), 'Why is the Common Law Efficient?', *Journal of Legal Studies* 6: 51–63.

Schmidt, D. (1991), 'Qualitätssicherungsvereinbarungen und ihr rechtlicher Rahmen', *Neue Juristische Wochenschrift* 44: 144–52.

Schwartz, A. (1992), 'Relational Contracts and the Courts', *Journal of Legal Studies* 21: 780–822.

Soskice, D. (1997), 'Divergent Production Regimes: Coordinated and Uncoordinated Market Economies in the 1980s and 1990s', in H. Kitschelt, P. Lange, G. Marks, and J. D. Stephens (eds), *Continuity and Change in Contemporary Capitalism*. Cambridge: Cambridge University Press, pp. 271–89.

Teubner, G. (1987), 'Evolution of Autopoietic Law', in G. Teubner (ed.), *Autopoietic Law: A New Approach to Law and Society*. Berlin: de Gruyter, pp. 217–41.

Teubner, G. (1992), 'The Two Faces of Janus: Rethinking Legal Pluralism', *Cardozo Law Review* 13: 1443–62.

Teubner, G. (1993), *Law as an Autopoietic System*. London: Blackwell.

Teubner, G. (1998), 'Legal Irritants: Good Faith in British Law or How Unifying Law Produces New Divergences', *Modern Law Review* 61: 11–32.

Ulmer, P., Brandner, E., and Hensen, H.-D. (1997), *AGB-Gesetz*, 8th edn. Köln: Schmidt.

Westphalen, F. G. von (1998), *Vertragsrecht und Klauselwerke*. München: Beck.

Williamson, O. E. (1985), *The Economic Institutions of Capitalism: Firms, Markets, Relational Contracting*. New York: Free Press.

Williamson, O. E. (1991), 'Comparative Economic Organization: The Analysis of Discrete Structural Alternatives', *Administrative Science Quarterly* 36: 269–96.

Williamson, O. E. (1993), 'Calculativeness, Trust, and Economic Organization', *Journal of Law and Economics* 36: 453–86.

Willke, H. (1992), 'Societal Guidance through Law', in A. Febbrajo and G. Teubner (eds), *State, Law, and Economy as Autopoeitic Systems Regulation and Autonomy in a New Perspective*. Milan: Giuffrè, pp. 353–87.

Willke, H. (1995), *Systemtheorie III: Steuerungstheorie: Grundzüge einer Theorie der Steuerung komplexer Sozialsysteme*. Stuttgart: UTB.

Winter, S. G. (1995), 'Four Rs of Profitability: Rents, Resources, Routines and Replication', in C. A. Montgomery (ed.), *Resource-Based and Evolutionary Theories of the Firm: Towards a Synthesis*. Boston: Kluwer, pp. 147–78.

Wolf, M., Horn, N., and Lindacher, W. (1994), *AGB-Gesetz*, 3rd edn. München: C. H. Beck.

Ziman, J. (1999), 'The Marriage of Design and Selection in the Evolution of Cultural Artefacts', *Interdisciplinary Science Review* 24(2): 139–54.

Zweigert, K. and Kötz, H. (1992), *An Introduction to Comparative Law*. Oxford: Oxford University Press.

The Evolution of Education:
Change and Reform

JOAN SOLOMON

THIS PAPER CONSIDERS EDUCATION and the courses it proposes as cultural entities, and explores how education can emerge, evolve, or change in response to external triggers, using three different evolutionary analogies. In each case the topic is the emergence of Science, Technology and Society (STS) courses in British tertiary and secondary education. This kind of education seems to provide a particularly relevant subject for this inquiry. Not only was it an educational innovation in a new field, but it also challenged current views on the nature of acceptable school science by calling for political and ethical points of view from the students studying it. This was new, and could be seen as challenging the deep cultural norms for school education.

One phase of this evolution seems almost Lamarckian; a change in the cultural environment inspires a substantial educational 'reform' as Orpwood (1999) would call it. A second phase is like Darwinian natural selection in which small-scale changes are tried out by the teacher who observes difficulties in the classroom and, even during the process of instruction, drops one method, adopts another, tests it, and retains the best. Using Donald Campbell's paper on 'Blind Variation and Selective Retention' (1960), this kind of educational change is shown to be similar to what he calls the 'learning' process of biological species as they evolve in response to the selection/retention processes in the habitat in order to survive. Finally, a third wave of educational reform is described which is clearly social Darwinist, with a crude process of reinforcement used at the expense of respect for variation and natural selection. Here Campbell's 1965 paper is used to show why deliberately altering the habitat to damage those educational species which do not conform to the requirements of the powerful educational movers—politicians, industrialists, or others from outside the classroom—creates a very dangerous environment, not just for the intended STS course, but for the whole of education. It is argued that this triple process of evolutionary analogy, applied over a comparatively short period of time, seriously damaged the development of STS in particular, and science

Proceedings of the British Academy, **112**, 183–200, © The British Academy 2002.

education in general. This sets the whole process of curriculum innovation in a valuable new light.

EDUCATION AS A CULTURAL ARTEFACT?

People often argue that the human brain does not now need to evolve further, as it did between the emergence of early *Homo erectus* and *Homo sapiens*, because, with access to writing, the media, and IT, we can transmit ever-increasing quantities of high-value knowledge from one generation to the next without having to wait for the uncertain processes of gene mutation to bring about greater storage capacity or more effective operation of the brain. So we might conclude that the process of expanding and improving thinking processes, which lies at the heart of education, has now finally left the realms of genetics and is neither more nor less than a completely sociocultural artefact.

To claim that education is a cultural process may not be new or surprising. Most of us are learned enough to know, for example, that science education in the countries which follow the Cartesian tradition, such as France, Spain, Portugal, and Italy, is different from science education in British and the Scandinavian countries with their more empirical/humanistic traditions. There are also some strange effects of gender differentiation across these two sets of countries. In the Latin countries girls are far more likely to take physics and engineering than they are in the British/Scandinavian block. As if to support the cultural thesis even further, it seems that, while practical veterinary work and field studies in the environment are very popular with our girls, the most popular of the specifically mathematical and physical tracks for girls within the British/Scandinavian block of countries is astrophysics, which certainly cannot be described as very practical. Hypotheses that girls are attracted by the more experimental laboratory aspects of science, or the converse, both fall down in this analysis, and most feminist work has now been forced to take a purely 'cultural' perspective (Harding 1991).

Until recently theories of teaching and learning did not go far in describing what a cultural approach to education might be like. Cognitive psychology has often described learning in far too monolithic and logical a way to permit of cultural variation. For a long time, the hegemony of Piaget made it difficult to see the processes of education other than as the maturation of young minds according to an immutable and logical schema of internal processes across all contexts. Even though Piaget's genetic epistemology took some account of social features, these were not held to have a strong influence on the child's learning at school. One might say that, in the Piagetian scheme, children were seen as shielded from almost all environmental effects, and hence that the Darwinian processes of adaptation could not take place. In fact this became a bone of quite public contention between Piaget and Bruner in the 1970s and 1980s, as the latter showed empirically that children from developing countries very rarely became top-level formal thinkers. Bruner claimed that where young people did not need to employ abstract thinking in their daily lives, in particular for making important career decisions, these skills simply did not develop. So the environment, social and cultural, had a strong effect on both their learning potential and their motivation.

Even the much-scorned 'operant conditioning' psychology of B. F. Skinner would have demonstrated cultural effects from different contexts rather more clearly than did Piaget. Skinner described in detail how a child might be taught to dig by reducing the task to simple acts capable of being demonstrated, copied, and mastered one after the other (Skinner 1968). More complex tasks were only more difficult to learn, and to teach, because they needed to be subdivided into a greater number of parts. Here there was no development of logic either for, or through, learning as there had been in Piaget's approach: indeed there was no individual cognitive effort required at all on the part of the learner, other than accurate copying and ordering. So, for Skinner, cultural effects in education were reduced to a mere vocabulary of different contexts.

The Russian educationalist Lev Vygotsky, on the other hand, made room for both the natural processes of cognitive development and the cultural ones. The latter included actions taken by the teacher, with Vygotsky claiming that the two lines of development merge into each other in a way that makes it difficult to distinguish between them unless there is a sudden change which produces extreme effects. This brings us back to the use of evolutionary analogies. In the same way that Tim Ingold has argued in this book that culture and environment do not comprise a secondary force superimposed upon the genotype, Vygotsky maintained that the sociocultural development of behaviour, including cognitive behaviour, consists of changes which occur only if they are both cognitively possible to the child at that stage of general development, and also culturally appropriate to how society wants things to be.

> Culture, generally speaking, does not produce anything new apart from that which is given by nature. But it transforms nature to suit the ends of man. (Vygotsky 1994 [1929]: 59)

It follows from this that, when any community greatly prizes education as a means of transmitting its culture, including knowledge, art, wit, and behaviour, a very considerable effort will be expended in bringing about the transformation of learning to suit the purposes of the community. It is this purposeful cultural transformation of what nature gives our children which we call education, and the effort to carry it forward often engenders a state of public anxiety which continually drives the community, its politicians, parents, and teachers to try to improve upon their educational processes. Sometimes, as we shall see, this involves heavily enhanced competition in order to ensure that the less favoured outcome is eliminated.

A CULTURAL TREND

Here we consider educational change which is clearly culturally influenced, but in a way which owes nothing to government policies and very little to small-scale trials in the school classroom or university lecture hall. The only evolutionary analogy that springs to mind is the passing of a huge meteorite or a local volcanic eruption that has so changed the educational environment that new mutant organisms of a certain kind have the capacity to thrive there. Dinosaurs on the other hand, and their educational analogues, are in danger of extinction if they cannot adapt to the change.

The first wave of STS arrived early in the UK. It arose out of the anxiety of a whole generation who watched the dreaded mushroom cloud envelop Hiroshima at the end of the Second World War. In particular, the scientists felt that they had a responsibility to explain the dangers of radioactivity to lay people. A group of young university scientists, led by Dr Bill Williams of Leeds University, rented an empty railway-carriage, furnished it with educational materials, and travelled across the country teaching the public about radio-activity. Like other contemporary movements such as the British Society for Social Responsibility in Science, Pugwash, and those who ran the *Bulletin of the Atomic Scientists* in the USA, the scientists who started the STS movement in the UK believed that their duty was to educate lay people so that they could exercise their democratic rights of decision-making in an informed way. At that time, the greatest emphasis in the UK was on nuclear power and the testing of nuclear bombs. Many left-wing scientists belonged to SANA—Scientists Against Nuclear Armaments—and took part in the protest marches against the testing of nuclear bombs.

In the USA this was a time of intense anti-communism, McCarthyism, which made any political protest a dangerous activity. The focus of early STS here was more on environmentalism than disarmament, but there is reason to believe that it was of the same general kind. Rachel Carson, herself a scientist like the originators of other first wave STS groups, wrote eloquently about the damage that was being done to the populations of plants and animals, and of the inevitable subsequent effects on all forms of life. She wrote about the science of ecology, which was a new scientific discipline at that time, originating partly in England and partly elsewhere. Her main point was that the science being applied by the agricultural industry was hopelessly out of date. In ecological terms, humans were just another species at risk from the new pesticides.

The 'control of nature' is a phrase conceived in arrogance, born of a Neanderthal age of biology and philosophy, when it was supposed that nature exists for the convenience of man. The concepts and practices of applied entomology for the most part date from that Stone Age of science. It is our alarming misfortune that so primitive a science has armed itself with the most modern and terrible of weapons, and that in turning them against the insects it has also turned them against the earth. (Carson 1962: 243)

By 1970, the STS group in the UK had received enough funds from the Leverhulme Foundation to start an organisation called Science In a Social Context, or SISCON for short. This encouraged the teaching of courses in STS in universities and polytechnics. Many of the SISCON teaching materials are still in existence, covering subjects such as 'Limits to Growth', 'The Atomic Bomb', 'Science, Technology and the Modern World', etc.

We could claim, in a rather general way, that in the 1970s the reaction against the severely abstract nature of Enlightenment science, a reaction that we now call postmodernism, was only just beginning to make its mark. So the academic culture was going through an epistemological change which affected philosophers and scientists almost as much as the environmental disasters did.

STS began in higher education and only later spread to the schools. The first international conference was held in Amsterdam, where STS had arisen directly out of a political need. The government there wanted to hold a national referendum on whether or not to invest in nuclear power. It seemed that a realistic preamble to this event would be an extended programme of public education in the physics of the issue. The Dutch government decided on an eight-year educational programme, and this was still under way when the conference took place in 1976. The serious, logical but naïve nature of this decision seems a remarkable example of long-termism as we would call it today.

This first phase of STS was in essence contemporary: as John Ziman wrote in *Teaching and Learning about Science and Society* (1980), 'The STS movement belongs to our own times, and to our own form of civilisation.' It was a reaction to what has been likened to a passing meteorite, which changed the environment for science education in a way that even the third dangerous phase of educational change was unable to reverse completely.

THE DARWINIAN ANALOGY IN THE SECOND PHASE
OF CHANGE

Donald Campbell (1960) called his evolutionary model 'blind variation and selective retention' (BVSR) and applied it very widely beyond the normal confines of biology. It was based on Darwin's theory of natural selection in a fairly direct sense. In biology one could speak of a kind of 'learning' on the part of the organism, which takes place by means of random variation through genetic mutation, followed by the brutal process of selective survival of some, or none, of the mutant individuals. For example, learning about what structure of limbs favours a quick turn of speed, or how to glide from one branch of a tree to another by means of a membrane of skin stretched from wrist to torso, is produced by BVSR mechanisms facing the rigours of the physical environment. This is similar to the success or failure of engineering artefacts—the different shapes of aeroplanes' wings which are tried out in the environment of wind tunnels (Vincenti 1990)—or to what might be called *the struggle of conjectures* to succeed in solving problems within an open learning environment (Popper 1972). For fairly obvious reasons large-scale educational reforms in the UK, or any other country, are not guided by such a naïve free struggle between a plethora of educational conjectures. Nevertheless, there was a time of small-scale BVSR activity in STS education.

Campbell was at pains insist that BVSR was a quite general learning theory which could be used whenever there was variation in a system which might make it fit better or worse into the surroundings. He wrote of BVSR that it was 'fundamental to . . . all genuine increases in knowledge, to all increases in fit of system to the environment' (1960: 380). He described his theme in three ways which may suggest both simpler and faster reactions.

(1)   A blind-variation-and-selective-retention process which is fundamental to all inductive achievement, to all genuine increases in knowledge, to all increases in fit of a system to its environment.

(2)   The many processes which shortcut a full blind-variation-and-selective-retention process are in themselves inductive achievements, containing wisdom about the environment achieved originally by earlier blind variation and selective retention.

(3)   In addition, such shortcut processes contain in their operation a blind-variation-and-selective-retention process at some level, substituting for overt locomotive exploration, or the life and death winnowing of organic evolution. (1960: 380)

Learning, like biological evolution, can be described as a process which proceeds in a series of 'breakouts' from the limits of what has been known before, and is then accumulated in a bank of accessible new strategies, which may be similar to genes in some respects and have sometimes been called *memes* (Dawkins 1976). In the case of changes to the processes of education or teaching, these memes may have a very short shelf life. Those which are used for teaching and learning French irregular verbs may be entirely different from those used to teach the Principle of Conservation of Energy. It is the existence of variation at the beginning of the process, existing in the teacher's reflection on ideas at work in the classroom, and the possibility of later selection amongst them as she sees how they work out, which together produce a BVSR style of learning.

To understand this better we may begin by considering Donald Schon's (1983) famous notion of 'reflection-in-action' as a possible example of BVSR. He worked out the theory of this continuing process in considerable detail; just equating reflection with cognition certainly does not do justice to his far-reaching argument. He wrote: 'As we try to understand the nature of reflection-in-action, and the conditions that encourage or inhibit it, we study a cognitive process greatly influenced by "cognitive emotions" and by the social context' (1983: 322). The first of these influences mentioned by Schon puts together two almost opposite terms. What could it mean to practise 'cognitive emotion'? Schon explains that he uses this term to describe the practitioner's 'feelings about his [sic] own performance'. We might put this more simply as reflection on the *values* on which professional action is based.

Handal and Lauvas (1987) have written eloquently on what they call teachers' 'practical theory', which is dynamic, a basis for action, and yet also subject to change as the teacher experiences new situations and acts on old values, or even on new ones. 'The practical theory (of teachers) refers to a person's private, integrated, but ever-changing system of knowledge, experience, and values which is relevant to teaching practice at any particular time' (Handal and Lauvas 1987: 79).

The second factor Schon mentions is external. He called it 'the social context', which might, at any instant, comprise pupil behaviour, classroom size, the equipment, even the weather (most British teachers agree that high winds blow excitement and bad discipline into the classroom). This general point was also made by Deanne Kuhn (1986) in a study of the contributions of psychology to the goal of education for thinking. She wrote that it was necessary to consider the teacher's 'thinking skills in the context of specific, content-rich domains'. This translates into the context of teachers' thinking in the midst of the busy learning classroom.

In terms of Campbell's theory we can see this as a BVSR process acting on ideas for teaching. The variations in the mind of the experienced teacher are not 'blind' so much as untried, and one part of the selective retention process is governed by what might be called an 'ever-changing system of knowledge and values'. This is clearly a small-scale creative phase, and it runs almost without interruption into one in which the social environment—the students' reactions—provides direct feedback. Here begins the full selective/retention phase that offers the teacher evidence upon which she can decide whether to abandon the new teaching idea almost as soon as it begins, or to persevere with it.

Gary Cziko, who includes education in his book on general and universal selection theory (Cziko 1995), argues that all education should be aimed at the selectionist growth of fallible knowledge, as 'learning from one's own mistakes', which he considered a restricted kind of BVSR often called 'trial and error'. It is hard to warm to such an idea when no previous learning experience, which Campbell had spoken of as 'accumulation of wisdom about the environment', has been allowed to affect the system. Even B. F. Skinner, whose method of operant conditioning hid the goals of learning from students at every turn, so that they could offer no conjectural variation of strategy whatsoever, knew enough about the psychology of learners to make sure it would be 'a fortunate history of successes' not failures, in order to make for satisfying, and motivated learning (Skinner 1968). The programmed learning that he advocated would not countenance a success rate in any written question of less than 95 per cent. However, this kind of success is only effective for 'surface' or rote learning, where the student's reward would never be the interest of the work, a deep understanding of the system, or the intellectual satisfaction that good learning brings. Operant conditioning is only effective in education where the total reward is manipulable by the teacher—a tube of sweets or a few more marks in the next test.

It remains only to see how this evolutionary/educational theory applies to the conditions in which STS education found itself during the early mid-1980s. In 1983 a considerable amount of funding was raised from industry and from the Association for Science Education to back a new project, the Secondary Science Curriculum Review (SSCR), which was committed to a 'periphery to centre' model of innovation. That meant a network of local 'working groups' of teachers which, as its evaluator David Ebbutt wrote in 1985, was expected to produce 'varied outcomes of a five-year study of the secondary science curriculum that has involved science teachers in the complex tasks of developing solutions to some very major tasks' (Ebbutt 1985: 645).

This looked like a series of small-scale BVSR processes amongst the teachers in the local working groups. However the results had to be evaluated, at every stage, by teachers in other working groups, the central Review Group, and/or 'external agencies' such as employers, parents, advisers, and learned societies. These agencies could not perform the kind of on-the-spot evaluation-in-action that classroom teachers did for their own ideas. The major problem was the way in which the Central Review team tried to address the difficulty of this mixture of criteria. In the event all they did was to insist that the outcomes should also:

(1)   meet the Central Team's views on increasing educational opportunity;
(2)   be consistent with the Central Team's report, *Science Education 11–16*;
(3)   be consistent with the Central Team's view of learning; as well as
(4)   reflect contemporary thinking about the chosen topic area.

Criteria for survival do not take kindly to mixing in this wishful way. In addition, the Central Team had no governmental mandate, and did not seek any. In the mid-1980s the teachers had seemed a powerful force not afraid to take on the government through industrial action when they wanted more pay. But the Thatcher governments managed to break the power of the teachers' trade unions as they had done already with the miners' unions. One of the remits of the SSCR project was to produce a national curriculum for science, and this they manifestly did *not* manage to do. When the government was ready, it began to put a national curriculum in place, and even invited the teachers to help in this process, although the SSCR had never included government officials in theirs. In retrospect it is easy to see that a sound educational initiative which is nationwide will require a whole team of players, from parents, through teachers, to politicians. These will need to have the same, or at least similar, criteria and be able to work together.

THE GOVERNMENT ACTS, AND SOCIAL DARWINISM TRIUMPHS

In order to apply evolutionary thinking to the great sweeps of educational reform that have affected Britain and other countries during the last century, we need to consider some of the later writings by Campbell. In a paper written in 1965 he begins by describing several sorts of social evolutionary theory, most of which he rejects because they do not conform to his BVSR model. That argument is pertinent to this study because education is so clearly a sociocultural effect that we might hope to learn from his analysis how good education could be selected from bad without recourse to endless ideological controversy or the blind, ineffective trial-and-error of too many conjectures.

The social Darwinism connected with the names of Herbert Spencer and Adolf Hitler has been almost universally rejected as being intolerably elitist, brutal, and racist. However this rejection was not because Darwinian theory should not be applied to humans. On the contrary, it was the fact that social Darwinism advocated direct *actions* that society should follow in *order to reinforce the selection processes*, thought by some to be no longer operating with sufficient severity to ensure the survival of (*what were considered to be*) the fittest which caused such revulsion. That sort of thinking argued that the unsuccessful and unemployed should be denied welfare, and that slow learners and the chronically unfit should be sterilised to protect the glory of the species at its best. Here there was none of the respect for the creative potentiality of variation which is so essential in BVSR, and the crude methods used to reinforce selection are reminiscent of a more precarious human existence at earlier times when kindness to the weak was a rarity.

There may be at least four reasons why such sociocultural effects do not really follow the simple variation/selection process model. The first three of these have been adapted from Campbell's 1965 paper.

(1) Sociocultural evolution takes place over a much shorter timescale than biological evolution, so a society may evolve into a whole new 'species' within a single generation.

(2) There are often 'vicarious selectors' at work, which refer to previous times and to a habitat which no longer exists.

(3) There is a potential conflict between the introduction of variations that produce change, and the value of retaining the cultural accumulation which is familiar to so many of the present population.

The fourth reason arises out of these three. The vicarious selectors at work in (2) and the conflict mentioned in (3), together with an unsubstantiated belief that Darwinian evolution always produces 'the best' (see also Midgley 1985) is apt to tempt some into an active reinforcement of the forces of selection.

(4) If it seems that the processes of variation and selection are at work, the latter may be subject to political manipulation in order to increase their effectiveness.

HABITATS FOR EDUCATIONAL REFORM?

If we are to understand the extreme and damaging educational changes of the 1990s in Britain, we need to begin by identifying both the organisms whose evolution was being tampered with, and the 'habitat' in which they had to exist. On a small scale, the classroom does regulate through gradual adaptation. When research explores science students' understanding of a topic like 'The Nature of Science' (Brickhouse 1989; Solomon *et al.* 1996), a topic which has not been tightly specified by the curriculum, it is not difficult to show that the teacher plays a very influential role in directing the general tenor of the students' thinking—even without explicit teaching of the topic. Here we have a curious implicit and quite reflexive process not unlike the workings of the hidden curriculum, through which changes take place so long as counter-examples from the wider educational environment do not select them out.

When the government imposes its own educational reforms, the children themselves are neither the habitat in which educational reform is regulated, nor the organisms which are selected. Of course their knowledge, manners, dispositions towards learning, and mechanical ingenuity may all be outcomes of their previous educational history, and will, in turn, affect what they retain of new instruction, but they themselves are not the instruments of selection and retention in the process of educational reform. School children have never yet closed down an educational system, even when it was both physically brutal to them and also élitist, as it was in English public schools for so very long. College students did try to do this in continental Europe in 1968, but not very much was achieved. Indeed, children still at school are almost the only group in society that usually has no voice at all in the great movements of educational reform.

Power for large-scale reform in education resides in a very large range of constituencies, as we have seen. This diversity makes for a complex and dangerous habitat for the evolution of new methods of education since it is almost impossible to please everyone; so the method adopted was that of the fair but mindless multiple-choice testing. These constituencies may hold quite different views about the outcomes of education, which could, in principle, be used to condemn to extinction all or any educational innovation if the actors were influential enough in government circles or on the media. In our evolutionary analogy there are also biological organisms unfortunate enough to have emerged in a similarly mixed and dangerous habitat, such as the South American sloth or the immensely long-surviving, but now extinct, ammonite. The varieties of dangers surrounding these organisms are such that they can never advance into a well-adapted and more specialised form. Instead, they were condemned by the many different threats of their environment to be generalised, well-defended, and rather static species. That part of the analogy with education is almost comically striking, and matches well with Campbell's comment (mentioned earlier) that in sociocultural systems there is a potential conflict between the variations which produce change, and the value accorded to the retention of a cultural accumulation which was prominent in an earlier phase of educational thinking and practice.

In highly centralised educational systems, such as those in the UK and France, the government specifies what it perceives to be the cultural preference with respect to education, in considerable detail. In less centralised systems, like those in the Scandinavian countries, the imposed detail may be missing except at community level. But that, equally, is a reflection of national cultural preference. Struggling to survive in this *mêlée* are the schools and their head teachers whose need, like that of the living organism in an ill-defined habitat, is to find a safe niche for existence, and to be endlessly on the alert for signals of danger. This is why the variations of educational culture are often more clearly to be read in the statements made by school head teachers than in the writings of academic researchers and philosophers of education, who live in far less threatening surroundings.

As Carr and Hartnett (1996) point out, at the beginning of this century there seemed to be just two distinct school models for emerging secondary education. One was the public school with its head teachers cast in the powerful élitist mould that Matthew Arnold had so applauded, and the other was the small grade schools providing education confined to the needs of the local community. It was the first variety of schools that was most copied, until and well beyond the rise of Halsey's controversial community schools some seventy years later. When schools became comprehensive in the 1960s they often included a 'grammar stream', which could just about continue to emulate the Arnold model, but this was increasingly unconvincing.

Modern head teachers regularly speak to and of their schools as they try to define their social and moral purpose, implicitly distinguishing theirs from other schools in a frankly competitive mode. In a country like England the purposes may indeed vary considerably. Social differentiation has long been a peculiarly English disease, endemic to our cultural landscape. The early state secondary schools were called upon to be vigilant in fitting boys and girls for retail and technical employment, 'the future career of the pupil is the leading thought to guide us in determining the duty of a school' (letter to *The Times* 1900). This seems to descend directly from the teaching of Adam Smith in *The Wealth of Nations* about the division of labour and hence a corresponding division in education.

This variation amongst the nation's schools is permitted not by educational learning theory, nor even by the pressure of international testing, but by the hidden strength of political and cultural purpose. While Adam Smith in Britain was calling for the breaking down of manufacture (his famous example was that of the humble pin) so that less labour, skill, creativity, and cost would be involved, the respect for invention in the USA was encouraging initiative and inventiveness in its workforce so that any citizen could, in principle, become a millionaire, or run for President. From Germany, guided as usual by their adherence to the education ideology of von Humboldt, Smith's social and educational perspective was soon being attacked as being 'in many ways profoundly immoral' (Winch 1998).

One more point emerges from Campbell's analysis of the sociocultural system. His 'vicarious selectors', which refer to previous times and to a cultural habitat which no longer exists, illustrates the commitment to an older cultural accumulation which is still familiar to the present population from their own youth. Within the barrage of criticisms, which reach a crescendo during any movement for educational reform such as that which is now taking place in the USA, we hear extraordinary comments, such as those by K. S. Louis (1998) who actually complained that students are being *forced* to take courses of 'AIDS-awareness education' rather than in economic or political geography. This is an arresting example of potentially damaging and out-of-date vicarious selectors. In Britain there are few educational debates that do not include an emotional call for the elimination of Media Studies or European Studies, both of which so clearly belong to the modern world. Communication comes to us and our pupils from the screen rather than the book, and emerging subnational groups claim our interest considerably more than do the old and sometimes crumbling national or super-national states which inhabited the pages of former history text books.

EDUCATIONAL PRESSURE ON THE SCHOOLS

When expansion in education faces budgetary restraints it seems that Britain always tends to succumb to a severe inspection system coupled with payment by results. Our schools also live within cultural environments, rural or urban, affluent or poor, educated or deprived, all of which might profoundly affect the education which is locally required, but centrally produced.

Schools are clearly social institutions. The figure of the be-robed head teacher, who lectures his pupils and staff in morning assembly on the 'ethos' of the school, is more than a mere caricature. His purpose is to embody the thinking of an institution. Ludwig Fleck (1935) was the first to recognise social institutions as being 'thought collectives', an idea later picked up and acknowledged by Thomas Kuhn in his emerging philosophy of science, which was based upon the group paradigm. Mary Douglas, expanding on this theme of social institutions in 1987, warned that not 'just any busload of people' forms a society: they need to be a like-minded group. This is precisely the aim of the head's morning lecture: it is not so much a rehearsal of where the school stood in the past, or of where it stands now, as an attempt to construct the common institutional mind. As Fleck put it: 'The general structure of a thought collective entails that the communication of thoughts within a collective, irrespective of content or logical justification, should lead, for sociological reasons, to the corroboration of the thought structure' (Fleck 1935: 103).

This does seem to have some effect within the school. A small exploration into the factors which facilitate change in science teaching commissioned by and published in *New Scientist* (Solomon 1987) suggested that the Head of the Science Department, the school's own voice on the merits of all and any innovation in science teaching, was already forcing teachers into an institutional mould. The study showed that no teacher's classroom innovation which had gone against the practice supported by their Head of Science and his/her team of technicians, had any chance of succeeding in effecting even quite a small permanent change (see also Vesilind and Jones 1998). This is an inevitable concomitant of the mould of like-mindedness. Foucault (1980) attacked all social institutions for the way in which they straitjacket minds, and Mary Douglas added that institutions frequently fix processes which should essentially be dynamic, and yet choose to hide their influence. Whatever management criticisms such institutional moulds attract, any bystander moving from one school to another can often observe their results.

At first it was the head teachers who were most vociferous in their criticisms of the new 1989 Education Act. The ultimate threat of extinction of their school, either by the inspectors' published verdict or by the school league tables, is selectionist in a raw and uncaring mode. Funding is based on the numbers of pupils attracted to the school in the same way as profit accrues to those who manufacture the most commodities. In the fashion of Adam Smith, education has been linked to the operation of crude market forces. Many commentators saw at once that this process would suppress the creative variation amongst schools at the very beginning of what might have been a larger-scale BVSR evolutionary process. However, they often forgot the older selective environmental pressures coming from the community in which the school was embedded, such as social deprivation, lack of student discipline, and illiteracy in the home. Where before these struggling schools were given extra funds to reduce class size and improve the chances of good teaching and learning, a social-Darwinist course would have cut their funding to hasten the selection process. This did indeed happen.

In the selectionist ideology used to explain this way of raising standards, it was supposed that where there was a choice of schools the struggle to survive would stimulate each school to improve their pupils' examination grades in order to attract more pupils and more funding for survival. As Gillian Sheppard, the Secretary of State for Education stated in Parliament in 1996, as though the proposition was quite self-evident, 'The existence of a range of different schools drives up standards for all our children.' In reality this did not happen. A careful and interesting report by Levacic (1996) showed that this quasi-market competition did not affect school performance in the way it was intended to. On average the examination performance did actually improve, if the marking of the new tests is to be trusted, while on average the school budgets declined. In socially deprived environments standards remained low. The grant maintained schools were more favourably funded and yet research shows that they did not attract more pupils than other local schools when other environmental factors such as distance and bus routes were taken into account. As concluded by the author, this study suggests that successful adaptive changes for schools are not based on surface changes to image.

It would be satisfying to believe that it was other features of the schools— their encouragement of creativity, of social responsibility, and of care for less able children, not to mention their locality—about which parents might want to express choice. However, British education has never been guided by any general vision or educational philosophy. Arnold's view of the grace and elegance of undergraduate life in Oxford is trivial when compared with the well-worked-out democratic philosophies of Comenius, von Humboldt, Dewey, or Grundwig. Some few of us have strong idiosyncratic views and attempt to choose schools for our children with care, but there is no thoughtful consensus to help us in this task. Parents who have themselves suffered from early removal from a loving home to a stark boarding school, or those who had learnt very little at a third-rate neighbourhood school in which bullying was rife, frequently send their own children to the same kind of institution in order to make them tougher. It must be concluded that we suffer badly from the lack of an educational value system. It is this philosophical silence that makes parental choice so blunt an instrument in the selection process by which schools survive in the 'pupils equals money' stakes. It is also this which has led some British parents to follow government rhetoric that insists that marks in the league tables of schools should be the decisive selection factor for their survival. It has not always worked in this way. Levacic showed that, where geographical isolation has prevented the movement of pupils to another school, there is no evidence that this has been a factor in letting standards drop. In order to make the government's ideology of competition in a market of parental preference work, the government had to provide itself with other powers for closing the neighbourhood school, such as the notorious system of 'failing schools' and 'special measures'.

To conclude, we may decide that where no values other than test grades and inspection reports guide parental choice of school, we have no more nor less than a dubious evolution in the manner of social Darwinism. Schools in neighbourhoods which are poor are no longer helped to overcome disadvantage. They become 'failing schools' and are either closed down, or continued in a model of competition for examination grades in which they, and the bookless homes from which their pupils come, are ill-equipped to succeed.

THE REBIRTH OF STS EDUCATION?

Two particularly heavy blows were struck at the early STS movement. The first was a hostile report from Sir Alec Cairncross in 1978 on STS courses at tertiary level, to be followed, at the end of the decade, by the arguments about raising educational standards in schools and going 'back to basics' (which was reinforced by Prime Minister Margaret Thatcher's personal problem with understanding what the word 'society' might mean, once memorably announcing 'There is no such thing as society, only people!'). In 1983 her Secretary of State for Education Sir Keith Joseph prohibited the teaching of social or economic issues in secondary school science. At first schools and teachers took little notice, but, in the end, frightened head teachers, tests, and leagues tables forced them to pay attention.

As Eva Jablonka (2000) described in a chapter devoted to modern Lamarckian systems and the kinds of metaphors and models generated by them, explaining cultural inheritance is not well served by gene models of Darwinian evolution. The isolated and almost digital nature of genes which have been so successful in describing biological inheritance have supported the metaphorical use of similar 'memes' for describing cultural and technological change. In technology it is not hard to find pieces or mechanisms which do seem to fulfil the role of memes, as they turn up in one kind of machine and then another. However non-technological cultural trends, like those in educational thinking, do not take place in discrete steps so the meme model proves to be of little value.

According to modern biology the environment not only affects how genes are expressed in a particular generation but, perhaps surprisingly, it turns out that some of these environmentally induced changes can even be transmitted to succeeding generations. The variations are often behavioural, thus having marked effects on the phenotype. This is all in contradistinction to Darwinian theories, but Jablonka recommends them as providing better analogies for cultural and technological evolution than the reductive on/off calculus of genes or memes.

> Natural selection is a general principle of evolutionary change at many levels, including the cultural level. However, adherence to the genic model of heredity is problematic for students of cultural evolution. Unlike genetic variations, cultural variations can hardly be described as non-directed . . . Furthermore, unlike the genetic system of DNA replication, the 'inheritance' of behaviour patterns and the product of behaviour follows diverse and changing routes, occurs at different levels of social organisation, and involves different types of potentially transmissible information. (Jablonka 2000: 30)

The variety of STS courses emerging in the early 1980s were a recognition that some educators had begun to see the whole business of education as concerned with much more than a mere body of transmitted knowledge. In the 1970s and 1980s, alongside the rise of STS and yet completely dissociated from it, Malcolm Skilbeck examined the aims of school curricula in a series of books and articles. He proposed that one of the two aims of all education was to provide the next generation with skills for critiquing their own culture.

> [H]istory, geography, politics, sociology and morality may be presented as problematic, controversial and many-sided, or as so much settled knowledge to be learnt and reproduced according to the conventions of the essay and the examination question. A curriculum plan in a school can aim to foster critical reflective thinking; it can stimulate and provide opportunities for participation in practical projects by which the community betters itself: it can encourage pupils to see themselves as the organisers of their own society. (Skilbeck 1975: 34)

Skilbeck rarely mentioned science but developed a concept of education as a preparation for social reconstruction which clearly encompassed citizens' decisions about the new technologies just as STS did. We can see Skilbeck's discussion of education as a preparation for community action as part of the same cultural trend that produced STS.

The influence of STS continues to exist, but only weakly. It is changing, as systems with an untramelled capacity for creative variation will always do. Perhaps it is on this cultural scale that we should look to see a larger BVSR mechanism at work, albeit haltingly; one which makes slow uneven progress.

Culture, as Vygotsky pointed out, has to work *with* our natural learning, our way of associating ideas. And yet it is itself a product of these ideas, and a fabricator of other ones. Occasionally this produces a feedback system in which change is fast and furious as it was during the 1970s; at other times the feedback from the culture is out of step and progress seems almost to stop at it did in the 1990s. As with the effects from the close passage of a meteorite, there is little we can do directly to influence outcomes.

And do the old dinosaurs get completely extinguished? The STS movement never did quite die out. Like most species that are assaulted by a huge change in the environment, a few of the less specialised organisms survive. For example in the SATIS (Science and Technology in Society) and Science Across Europe projects, their industry connection protected them from total extinction. They hid from the more hostile changes by concentrating on economic changes and statistical analysis in place of the consideration of ethics and civic action. Much the same happened to some of the university-centred STS courses. Perhaps the best evolutionary analogy for this is closer to that of the strange and ancient coelacanth, which can occasionally be fished up from the depths of some ocean, and may even have a future if the environment moves to its advantage.

Now, in our post-Thatcher era, with a still frail but surviving STS movement, the emphasis is moving towards considering ethics in contemporary cases of science-based controversies, evaluating evidence, and considering ethical matters, and moving away from purely economic considerations. The British national curriculum in science for the year 2000 gives some cause for hope, even though the era of social Darwinism has not yet disappeared. The STS coelacanth may be mutating and stirring as the cultural habitat slowly becomes rather more favourable. Global climate changes may, literally as well as metaphorically, be favouring a return to an STS education, in which social responsibility once more has an important place on a local as well as an international level.

REFERENCES

Brickhouse, N. (1989), 'The Teaching of the Philosophy of Science in Secondary Classrooms: Case-Studies of Teachers' Personal Theories', *International Journal of Science Education* 11: 437–49.

Campbell, D. (1960), 'Blind Variation and Selective Retention in Creative Thought as in Other Knowledge Processes', *Psychological Review* 67(6): 380–400.

Campbell, D. (1965), 'Variation and Selective Retention in Socio-cultural Evolution'. In H. Barrington, G. Blankston, and R. Mack (eds), *Social Change in Developing Areas*. Cambridge, MA: Schenkman, pp. 21–49.

Carr, W. and Hartnett, A. (1996), *Education and the Struggle for Democracy: The Politics of Educational Ideas*. Buckingham: Open University Press.

Carson, R. (1962), *Silent Spring*. London: Hamish Hamilton.

Cziko, G. (1995), *Without Miracles*. Cambridge, MA: MIT Press.

Dawkins, R. (1976), *The Selfish Gene*. Oxford: Oxford University Press.

Douglas, M. (1987), *How Institutions Think*. London: Routledge and Kegan Paul.

Ebbutt, D. (1985), 'Evaluation and the Secondary Science Curriculum Review—Setting the Scene', *School Science Review* 66(237): 645–50.

Fleck, L. (1935), *The Genesis and Development of a Scientific Fact*, English trans. 1979. Chicago: University of Chicago Press.

Foucault, M. (1980) *Power/Knowledge*. Hemel Hempstead: Harvester Press.

Handal, G. and Lauvas, P. (1987), *Promoting Reflective Teaching; Supervision in Action*. Buckingham: SRHE and Open University Press.

Harding. S. (1991), *Whose Science? Whose Knowledge?* Milton Keynes: Open University Press.

Jablonka, E. (2000), 'Lamarckian Inheritance Systems in Biology: A Source of Metaphors in Technological Evolution', in J. Ziman (ed.), *Technological Innovation as an Evolutionary Process*. Cambridge: Cambridge University Press.

Kuhn, D. (1986), 'Education for Thinking', *Teachers' College Record* 87(4): 495–512.

Levacic, R. (1996), 'Competing for Resources: The Impact of Social Disadvantage and Other Factors on English Secondary Schools' Financial Performance', *Oxford Review of Education* 24(3): 303–28.

Louis, K. S. (1998) '"A Light Feeling of Chaos": Educational Reform and Policy in the United States', *Daedalus* Fall: 13–40.

Midgley, M. (1985), *Evolution as a Religion*. London: Methuen.

Orpwood, G. (1999), '"But Will it Be on the Test?"—The Role of Assessment in Science Curriculum Change', STEU Seminar, 3 June, Kings College, London.

Popper, K. (1972), *Objective Knowledge: An Evolutionary Approach*. Oxford: Oxford University Press.

Schon, D. (1983), *The Reflective Practitioner*. Cambridge: Maurice Temple Smith.

Skilbeck, M. (1975), 'The School and Cultural Development', in M. Golby, J. Greenwald, and R. West (eds) *Curriculum Design*. Milton Keynes: Open University Press, pp. 7–19.

Skinner, B. F. (1968), *The Technology of Teaching*. New York: Appleton.

Solomon, J. (1987), 'Signs of Change in the Science Class', *New Scientist* 5 Feb.

Solomon, J., Scott, L., and Duveen, J. (1996), 'Large-Scale Exploration of Pupils' Understanding of the Nature of Science', *Science Education* 80(5): 493–508.

Vesilind, E. and Jones, M. (1998), 'Gardens or Graveyards: Science Educational Reform and School Culture', *Journal of Research in Science Teaaching* 35(7): 757–75.

Vincenti, W. (1990), *What Engineers Know and How They Know It*. Baltimore, MD: Johns Hopkins University Press.

Vygotsky, L. S. (1994 [1929]), 'The Cultural Development of the Child', in R. Van der Veer and J. Valsiner (eds) *The Vygotsky Reader*. Oxford: Blackwell, pp. 57–99.

Winch, C. (1998), 'Two Rival Conceptions of Vocational Education: Adam Smith and Friedrich List', *Oxford Review of Education* 24(3): 365–78.

Ziman, J. (1980), *Teaching and Learning about Science and Society*. Cambridge: Cambridge University Press.

The Evolution of Merged Culture, Genes, and Computing Artefacts

THE EVOLUTION OF CULTURAL INFORMATION implies certain concepts. First is that of culture as essentially contents of human minds. Second is that of information, albeit the information that flows through human minds as humans interact with each other socially. Culture is not information generated within human minds solipsistically; it is only when this solipsistic internal material is articulated socially and made to interact with other humans that it becomes culture. A third notion is that of evolution, as the human carriers of this social information interact with their environments and change the information characteristics of culture.

But this cultural information is not the only information around in the world that has evolutionary characteristics. Nor is it the only information, or carrier of information, with which humans interact. Humans in their cultural mode are also biological entities. Biological entities also carry another type of information, genetic information, DNA. But only a few biological entities are cultural creatures able to interact with each other culturally and change their behaviour accordingly. Such flexibility of behaviour at the level of the phenotype due to culture provides such carriers of genetic information with a greater capacity for adaptation to the environment and hence of survival. Humans have the greatest capacity for culture but other cultural animals include for example, chimpanzees and similar primates, wolves and some species of birds, as Wilson pointed out several years ago (Wilson 1980: 76–81).

Humans interact culturally not only with biological entities that are cultural but also those that are not cultural, that is with organisms that do not pass learnt information on to their cohorts. Biological entities, as both genetic systems and cultural systems, form part of the environment with which humans interact and evolve culturally. Non-biological systems that are inanimate and do not process information also constitute part of this environment.

There are systems normally considered inanimate that also process information. These are human-made entities, such as computers. These computing devices are now multiplying rapidly in number and increasingly form part of

Proceedings of the British Academy, **112**, 201–213, © The British Academy 2002.

the environment within which human culture evolves. Initially the 'artefactual' information in these devices was simply cultural information put there for storage by humans (say, supplanting earlier storage devices like paper and books), and processed in a rudimentary manner. But artefactual information is increasingly being processed through such techniques as genetic algorithms, fuzzy logic, and expert systems that continuously adjust their behaviour according to the inputs from their environments in a non-trivial manner. These devices learn and pass this learnt information to other devices.

Further, the number of computing devices, say in the form of micro-controllers, even today is in the billions range, an information environment which has as many entities as the human population. Soon such computing entities will swamp in number 'cultural information processors' in the form of humans. Especially when these devices have learning capacities and pass on their information from computing device to computing device, a chain of artefactual information is established that is parallel to genetic information systems and cultural information systems.

The autonomous characteristics of these computer lineages are increasing as more and more artefactual information functions are made less human-dependent. Consequently, the environment within which cultural entities evolve becomes one in which these artefacts' contribution has to be taken into account. Humans increasingly interact with artefactual entities and change their behaviour, as at a trivial level I do as I type this paragraph, changing my behaviour according to the cues my computer gives me. With less trivial devices my behaviour would change more profoundly.

So the evolution of cultural entities has to be considered as influenced by an environment that includes two other information carriers, namely genes and computing devices. Culture will increasingly co-evolve with the environment comprising these two information realms. And, one could add, each of these latter information realms in turn will co-evolve with respect to the two others in the tripod. So, increasingly, cultural entities have to be seen as part of a larger co-evolving whole, which includes the other two areas of genes and artefacts.

Are there general properties of this co-evolving whole that we can discern?

GENERAL PROPERTIES

First is timing and sequence. Genetic systems were the first information devices on earth, with culture coming later and artefactual devices much later. There is thus a nested hierarchy of the three. There is also in this sequence a seeming intentionality within which information envelopes emerged. Culture emerged because it allowed greater adaptability in interaction with the environment for organisms, carriers of genetic information. Reactions with an environment and consequent changes in behaviour of the information carrier were now more rapid. Similarly, artefactual devices give cultural processing entities (say, us), an expanded and more rapid response to the environment.

There are also many commonalities in the three systems. In a world driving towards chaos and increased entropy, each of them constitutes a reversal. They constitute order, negentropy; in the sense Schrödinger once defined life as a reversal of entropy (Schrödinger 1945). These lineages tunnel through time in a direction different to that given by the Second Law of Thermodynamics. They can do so only under specific conditions. They must constitute open systems that import and export energy and matter allowing for a local reduction of entropy. That is, the particular physical carriers of information—cells, brains, or computers—should allow for import and export of energy allowing for local reductions of entropy.

Each information realm has lineages that come from the past and are carried on to the future. Thus each carries information from the past, that is, it has a memory. To this memory it adds on further information whilst also excising older information. In interaction with a hostile environment some information carriers—organisms—are eliminated. Those that are not, move forward in time, carrying their past and any added information. Part of this process occurs under what Maturana and Varela called autopoiesis, self-construction (Maturana and Varela 1975). This process also leads to speciation as new information carriers that do not interact with existing carriers are formed. Given sufficient time, the lineages split up, fitting into a variety of niches. With the passage of very long time spans, say 3–4 billion years, these carriers can have very complex information coded within them, the result of successful interactions with past environments. There is also phylogenesis built into evolutionary systems. A carrier of large amounts of information cannot appear overnight; it takes time and repeated interactions with changing environments.

But given a new niche, say, after the elimination of existing carriers due to a catastrophic environmental change, one can have very rapid growth of varieties of new carriers, including some complex ones. This allows for processes of punctuated equilibrium, sudden disjunctures.

And, as a lineage arises only from particular interactions with particular environments, it codes within it a particular approach to the environment. This has been called a particular 'world view' or a particular hypothesis about the environment (Wuketits 1990). Thus the world view of the genes of a worm differs from that of a moth because they have to capture cognitively different realities—meaning different spectra, different acoustic frequencies, different molecules for smell, etc. (Greene 1985). And if we were to trace a lineage from, say, a billion years ago, and trace the twists and turns it had taken as it bifurcated into different species and sub-species, we could picture the cognitive window of the lineage changing with time. It is like a ride through time taken with a screen (if one were to limit oneself to only one sense) in front. The screen projects different images as the lineage careens through time.

Some of these general characteristics of biological evolution one finds in the cultural realm too. Here, information is passed through from human mind to human mind down lineages. This transmission may be at times mediated through temporary stores of information, such as books, adjuncts to the cultural carrier, the brain. But such stores become parts of the cultural system only when their contents pass through a live human brain, the artefact of culture. A Dead Sea Scroll may remain under desert sand for 2,000 years, or, for that matter, lie in a university vault for decades, but it becomes cultural information only when it is decoded into cultural material that fits into the fabric of meanings in real human minds. Without human minds, stored cultural artefacts are, to all intents and purposes, dead cultural information.

Cultural information is passed through from generation to generation and is gradually modified. Part of it is kept as a memory and new information is added or some old information is excised. The hunter-gatherer moves around in the Amazon continuously sampling his environment, testing it (most famously for medicinal and other purposes), and adds to his store of cultural information. Shifting to a new environment, say a desert, such a group would have to excise, as useless, part of its existing knowledge and acquire new knowledge. The information now transmitted orally to their progeny as useful is now different from that passed down in the wet tropical Amazon. It would still have some common cores of information from the past, like, say, most of its language, with new words added from its interactions with the new environment, some ways of bringing up children, and methods of preparing food. Some of these core items could even be traced back a long time, say, knowledge of making stone tools to Palaeolithic times. But to this core have been added fresh items that arise from successful adaptation to the newer environment. If the new niches to which these subgroups migrate are isolated for sufficient time, they begin to acquire new cultural information that could be impermeable to the groups that they left generations ago. Given sufficient time new cultural forms such as languages, forms of food preparation, and child rearing emerge. The cultural world now begins to differ from subculture to subculture, giving rise to different processes of cultural cognition, to differing realties that are socially constructed by the different groups (Berger and Luckmann 1967).

These 'world views' constructed in cultural lineages have been the subject of extensive study by social scientists in their studies on ideologies, forms of social cognition, social constructions of reality, and their work on the evolutionary epistemology of science. These general cognitive characteristics are true of the historical evolution of broad symbolic systems in general, whether they be scripts, languages, arts, or sciences, all of which are cognitive systems and cultural cognitive maps that evolve in interaction with the environment (Artigiani 1988).

Such world views are associated not only with broad cultures as a whole but also with social classes that arise from the major social fault-lines. These latter class-wide social constructs of reality and their evolution have been studied by Lukács (1923) in his work on history and class consciousness. Social classes, as well as narrower social groupings, have evolving social epistemologies that change with the environment. And, corresponding to the differing flow lines, there are differing cognitive systems, different social epistemologies. This also leads to an incommensurability in the different cognitions from the different flow lines, as, say, demonstrated in the differing consciousness of different classes or, in the case of formal knowledge, in the cognitive incompatibilities of different disciplines in science (Pickering 1981).

The processes of speciation, the development of social world views, and creation of lineages and sub-lineages can be seen in a most demarcated form in the practice of science as documented by the school of the social construction of science. The problems of science are delivered by the information of past practitioners. As scientists interact with new problems, new information is added on to create new lineages or sub-lineages. Thus, the pursuit of problems in natural philosophy led it to branching off, say, into physics, chemistry, biology, and so on. And, later, given different problems resulting in different solutions further splitting into sub-disciplines occurred, such as, say, biology splitting into taxonomy, molecular biology, evolutionary theory, etc. Some of these new areas are partly incommensurate with each other. With time, cultural lineages split and speciate.

The social factors, with which disciplines advance include those of networks of practitioners or theorists constituting 'invisible colleges', laboratory groups (Latour and Woolgar 1979), and key gatekeepers in a discipline, such as editors and referees. Sufficient case studies now exist to describe in detail the social and contingent nature of the knowledge so produced. These cultural choices are engrained in the final bundle of information that ultimately emerges as science. Sometimes this speciation in science takes the form of sudden jumps, radical cognitive shifts, as new paradigms replace old ones, perhaps paralleling the punctuated equilibria in biological information processes.

But genetic information and cultural information are not the only types of information that interact with environments and change their contents. A third information lineage has emerged, that contained in computing artefacts. They have existed barely for half a century—although one can push back the emergence of such artefacts in an incipient form to office machines of the nineteenth century, or to the Napier's Rods of the seventeenth century, or even to the abacus.

Since the 1940s computing artefacts have been growing rapidly; more importantly, since the invention of the chip, following 'Moore's Law' they have been doubling their capacity every eighteen months. Today the number of chips, especially of micro-controllers, are in the billions, and will soon surpass in number the human population as information processors (Calem 1994). In quality they have moved beyond their initial role of mere mechanical devices that carry out faster the detailed instructions of human programmers. Artificial intelligence (AI) approaches such as genetic algorithms, fuzzy logic, expert systems, and learning systems have tended to give autonomous characteristics to computers. No longer can the human programmer know beforehand the outcome of an AI-enabled computing device. They are opaque to humans, and constitute a 'significant other' for human interactions.

Even with simple programmable devices, it should be noted there is in practice an opacity to humans. This is because of the enormous number of such devices doing a multiplicity of tasks in any given second. It is no longer possible for humans to track their detailed activities. Even if the entire human species were harnessed to these activities, it would not be able to duplicate even a minute fraction of the contemporary activities of information artefacts. There is, therefore, a double opacity, one connected with the large number of relatively unintelligent devices and the other with devices that have a capacity for intelligent behaviour.

Initially, computing artefacts work on the output given by human culture. For example, they help humans process numbers, images, and so on. This is cultural fodder that would normally pass through human minds. It is parallel to human cultural processing initially working on the problems given by the genetic and biological systems. For example poets and artists can rhapsodise only on the sights, sounds and smells given by their genetic machinery. They cannot visualise colours beyond red and violet or sounds below 50 cycles per second or greater than 20,000 cycles. But we can think beyond these limits in the abstract. And, just as human culture can transcend limits set by genes and arrive at new information combinations, fresh forms of cognising the world external to the lineage, so can artefactual information.

Artefactual information operating on initial cultural information thus brings on new information admixtures not seen before. Computing artefacts turn out, for example, new music forms (as some AI-based music creation attempts), or new types of visual expressions to be consumed by humans. But as information is handed down a chain, from computing device to computing device, increasingly unaided by humans, a new autonomous information lineage with its own characteristics tends to emerge.

These new artefactual lineages will initially follow the contours, classifications, and boundaries given by their human makers. But as the autonomy and processing power of computing devices increase both quantitatively and qualitatively, new boundaries between lineages, new classifications, and new contours will emerge. Processes of speciation now occur, splitting the earlier human-given lineages into new sub-lineages. But each such lineage samples only some aspects of its environment, cognises it, and operates on it. That is, associated with each artefactual lineage, is a particular world view, its own hypothesis on the environment, just as genetic and cultural systems have their own world views, cognitive windows to the external world. There is also some evidence that largely interconnected computer systems go through sudden disjunctures, sudden punctuations in their evolution as do biological and cultural systems (Huberman and Hogg 1988). These three realms that have been hitherto separated—at least in a nominal, conceptual sense—are about to be merged into one composite through advances in biotechnology and information technology. Let me explain.

MERGING

Genetic information that is being operated on in biotechnology to bring about new organisms or changes in existing organisms does not exist in a cultural vacuum. What the biotechnologist does is a cultural act. He transfers his cultural knowledge on how genes operate on to the genetic field and changes genetic structure. He also transfers society's wishes—that is, cultural information, on what genetic characteristics are desirable (say, an extra gene for intelligence, or the excising of the gene responsible for a disease)—to the genetic field and thereby alters it. Biologists recognise two types of genetic information. First are structural genes, genes that build a particular type of nose or a particular type of thumb, and second are regulatory genes, which say 'now start the construction' or 'now stop it'. The new cultural information that is mapped on to the genetic field is a type of information that eventually produces the particular biological organism, the phenotype.

But genes are not just operated on by human biotechnologists. Increasingly the vast amount of data that is being spewed out of the genetic field is stored in computer form, analysed through them, and operated on by them. For example, large banks of computers, some using advanced pattern-recognition means derived from AI techniques, are doing the mapping of the human genome. In the not too distant future, the fishing out of a desirable gene would be done out of a data bank of phenotypic characteristics and their associated gene sequences, down to the detailed chemical composition of the required gene. One could also imagine virtual experiments being done on the electronically stored chemical sequences to yield new artificial genes, with new biological properties hitherto unknown in nature. In the not too distant future, one can also imagine dry runs on evolution mimicking Darwinian processes being done on gene banks stored in computer databases, in a similar manner to genetic algorithms doing runs on possible solutions to problems in the computer field. But, instead of just mimicking biological evolution for solving other problems, such dry runs on real genetic information would be artificial evolutionary biology, evolutionary runs leading to real biological creatures in wet ware, as it were, in real blood and flesh.

So genetic information is getting intimately mixed up, in fact merged with, cultural information and artefactual information. But if we look from the perspective of culture too, we see the same process occurring. We perceive the world partly through inputs from our five senses and through the memory and processing power of the mind, six windows (incidentally, from a cross-cultural perspective, corresponding directly to the 'six senses' of Buddhist psychology). But our senses limit what we can perceive in the world, limiting us to particular colours, particular sounds, and particular smells. Other animals (your dog or your bat) perceive different sounds or different smells, and have different internal worlds. To be a bat is to be epistemologically and cognitively in a different space, at a different cognitive location, grounded in a different world (Nagel 1974).

We can transcend these limits and think abstractly of, say, frequencies and molecules beyond our sensing devices. Presumably so could also animals to some extent. But this is not the same as direct perception. The cultural stream of information racing through our minds would have a different flavour in the two cases—concrete cognition and abstract cognition. Now biotechnology, to the extent that it can alter the genetic matrix associated with perception and thought (and regularly we read of new genes being discovered related to different mental faculties), allows one to change this grounded cognition. Initially, such genetic intervention would be to correct genetic faults, say of a lack of colour vision. But it is not too far-fetched to think of sensory enhancement not only by adding new spectra to the senses but also by adding genes for different intelligences. Because of the new genetic lenses that are added, this brings new filters in our cultural perception. Our cultural information output is changed by the added genetic information, both cultural and genetic information are now merged.

Our culture has been partly stored in artefacts, such as books, before they stream through our minds and become culture. With computing devices, not only is cultural information stored, it is also partly processed through artefacts. When I stare at my computer screen I change my behaviour according to the cues that it presents me. My internal cultural information is transformed by artefactual information. Both cultural and artefactual information gets merged. This merger occurs in dynamic real time in such instances as when kids play computer games, persons explore the Internet, and scientists using computers process data. Once these devices use AI techniques the texture of merged information increases in quality. With tens of ubiquitous embedded computing devices already present in Western homes and thousands promised in the coming decades we will be taking many cognitive cues from artefactual devices. The merging will increase in quantity. Such ecologies of artefactual devices will surround us like a jungle, continuously feeding us information that will merge with our cultural stream, enriching it.

Computing artefacts are initially projections of our scientific thoughts—that is of our cultural information—concretised into hardware and software. So artefactual information is initially our cultural information. But, with increasing processing power and number of artefacts, the information throughput of such devices increases qualitatively and quantitatively. They now spew out information never before seen on earth that in turn interacts with cultural information. Artefactual and cultural information are merged in a richer mode, resulting in a two-way conversation between the two realms.

Computing artefacts are made of silicon-based chips. There is, however, research being done to incorporate biological elements within these artefacts. This research into biochips is still in its infancy but will result in the direct merging of biological systems into computing hardware. But genetic systems in the form of strands of DNA have been already used as computing devices in some experiments (Manning 1996). Indirectly, biological models have also inspired the search for software that mimics brain functions. Hebbs's pioneering research into how the brain functions led to modelling it on the perceptron (Kaminuma and Matsumoto 1991), which approach later led to today's successful neural networks (Milner 1993). In a less direct way, biological evolution is also mimicked through genetic algorithms that arrive at their solutions by evolutionary processes. Biological information processes are thus mapped within artefactual ones, both directly and indirectly, thus merging the two. With the merger of the three streams it is no longer enough to consider their evolution as separate entities. They have to be seen as one evolving whole.

THE DYNAMICS OF MERGED EVOLUTION

Through the new technologies, information from one stream is ferried across to another and made to merge. Information in the three streams now becomes translatable into one another, and information as an entity becomes a common currency of discourse between the three realms.

We noted a time sequence in the three lineages; the cultural came after the genetic and after that the artefactual. They form a nested hierarchy; the artefactual is above the cultural that is above the genetic. There is also a time element: genetic information lasts for a long time counted, say, in geological terms; cultural information changes faster and artefactual information still faster.

The merging through the new technologies changes the hierarchy of reaction times among the three nested lineages; and the associated survivability of information gets disturbed. The later lineage, whether it be culture or artefact, is faster than the earlier one, whether it be gene or culture. With the merging, this sequence of reaction times is disturbed. Because of influences from the outer elements, evolution in the inner lineages (respectively genetic and cultural) now becomes faster. Genetic information changes faster now with cultural and artefactual information incursions, and cultural information changes faster with artefactual information incursions. Also, as a consequence, the information from the outer layer that had a relatively shorter lifetime now lives longer in the inner one. So, artefactual information lives longer when embedded in cultural information, and cultural information lives longer when embedded in genetic information, and artefactual information lives longer than cultural information when embedded in genetic systems.

In becoming a single evolving whole, the historical sequence of biology giving rise to culture, giving rise to artefact, and to each inner core lineage acting as it were 'hand-in-glove', becomes changed. Being its inner core, genes constitute the partial 'hand-in-glove' of cultural information, initially setting the template for the latter, for example giving the senses one can sample the world with. In the same way, culture is partially the 'hand-in-glove-puppet' of artefactual information, setting the initial outlines for the artefactual lineage. When the mixing of genes into new combinations is done through artefactual information, it is indirectly done through culture, which in turn is influenced by genes. The artefact now reaches back and changes culture or gene, culture reaches back and changes the gene, and the glove turns back and changes the hand.

Instead of a unilinear sequence of information cores and later envelopes, recursive loops between them are established. Genes now reach back indirectly through the chain of culture and artefact, and through them partly redirect their own mixing. Similar recursive loops occur, for example, from culture to artefact alone, when, say, a computer system's output helps a human scientist to change the computer system's design. These recursive loops help bind the three streams together. They also now become determinants of evolution in all three lineages.

Phylogenesis of the different lineages is also affected. Earlier, as in biological systems, a phylogenetic tendency for greater diversity and greater and greater information existed with the passage of time. This phylogenetic tendency is now increased, as a greater shuffling of information is now possible, leaving room for more combinations. This would be like the introduction of sexual reproduction in evolution that brought in a greater shuffling of genetic material. The rate of evolution would be speeded up analogous to the speeding up of evolution that was brought about by the introduction of sexual reproduction in the biological field. The information contents of the three lineages are now to be viewed as a single reservoir of information whose shuffling yields entirely new patterns.

The world views arising from the evolutionary epistemology in the three lineages also incorporate tendencies and biases in their different interactions with the environment. They constitute human values embedded in the cultural lineage and their equivalents in the case of the other two egocentricities. These world views could, therefore, provide for a common factor through which to enter into the realm of 'values' in each stream. This could be a window into an objective examination of the 'subjectivities' of each lineage, and hence provide for a common general perspective and a valid framework of the 'ethics' of each lineage vis-à-vis its environment. It could thus become a framework for a truly universal 'eco-ethics' in the largest sense of the term.

What will the future of these windows be in the era of merged evolution? Merging means that there are cognitive windows being added on to the existing cognition system of a single lineage or sub-lineage. The ferrying in of information from lineage to lineage alters the structure and content of information in a lineage, resulting in the lineage's cognition of the world changing. In the process of merging, the lineages' cognition is enlarged or diminished, new features are added on, and are others excised. Generally, the cognition becomes richer and more varied. The battery of possible interactions with the environment, and hence the richness of the cognition, increases with the phylogenetic ascendancy of the lineages, which is brought about by the increased introduction of new information to the lineage.

In addition, the three lineages in the process of merging have to be considered also as one evolving whole. This macro-lineage of the three together has also, therefore, its own cognition of the world. The macro single lineage is built up through the mergings of the three. So, at another level, the three have to be seen as a single system that has its own single composite window on the world.

This composite window cannot be described in terms of the cognition perspectives of any one lineage. This would be similar to a human being capable of adequately describing their cognition of the external world in terms of one information interface only, say of sight, sound, touch, smell, or taste. A human's cognition is a composite of all the information inputs into it. So the cognition of the information sub-lineage associated with the human species is a lineage built up from these sensory inputs and which changes historically as the human species tunnels through time. Further, the lineage of humans is different from say that of bats, because the two sample different segments of reality through their sensory organs. In a parallel manner, the three merged lineages now present an evolving single set of windows with changing cognitions of the external world.

The broad characteristics of merging that have been sketched above imply that the evolutionary implications of the new technologies are many. They change key characteristics of each lineage such as speciation, memory retention, flexibility, and speed of reaction to the environment, hierarchies in nestedness, rates of evolution, and 'world views', as well as developing into one single macro-lineage.

These changes encroach directly on the 4 billion-year history of biology and, say, the 10,000-year history of human culture. In mixing together the constituents of these two histories with a newer one into one whole, history as we know it changes dramatically. Biology, history, and artefacts now become one entity.

The carriers of information in a single lineage interact with each other and so constitute communities. In the merged situation they constitute for other carriers 'significant others' with whom they communicate. The image that emerges is of an ocean of communities, existing at different levels, the genetic, the cultural, and the artefactual. They interact with, and in, different environments—the genetic, the cultural, and the artefactual—and change their states. Currents and bubbles of information rise, fall, and circulate, according to both the internal dynamics of each community and inter-lineage dynamics. There are processes of localisation and globalisation in and across all three realms. There are continuous processes of organisation of communities within the system, sideways, upward, and downward. Truly a witch's brew—or, if you wish, a wizard's brew—of communication possibilities, of shifting dynamic communities results.

These dynamics lead to changes in the evolutionary characteristics of each lineage and sub-lineage, including the internal perceptions from within a lineage, namely, in the language of evolutionary epistemology, the different 'meanings' of and 'hypotheses' about the world. New sets of webs of meanings result. Thermodynamically, this is also an open system, with a constant increase of organisation within the system, accompanied necessarily by changes in inflows and outflows to and from the system. The study of social and cultural phenomena in the new millennium should necessarily take into account all these varied factors. A future theory of culture must incorporate the dynamics of all three realms. The world of communities will never be the same.

Note. Some of the issues dealt with here are treated more fully in the author's *Evolution of Information: Lineages in Genes, Culture and Artefact* (London: Pinter, 1992), and *Merged Evolution: The Long-Term Implications of Information Technology and Biotechnology* (London: Gordon & Breach, 1999)

REFERENCES

Artigiani, R. (1988), 'Scientific Revolution and the Evolution of Consciousness', *World Futures* 25: 237–61.

Berger, P. L. and Luckmann, T. (1967), *The Social Construction of Reality: A Treatise in the Sociology of Knowledge*. New York: Doubleday.

Calem, Robert E. (1994), 'In Far More Gadgets, a Hidden Chip', *New York Times* 2 Jan.

Greene, M. (1985), 'Perception, Interpretation and the Sciences: Toward a New Philosophy of Science', in D. J. Depew and B. H. Weber (eds) *Evolution at the Cross Roads: The New Biology and New Philosophy of Science*. Cambridge, MA: MIT Press.

Huberman, B. A. and T. Hogg (1988), 'The Behaviors of Computational Ecologies', in B. A. Huberman (ed.) *The Ecology of Computation*. Amsterdam: North-Holland Publishing.

Kaminuma T. and G. Matsumoto (eds) (1991), *Biocomputers: The Next Generation from Japan*. London: Chapman and Hall.

Latour, B. and Woolgar, S. (1979), *Laboratory Life: The Social Construction of Scientific Facts*. London: Sage.

Lukács, G. (1923), *Gesichte und Klassen Bewusstein* (History and Class Consciousness). Berlin: Malik.

Manning, E. (1996), 'DNA Strands Learn to Add', *United Press International Reports* 27 July.

Maturana, H. R. and Varela, F. (1975), 'Autopoietic Systems', Report BCL 9.4. Urbana, IL: Biological Computer Laboratory, University of Illinois.

Milner, P. A. (1993) 'The Mind and Donald O. Hebb', *Scientific American* January: 124–9.

Nagel, T. (1974), 'What is it Like to Be a Bat?', *Philosophical Review* October.

Pickering, A. (1981), 'The Hunting of the Quark', *ISIS* 72: 216–36.

Schrödinger, E. (1945), *What is Life?* London: Cambridge University Press.

Wilson, E. O. (1980), *Sociobiology: The New Synthesis*, Cambridge, MA: Harvard University Press.

Wuketits, F. M. (1990), *Evolutionary Epistemology and its Implications for Human Kind*. Albany: State University of New York Press.

Index